Fodor's

Short Escapes in Britain

Fodor's Travel Publications, Inc.
New York * Toronto * London * Sydney * Auckland

▼

SHORT ESCAPES IN BRITAIN

Design: Steve Phillips Design / Nancy Koch

Map Design: John Grimwade

Maps: John Grimwade, Greg Wakabayashi

Reporter: Helen Livingston

Editors: Marita Begley, Holly Ann Hughes

Research Editor: Paul Rogers

Research Associates: Terry Stoller, Ray Lipinsky

Cover Design: Tigist Getachew, Fabrizio La Rocca

Cover Photo: Bob Krist

Art Assistant: Lauri Marks

Legal Counsel: Gene Winter, John Stoller

Copyright © 1993
by Bruce Bolger and Gary Stoller

While every care has been taken to ensure the accuracy of the information in this guide, time brings change, and consequently, the publisher cannot accept responsibility for errors that may occur. Prudent travelers will therefore want to call ahead to verify prices and other "perishable" information.

ISBN 0-679-02468-9

First Edition

MANUFACTURED IN THE UNITED STATES OF AMERICA
10 9 8 7 6 5 4 3 2 1

ABOUT THE AUTHORS

Gary Stoller has been an editor at *Condé Nast Traveler* magazine since its start-up in 1987. Considered a pioneer of the concept of "investigative travel reporting," he wrote articles that were cited by judges when the magazine twice received National Magazine Awards. His articles have also won awards from the National Press Club and the Aviation/Space Writers Association. He has a journalism degree from the University of Colorado and now lives outside of New York City with his wife, Terry, and daughter, Kristin.

Bruce Bolger, an avid traveler and experienced walker, has explored the countryside in over a dozen countries spanning four continents. Currently a trade show director and management consultant, he has extensive experience in the travel and publishing fields. He is a graduate of the University of California at Santa Barbara and attended the University of Paris in France for a year. He speaks French fluently. He lives outside of New York City with his wife, Shawn, and children, Kate and Chris.

To my wife, Terry Stoller, and our beautiful new daughter, Kristin, for never giving up the fight during a turbulent year that ended in jubilation. And to my mother, Lillian, for all her love and support during the writing of this book and throughout my life.

◆◆◆

To my wife, Shawn Bolger, and children, Kate and Chris, whose loving support helped make this book possible. And to all the people who have worked so hard to create an entirely new kind of travel experience.

▼

Contents

▼

WHERE TO FIND EACH EXPERIENCE

Aberdeen

21 Stonehaven

SCOTLAND

Balquhidder 20

Dundee

Gartocharn 19

Edinburgh

Glasgow

Melrose 18   **17** Bamburgh

Gilsland 16

Newcastle

15 Barnard Castle

Hawkshead 14

Haworth 13 Leeds

Manchester

11 Hathersage

12 Waverton

25 Harlech

ENGLAND

24 Aberdovey
(Aberdyfi)

Birmingham

50 MILES

WALES

5 Wilmcote

22 Brecon   Wyck
Rissington **6** **3** Woodstock

23 Laugharne

Oxford

Cardiff

LONDON

Swansea

7 Avebury   **4** Richmond

Bristol

2 Hever

Luxborough 8

1 Bodiam

10 Boscastle

Southampton

Plymouth

9 East Portlemouth

▼

Introduction

When you come to Britain's great cities and towns in search of history, you can find monuments to the past everywhere along the grand avenues and back streets. But not even in the most silent corner of a city can you escape the sounds of modern life— trucks, cars, scooters, and machines—that forever encroach upon your effort to experience the past.

This guide is for everyone who would like to escape to the peace of the British countryside and soak up a more complete sense of the way life once was, and is today. It will take you away from the tourist crowds to unique places with spectacular vistas and remarkable histories. You can stroll alone through an ancient forest, walk along the towpath of a centuries-old canal, or picnic without neighbors on the grassy banks of a peaceful river. You can continue the mood at a recommended restaurant in a picturesque setting and then complete the experience at a charming country inn or a unique bed and breakfast.

Short Escapes brings you to special places little known even to the British. According to your tastes, you can tramp around historic landmarks, plunge deep into farmland or forest, or just sit undisturbed for hours looking down at gentle waves lapping against a shore. Through the quiet, you will be able to feel what it might have been like when Shakespeare roamed through the Forest of Arden, when Henry VIII courted Anne Boleyn, or when Britain braced for an impending German invasion during World War II. Many of the book's suggested walking tours cover country roads and footpaths in use for hundreds or even thousands of years.

The 25 experiences in this guide are scattered around seven different regions—each with its own distinctive character, flavor, and points of historical, cultural, or natural interest. All are within a day's excursion from Britain's major tourist spots, and some are accessible by

▼

train. Each experience is centered around a walking tour, which can be anything from a short stroll to a four-hour walk. The text that accompanies each experience takes an in-depth look at something special about the place, its past or present.

These experiences cost less than other forms of travel. Nobody charges admission to villages and the countryside, and rural hotels and restaurants match and even surpass their urban counterparts in comfort and luxury at much lower prices.

Short Escapes is more than a travel guide: It's designed to awaken the traveler's senses to the moods and flavors of a place and its people; to help evoke a real sense of the past and present. We hope that the 25 experiences will have the same uplifting effect on you as they had on us. We thrust ourselves into the soul of the country and learned about the land in a way you can't by reading about it in a book or observing artifacts in a museum.

In fact, we felt we had stumbled upon a new form of travel—one which combines the cultural and sensual enrichment of traditional travel with the spiritual pleasures of walking. We ended each day with a great sense of accomplishment and, like a local resident, felt we had participated in the place.

The rewards of exploring the countryside are great: You will return home having experienced the essence of Britain, knowing that you have felt its history, escaped from the hubbub of its cities and tourist attractions, and savored the beauty of the land and its people.

How to Use Short Escapes

We selected the 25 experiences in *Short Escapes* for their historic, cultural, or natural interest and for their general proximity to regions popular with travelers. Seventeen of the experiences are scattered about five regions in England—outside London, the Cotswolds and the Heart of England, southwest England, central England, and northern England. Four experiences are in Scotland and four in Wales. At each location, walking tours permit visitors to get out of their cars or the train and experience special places up close. All include private, easily accessible places to picnic or to enjoy a memorable view. When possible, itineraries provide optional walks for strollers and serious walkers.

Itineraries are organized by region and are selected so that travelers staying in one of the selected lodgings can easily enjoy multiple experiences during their stay. We personally followed every itinerary mentioned in this book and purposely omitted others which gave us difficulty.

Each experience comes with a narrative on historical, cultural, literary, or natural points of interest to bring your visit to life. In addition, there are suggestions on other unique places to explore nearby, so you don't have to be a walker to enjoy this book.

If you plan on making overseas calls to any of the telephone or fax numbers in this book, first dial 011-44 and then omit the zero before each number. If you call any of the phone or fax numbers from within Britain, retain the zero.

▼

FINDING YOUR WAY

We designed this book to make it as easy as possible to follow the directions. For your convenience, each walking tour begins with basic information on duration, length, and level of difficulty. The time it takes to complete an itinerary is approximate and is based on a walk with only momentary stops. All itineraries are loops unless otherwise indicated; walking time is based on a very leisurely 2 mph.

A walk marked "Easy" has few ups and downs, no areas of tricky footing, and no navigational challenges and is appropriate for anybody capable of walking. A walk marked "Moderate" requires a little more physical commitment and might have an area of tricky footing but requires no particular navigational abilities or physical endurance. Even the least experienced walkers can safely follow all "Moderate" itineraries just a short way to a nice view, picnic spot, or historic site, and then retrace their steps to the starting point. A walk marked "Easy to moderate" offers readers the choice of following the entire moderately difficult walk or an easy abbreviated version of it. For all walks, the text fully details whatever difficulties you might encounter along the way.

The numbered word directions for all itineraries enable you to complete a walking tour without using the map, but some may find it easier simply to follow the map and refer to the text when necessary. We strongly recommend that you use both the text and the maps, which provide navigational aids and show the places of interest, pubs, and restaurants along the way. At each numbered point on the map, the same number in the text gives the information you'll need to find your way and additional observations about the terrain and the sights you are passing. Experienced walkers might enjoy having a compass and a more detailed topographical map, which can be purchased at various stores throughout Britain (*see* the For Serious Walkers section, below).

Proceed carefully, and don't ever walk for long in any one direction unless you're sure of the way. You will never be too far from assistance. By American standards, Britain is densely populated and crisscrossed with paved roads, so you can almost always find help along the way. Should you ever get confused, feel free to knock on a door or flag down a car; use the map in this book to indicate where you began the

▼

tour. Most people will happily help you out. If you cannot find assistance, simply turn back and retrace your steps. You'll still have seen far more of Britain than most tourists ever do.

A few of the itineraries follow footpaths marked with colored trailblazes that indicate the way. Pay more attention to our word directions and maps than to the blazes. The same colored blaze is sometimes used for intersecting trails, causing confusion for walkers. And on some trails, blazes mysteriously disappear for a short time.

While we have made every effort to select well-established itineraries and have walked every single one, we cannot guarantee that some farmer, municipality, or commercial venture has not altered or deformed the character of an itinerary. If you encounter a dramatic change, such as a missing stile (steps that make it possible to pass over a fence or wall) or a barbed-wire fence that blocks your path, we'd like to hear from you.

PRECAUTIONS

Although most of the itineraries require no special athletic abilities, all travelers should be sure to dress for the weather and wear shoes or sneakers appropriate for walking. Weather conditions change rapidly in Britain, a country notorious for rainy weather. Always carry the clothing you'll need for a worst-case change in the weather. A daypack generally can handle whatever clothing two people might need, in addition to drinks and a picnic, and these small packs, when empty, fit easily into your suitcase.

The usual countryside obstacles—such as muddy and rocky trails, fallen trees, and poorly cut footpaths—pose the greatest risks. Since you can accomplish the longest of these itineraries in about half a day, you need not race through your walking tour. Take the time to enjoy the beauty, and watch your step.

Finally, keep an eye out for hunters, and wear bright-colored clothing if you're walking through forests during the hunting season. Grouse season runs from mid-August to mid-December; partridge, from September to February; pheasant, from October to February; duck, from September to late February. Game shooting is forbidden on Sundays and on Christmas in England and Wales, and no shooting of any animal

▼

is permitted on Sundays in Scotland. In the regions you are visiting, you may wish to inquire at the tourist offices about the exact dates for hunting and the specific areas popular with hunters.

WEATHER

No rain fell during the 175 miles or so we walked while researching this book, but we were lucky: Rain is frequent and can occur at any time throughout the year in England, Scotland, and Wales. In northern England, temperatures are often two to five degrees colder than in the south; it's also colder in northern Scotland than in the southern part of that country. From April through September, average high temperatures in London can exceed those in Edinburgh, Scotland, by five to seven degrees. In both northern England and Scotland, the sun sets late in the evening during the summer but very early in winter. Be prepared for snow storms and dense fog during the winter months.

GETTING THERE

If you are driving to a short escape, use the directions in the Getting There section and the small regional map included in the walking tour map. A more detailed, commercially available road map will help.

Although those who travel by car have the greatest and most flexible access to Britain's hidden treasures, even train travelers can enjoy some of these short escapes. Wherever there is direct rail access, it is noted in the Getting There section. Intrepid train travelers can also reach some of the more remote itineraries by bus from a major train station.

You can get specific information on train fares and schedules in the United States from *Brit Rail, 1500 Broadway, New York, N.Y. 10036, tel. 212-575-2667.* Brit Rail sells a variety of discount passes to travelers who plan to do a fair amount of train travel.

Almost all itineraries have been selected in regions already popular with travelers. So if you plan on going to a popular tourist attraction as well, you won't have to go far out of your way to enjoy a short escape.

▼

OTHER PLACES NEARBY

For those who prefer to tour by car, we've provided suggestions on how to visit the highpoints of our experiences and have pointed out other places of interest in the region that are often overlooked by tourists. This way, you can enjoy the highlights of our itineraries and uncover other special places without driving more than a short distance. The location of many nearby points of interest can be found in the small inset map accompanying the walking tour map in each chapter.

DINING

For those who want to continue the mood created by their experience of the day, we've selected a few restaurants and pubs in the countryside near our itineraries.

To be included in *Short Escapes,* a restaurant must either have an excellent view, be rustic or historic, or serve good food popular with locals. Since many of the walking tours are in tiny villages and hamlets, expect food quality to be a step or two below that found in London or in other major cities. Another drawback is that too many countryside restaurants and pubs (and hotels and bed and breakfasts) serve traditional English food, with little variety on the menu and a lack of flair in the kitchen. It usually pays to call ahead to reserve a table, especially on weekends and holidays. You'll usually find the best (and most expensive) meals at the many country houses we've recommended. In restaurants and pubs with both a dinner menu and a pub menu, you'll get the best value (and often the same food) by ordering from the pub menu. Restaurants fall into four price categories based on the approximate cost of a dinner for two:

Very expensive .... **Over 55 pounds**

Expensive .... **33-54 pounds**

Moderate .... **21-32 pounds**

Inexpensive .... **Under 21 pounds**

The most inexpensive way to savor some of Britain's tastiest food is to shop for lunch in the local food stores and enjoy the fruits of your efforts on the walking tour. You can pick up baked goods filled with meat or vegetables, cheese, luncheon meats, bread, and fresh fruit in specialty shops or in local grocery stores. Bakeries are also prominent in the country and can be a valuable source of picnic supplies. If you happen to be in a town on market day, you can select your lunch from an ample variety of vendors.

LODGING

All country inns, bed and breakfasts, and other lodging establishments we've chosen are either rustic or historic, have an excellent view, or are a great value. Most have less than 20 rooms and are located in extremely quiet locations. We have checked each one for cleanliness and up-to-date maintenance.

In general, Britain offers plenty of top-quality expensive and very expensive lodgings, as well as a treasure chest of unique, inexpensive bed and breakfasts. Moderately priced hotels of good quality and value are rare; bed and breakfasts are usually a better bet. Make sure that you have enough cash or traveler's checks because most bed and breakfasts recommended in this book do not accept credit cards. In addition, many bed and breakfasts rent rooms without private bathrooms, so you may want to reserve a room with private facilities. If you can't live without a shower, be sure to request a room equipped with one—hotels, country inns, and bed and breakfasts often provide only a tub, even in rooms with private bathrooms. You may also want to request a double bed because many rooms are furnished with twin beds.

Try to reserve your room well in advance, particularly at bed and breakfasts with a limited number of rooms. Local tourist offices will also make reservations for you; if an office is closed, check on the window or door for a listing of local bed and breakfasts.

Regardless of the price range, most establishments include breakfast in the cost of the lodging. Keep in mind that the prices at many hotels and bed and breakfasts are negotiable, particularly during the off season or when business is slow. Lodging prices in this book are per-

▼

person and are based on double-occupancy:

Very expensive .... **Over 50 pounds per person**

Expensive .... **30-49 pounds**

Moderate .... **21-29 pounds**

Inexpensive .... **Under 21 pounds**

For the backpacking crowd, or travelers on a very limited budget, there are more than 350 youth hostels in Britain. We have not reviewed them in the following chapters, but most offer decent accommodations at an attractive price. For youth hostel information, contact: *YHA Headquarters, Trevelyan House, 8 St. Stephen's Hill, St. Albans, Hertsfordshire AL1 2DY, England, tel. 0727-55215, fax 0727-44126.*

You'll find that some hotels and restaurants well-suited for one itinerary may also be within easy access of another recommended itinerary. Some regions do not have a wide selection of restaurants and hotels in keeping with the ambience of this book. In such cases, we recommend establishments that come as close as possible to our standards and warn you of the shortfalls in the text.

Many of the hotels also have restaurants, so rates that include room, dinner, and breakfast are often available. Determining whether this arrangement makes sense for you requires a little judgment, because some items on the menu have supplemental charges that must be paid by guests who commit to a room-and-meal package. You can make your decision on the day of your arrival, after you've had a chance to review the menu and its prices.

TOURIST OFFICES

In the United States, you can obtain information about Britain by contacting the British Tourist Authority. The organization's main office is located at *551 Fifth Ave., New York, N.Y. 10176-0799, tel. 212-986-2200, fax 212-986-1188.* Information can also be obtained from three other BTA offices in the United States: *2580 Cumberland Pkwy. #470, Atlanta, Ga. 30339, tel. 404-432-9635, fax 404-432-9641; 625 N. Michigan Ave. #1510, Chicago, Ill. 60611, tel. 312-787-0490, fax 312-*

▼

787-7746; and *World Trade Center, 350 S. Figueroa St. #450, Los Angeles, Calif. 90071, tel. 213-628-3525, fax 213-687-6621.*

If you are looking for general travel information after you arrive in England, the best place is the *British Travel Centre, 12 Regent St., Piccadilly Circus, London SW1Y 4PQ, England, tel. 0719-300572.* The center will also book accommodations.

The above offices, however, will be able to provide little information about many of the experiences in this book. To obtain information on places relevant to this book, contact the local or regional tourist office listed at the end of each chapter. Keep in mind that many local offices are closed in winter or have limited hours in the off season. To take advantage of these offices, select the area you're interested in and request everything they have on the history, walking trails, restaurants, hotels, and bed and breakfasts in the region. Although these offices vary greatly in the quality of information offered, they often supply maps indicating locations of historical sights, hotels, bed and breakfasts, and restaurants, as well as walking tours. You should also ask for their most current hours of operation, so that you can stop in when you're there, and the most recent hours of museums or attractions you want to visit. Within two to three weeks, you should have the most up-to-date information you'll need to plan your experience.

As you enter every town, you'll almost always notice road signs indicating the tourist office (usually marked with the letter *I* for information). Volunteers there will often direct you to the restaurants or hotels you're interested in, and to places of interest. If you ask, they'll even phone ahead and make reservations.

FOR SERIOUS WALKERS

Britain has many famous long-distance footpaths as well as an extensive network of local paths and trails. The Ramblers, the country-wide walking club, is constantly battling to keep paths accessible to the traveling public. Farmers and landowners have been known to eliminate a stile or erect a fence to thwart walkers, so it's always best to carry an Ordnance Survey Map. For every itinerary mentioned in this book, we have provided the numbers of the corresponding Ordnance

▼

Survey Maps. The most detailed ones are most useful for walkers and have a scale of 1:25,000; others have scales of 1:50,000 and even 1:100,000. Keep in mind that each map covers a small area—you might need more than one to complete a long itinerary.

You can obtain these maps by mail, or by telephone, from the *National Map Centre, 22-24 Caxton St., London SW1H 0QU, England, tel. 0712-222466, fax 0712-222466.* The maps can also be purchased at stores in the area you are visiting. Local stores, however, are frequently sold out of the particular map you desire.

Because walking has become a national pastime in Britain, a huge collection of maps and literature exists. Local bookstores, news shops, and other stores stock loads of this information.

The Garden of England

EXPERIENCE 1: BODIAM

As you stand on the hillsides around **Bodiam Castle,** you see a very different landscape than you would have in the 14th century, when the castle was first built. Close to the English Channel, this was once a region of treacherous coastal marshes cut by a navigable estuary. Over the centuries, however, the water drained away and the land filled in, creating the lush, fertile **Rother Valley,** often called the Garden of England.

While rambling through the countryside here, notice the patchwork of farming and horticulture: sheep in one field, apple trees in the next, sweet-smelling hops in another. The fields are home to foxes, owls, swallows, and thrushes, and little belts of woodland are still "coppiced" in the traditional way—cut down to stumps for firewood and other uses. Beneath all the many layers of history, this is traditional English countryside and is best seen on foot and up close.

The Highlights: A moated castle above a river in hops country, two ancient churches, a Roman road leading into the historic county of Kent, World War II pillboxes.

Other Places Nearby: The battlefield where William the Conqueror began the Norman conquest of England, an attractive village with a steam railway, the remains of a 12th-century abbey, a house where Rudyard Kipling lived.

▼

Bordering the southeastern counties of Sussex and Kent, the land around Bodiam has always been of strategic importance. When the Romans colonized Britain, they built an ironworks here and a vital northward road, traces of which can be seen today. The Saxons later actually sailed in here: In 1822, a complete 9th-century Danish vessel, 65 feet long, was found buried in what is now farmland, though it apparently sank in open water long ago. Throughout the centuries of fighting between England and France, this land was a significant front line of defense against French attacks. And during World War II, the area was considered a line of defense against impending German attacks. **Pillboxes** still stand today as a reminder of a much-feared invasion that never occurred, and you pass two of them on this walk—one buried next to a tree in the former marshes, the other outside the castle.

The idea of a castle was formulated in 1385, when King Richard II ordered Sir Edward Dalyngrigge to "strengthen" Dalyngrigge's manor house against a possible French attack. Dalyngrigge complied by building Bodiam Castle on the gentle slopes of a hill above the estuary. While it was equipped with a primitive central heating system and other modern comforts of the time, it also looked indomitable, with its broad moat, massive curtain wall, mighty round towers, and frowning gatehouse. The average thickness of the walls is six feet six inches, and the drum towers rise more than 60 feet; entry was provided by a wooden bridge at right angles to the front gate, an approach intended to expose the right flank of any attacking army. But Dalyngrigge, who later became keeper of the Tower of London, may have built it more as a status symbol than a military stronghold. By the time the castle was completed in 1388, the British had taken control of the English Channel, and the French were no longer a threat to this area.

The castle's interior was demolished during the 17th-century English Civil War, but no damage was done to the walls, suggesting that the defenders of the fortress surrendered without much of a fight. That may have been a wise decision, because the final attack was in 1643, a time when the predominant weapons of war were powerful cannons

▼

that could have knocked down the relatively thin walls. No one has lived within the castle since, and in the mid-18th century, its interior was used to grow vegetables. It's a pity only the walls remain, because the castle once contained a fortified courtyard house with suites, servants' quarters, and a chapel. In addition, 33 fireplaces burned within the castle, and 28 bathrooms built into the walls drained into the moat.

On the walking tour outlined below, you approach the castle walls from a direction the tourists never take, getting an unusual perspective on this outstanding remnant of English history. You round a bend on the floor of the former estuary, and the castle suddenly peeks through the trees. Most visitors approach the castle from the heart of Bodiam, a quiet village—except when the tourists invade during the height of the summer season. The village offers little except a tea room, a pub that's also an inn, and **St. Giles' Church.** This church, which houses relics from a knight of 1360 and a priest of 1513, has a turret and sits in a grove of trees, slightly aloof from the village.

Nearby, you pass Kitchenham Farm, notable for its oast houses—distinctive round buildings with spirelike roofs used to dry the hops (an important ingredient of beer) that grew in the fields hereabouts. Until the mid-1960s, almost every farm in the area had its own oast house; today most have been converted into quirky dwellings, and the hop gardens have all but disappeared. One very famous name does remain in business in the area: The Guinness brewing company owns Britain's largest hops farm, a popular place for students to work each fall at harvest time.

Take note of the **Mill House,** Bodiam's old mill, which still stands with its broken waterwheel beside the **Kent Ditch.** The ditch is an old marshland river sometimes known as the Kennett that flows between tall levees and forms the boundary between Kent and Sussex.

When you reach the top of a hill above the farms just outside the town of Sandhurst, you'll see historic **St. Nicholas Church.** From the church grounds, savor the spectacular panoramic views of Sussex and the Rother Valley. Local tradition says that the church was located outside the village because so many victims of the Black Plague were buried in its churchyard during the 14th century. In the churchyard, look for a sundial from the reign of Queen Anne (1701-1714) and a collection of ornate memorials. A Saxon church may formerly have stood on this site, though no physical trace of a church from before the 12th

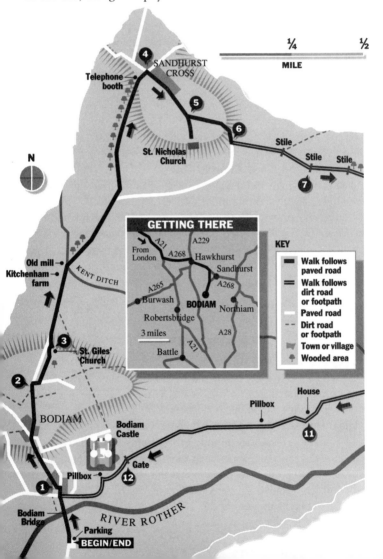

¼   ½
MILE

④ SANDHURST CROSS
Telephone booth
⑤
⑥
Stile
Stile   Stile
⑦

N

St. Nicholas Church

Old mill
Kitchenham farm
KENT DITCH

③ St. Giles' Church
②

BODIAM

Bodiam Castle

Pillbox   House

Pillbox

⑪

Gate
⑫

① Pillbox

Bodiam Bridge

RIVER ROTHER

Parking
BEGIN/END

GETTING THERE

From London
A21
A268
A229
Hawkhurst
Sandhurst
A268
A265
Burwash
BODIAM
Northiam
Robertsbridge
A28
3 miles
A21
Battle

KEY

▬ Walk follows paved road

= Walk follows dirt road or footpath

▬ Paved road

--- Dirt road or footpath

🏘 Town or village

🌲 Wooded area

▼

century has been discovered. The oldest parts of the present church are its 13th-century clerestory lancets, while the west tower dates from the 14th century. The glory of St. Nicholas Church is the 15th-century St. Michael window, radiant in gold and blue glass, depicting St. Michael choosing between a Christian and the Devil.

GETTING THERE
By car:

From London (50 miles away), take *M25* south to Junction 5. Follow *A21* south past Sevenoaks, Tonbridge, and Tunbridge Wells. Take *A268* east past Hawkhurst. Just before you reach Sandhurst, turn right, following signs to Bodiam and then Bodiam Castle. Pass the castle parking lot and go over a bridge. Just after the bridge, pull over at a roadside parking area on your left.

Walk Directions

TIME: 2 to 3 hours
LEVEL: Easy to moderate
DISTANCE: 4 to 5 miles
ACCESS: By car

This walk takes you in a loop around the countryside, beginning and ending outside Bodiam Castle. The walk begins on pavement and then follows dirt paths. There are a few stiles to cross but no difficult inclines. If you want to abbreviate the walk and complete it in about two hours, follow Points 1 through 4, enjoy the beautiful view, and retrace your steps to the parking lot. Set up a picnic on the land surrounding St. Nicholas Church or anywhere from Points 6 through 12. Picnic provisions are very limited in Bodiam, so stop in Sandhurst or another town nearby.

▼

TO BEGIN

Walk back over the bridge you crossed just before parking, with Bodiam Castle nestled in the trees to your right. Pass the castle parking lot. At Knollys Tea Room, cross the paved road in front of it and proceed a few steps.

1. Turn right between hedges, just before a low brick wall on the right. Follow a paved path up an incline until you emerge at the same road. Ignore a path to your left and follow the road uphill to an intersection. Make a right and proceed up the paved road.

2. Make another right at a sign for a church (St. Giles'). Then take the first left down a paved path (there will be a wooden fence to your right). *Go through the gates into the churchyard and follow the path as it circles behind St. Giles' Church.*

3. Turn left through a gap in a fence. Proceed down steps and then a path to the paved road. *Continue straight, past cottages, Kitchenham Farm, and the Mill House, Bodiam's old mill, standing with its broken waterwheel beside the Kent Ditch. Here you cross an ancient county boundary between Sussex and Kent. The Romans crossed the Kent Ditch, and for the next quarter mile you will follow the line of the old Roman road north from their vital Sussex ironworks.* Follow the paved road up a hill until you pass a Sandhurst sign and a telephone booth on your left.

4. Turn right at a signpost for Sandhurst's medieval St. Nicholas Church. Continue on the paved road until you reach an intersection.

5. Bear right to reach the church. *There are magnificent views of the countryside from here.* Go back to the intersection in front of the church and turn right. Go down a paved lane (there's a sign that says "Private," but you are allowed to walk down). Continue down the lane (with a barbed-wire fence to your right) as it curves to the right.

▼

6. At a stone "Public Foot Path" marker (on your left next to a tree), turn left. Cross a field. Continue straight, ignoring paths that cross diagonally. Head toward a fence (again ignoring the last diagonal path) and cross a stile. Walk along the path through the next field, aiming straight for a power-line tower.

7. Cross a stile to the left of a thick old tree trunk. Continue straight across the next field. Cross another stile into the woodland and follow the path through the trees. The path turns to your right and then there's a stile on your left. Cross the stile and follow the path across a field and toward the trees.

8. Go through a gate onto a dirt road and make a right turn. Follow the dirt road down to the right of a barn and then bear right at an intersection before a farmhouse. Pass two metal gates to your right and continue on the dirt road as it circles around a pond on your left. Continue alongside the barbed-wire fence on your right until the fence ends.

9. Cross a stile. Head down the field, alongside a hedge line to your left. Pass a power-line tower and go through a gate. Walk down the field, keeping the treeline to your left, and head toward a footbridge (to your right) at the bottom of the field.

10. Cross the bridge over the drainage channel. With the channel to your right, head straight for a squat brick square of the Kent Ditch pumping station. Follow a path and turn right over the drainage channel. Turn left at a footbridge and go over the Kent Ditch. Make a right turn and then a quick left onto a wide pathway that leads across a field. *When Bodiam Castle was built, this field was a marsh that was an arm of the sea.* Follow the path.

11. Pass a small house. Bodiam Castle hovers ahead. *To your right, about 200 yards past the small house, is a World War II pillbox standing vine-covered between the trees in what were once the Rother marshes.* At an intersection just past the pillbox, continue straight toward the castle

▼

(ignoring the path to your right).

12. Go through a wooden gate adjacent to the castle. Follow the path around the castle. There's another pillbox straight ahead, where two paths meet. Take the path on your left and follow it as it circles a field. Go through a gate into a parking lot and proceed to the road you drove in on. Turn left and walk over the bridge to your car.

PLACES ALONG THE WALK
■ **Bodiam Castle.** *Open daily 10-6, or 10-sunset when the sun sets earlier than 6. Closed Sun. Nov.-Mar. and Dec. 25-29. Admission.*

OTHER PLACES NEARBY
■ **Kent and East Sussex Railway.** This steam railway runs for seven miles from Tenterden to Northiam. Stations have been restored to reflect the character of a bygone era. *5 mi. east of Bodiam in Northiam, tel. 0580-65155. Trains run daily Jun.-Sep.; Sun. only Jan.-Mar.; Sat. and Sun. only Apr., May, Oct., Nov. Admission.*

■ **Northiam.** In this attractive village with a wide green, Queen Elizabeth I stopped for a feast in 1573. The house in which the food was prepared still stands, and the village government still owns the green high-heeled shoes the Queen left behind. *5 mi. east of Bodiam on A28.*

■ **Battle.** William the Conqueror won the decisive Battle of Hastings here in 1066. Stop at the Battle Abbey, a ruined Benedictine abbey built by William to commemorate his conquest. The ruins include a princely gatehouse, abbot's lodgings, and guest quarters that overlook the battlefield. *7 mi. southwest of Bodiam off A21.*

■ **Bateman's.** Rudyard Kipling spent the last three decades of his life inside this stone house, built in 1634 by a wealthy ironmaster. Kipling wrote *Puck of Pook's Hill* here—the hill can be seen outside the windows. Inside, his walnut writing chair and the 16th- and 17th-century oak furniture make it look as if he never left. *8 mi. west of Bodiam off A265 in Burwash, tel. 0435-882302. Open Sat.-Wed. Apr.-Oct., Good Friday 11-5:30. Admission.*

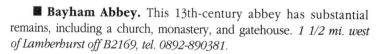

■ **Bayham Abbey.** This 13th-century abbey has substantial remains, including a church, monastery, and gatehouse. *1 1/2 mi. west of Lamberhurst off B2169, tel. 0892-890381.*

DINING

Both Bodiam and Sandhurst lack top restaurants, so you may want to hold your appetite until you reach London. Or, you can detour off *A21* on your way back to London and stop at Royal Tunbridge Wells, 17 miles northwest of Bodiam.

■ **Thackeray's House** (expensive). This mid-17th-century building was once the residence of Victorian novelist William Makepeace Thackeray. Skillful chef-owner Bruce Wass turns out winner after winner. Beneath the restaurant is a less formal small bistro, **Downstairs at Thackeray's.** It's less expensive and just as good. *85 London Rd., Royal Tunbridge Wells, tel. 0892-511921. Closed Dec. 24-30.*

■ **Knollys Tea Room** (inexpensive). This comfortable castle-side establishment makes a convenient stop for lunchtime snacks, desserts, and tea. *Main St., Bodiam, tel. 0580-830323. Open for morning coffee, lunch, and tea Tues.-Sun. 10:30-5:30 Easter to mid-Oct.*

LODGING

There are no unique lodging facilities in Bodiam or Sandhurst, but there are two excellent places to stay within 20 miles. London offers the best and the widest range of accommodations for all budgets.

■ **Spa Hotel** (expensive). This 76-bedroom Georgian mansion provides excellent views of the town and the forests of Kent. Facilities include an indoor pool, sauna, and jogging track. *17 mi. northwest of Bodiam, Mt. Ephraim, Royal Tunbridge Wells TN4 8XJ, tel. 0892-520331, fax 0892-510575.*

■ **Crit Hall** (moderate). This late-Georgian country house is one of the nicest bed and breakfasts in southeastern England. All three bedrooms have superb views of the Kent countryside; the Peach Room has the largest bathroom. A four-course dinner is available on request, and there is a licensed bar. *6 mi. northeast of Bodiam, Cranbrook Rd., Benenden, tel. 0580-240609, fax 0580-241743.*

▼

FOR MORE INFORMATION

Tourist Offices:

Tonbridge Castle, Castle St., Tonbridge TN9 1BG, tel. 0732-770929.

Monson House, Monson Way, Royal Tunbridge Wells TN1 1LQ, tel. 0892-515675.

For Serious Walkers:

The above walk can be found in Ordnance Survey Pathfinder Sheets TQ 62/72 (Map 1270) and TQ 82/92 (Map 1271).

The Home of Anne Boleyn

EXPERIENCE 2: HEVER

Although the London metropolis lies just a few miles away, Hever (pronounced *"Heever"*) seems like a tiny, remote kingdom hidden in the countryside. Few cars navigate the narrow roads that weave around the surrounding open fields and woodland, and the houses nestle privately, spread out among the trees. The peaceful village is actually quieter today than it was for many centuries—years when the town bustled with the activity generated by **Hever Castle,** childhood home of Anne Boleyn.

> **The Highlights:** The castle where Henry VIII courted Anne Boleyn, peaceful woodlands, a 14th-century church in a secluded village.
>
> **Other Places Nearby:** Winston Churchill's home, Chartwell; Knole, a manor house dating to the 1340s; Penshurst, a picturesque hamlet with old timber houses and a castle.

The site of the castle dates to 1200 when a Norman family named De Hever settled here. The family lived in a fortified farmhouse surrounded by a moat, with a wooden drawbridge providing access. The oldest parts that you can still see today—the gate house and the outer walls—date to 1270, when battlements were added. A couple of centuries later, in 1462, Sir Geoffrey Bullen, Anne Boleyn's great-grandfather and a former Lord Mayor of London, erected a house within the walls.

▼

It's not known where Anne Boleyn was born, but she spent much of her early years at Hever Castle. Inside the fortress you can see the bedroom she shared with her sister and her governess. In the Long Gallery, take a look at the exhibition devoted to her.

Although Anne's name became forever entwined with Henry VIII's, the king at first fancied her sister, Mary, whom he courted at Hever Castle. Mary became one of his many mistresses. In 1514, however, Anne returned from France after serving as a bridal attendant for the king's sister, who married King Louis XII, and Henry's roving eye turned to Anne. She was not known for her beauty but had extraordinary black eyes and a lively wit. She was bent on becoming the queen, however, not just the latest mistress, and the king assiduously courted her for six years, at Hever Castle and in London.

After she became pregnant, Henry, hoping ardently for a son to succeed him on the throne, finally married Anne in 1533. This was no small event, for he had to break England's ties to the Catholic Church so he could divorce his first wife, Catherine. But the baby was born a girl—the future Queen Elizabeth I—and Anne's grip on the disappointed king began to loosen. Accusing her of adultery with four men—which may or may not have been true—he had Anne beheaded on the Tower Green on May 19, 1536. (The king didn't personally witness the execution but stood atop a hill in what is now Richmond Park waiting for a flare signalling a successful execution. You can visit that same hill in Richmond today—*see* Experience 4). Henry VIII also accused Anne's brother of adultery with his sister and executed him, too.

In 1538, their father, Thomas, died and was given a quiet burial in nearby **St. Peter's Church,** built in the 14th century. A magnificent brass memorial tablet in the church signifies him as a Knight of the Garter.

After Sir Thomas's death, the Crown expediently grabbed possession of Hever Castle, and Henry gave it to his fourth wife, Anne of Cleves, as part of a divorce settlement in 1540. Two families owned the fortress during most of the next two centuries, and smugglers later used it as a safe house when they came north from the English Channel

▼

coastline. At the end of the 19th century, farmers stored grain and tools inside, and their animals wandered within. In 1903, American millionaire William Waldorf Astor, who served as U.S. ambassador to Italy, bought the neglected castle and spent large sums to restore it. He installed plaster ceilings and brought in master craftsmen for wood paneling and oak, teak, and walnut decoration; radiators and light switches were hidden behind the paneling.

Astor also had the castle grounds—once a mixture of meadows, orchard, and marsh—turned into beautiful gardens. The main attraction is the formal Italian garden, with a maze, columns, statues, vases, and sculpted fountains. More than 800 workers spent almost two years digging a huge lake at the back of the garden. Behind the castle, Astor built for guests a Tudor-style "village of cottages," which was actually a huge country house linked to the fortress by a bridge over the moat. The Astor family resided at Hever Castle for 80 years.

The grounds and the castle have been the setting for various TV shows and films, including *Anne of 1,000 Days, Lady Jane,* and *King Ralph.* On a rainy Sunday morning in 1967, a BBC television crew filmed a reenactment of the Earl of Leicester proposing to Queen Elizabeth I on its grounds. Twenty years later the BBC returned for a very different kind of news event: hurricane-force winds devastated the castle grounds destroying 150 trees.

A miniature course in English history could be drawn from other sights in the area: **Penshurst Place,** a 14th-century manor house; 15th-century **Knole,** a huge country house; 18th-century **Chiddingstone Castle;** the elegant 18th-century spa town **Royal Tunbridge Wells;** and **Chartwell,** the Victorian country house where Winston Churchill lived from 1922 to 1965.

GETTING THERE

By car:

From central London (35 miles away), take *A23* south to *M25* east. Get off *M25* at Exit 6. Follow *A22* south for just over a mile to *A25* east. Proceed on *A25* east through Oxted and Limpsfield to *B269.* Take *B269* to Crockham Hill where you connect to *B2026,* following signs to

Edenbridge. Go through Edenbridge and turn left onto a minor road signposted to Hever. The road leads to Hever where you turn left onto Hever Road. Follow signs to the railroad station.

By train:

From London's Victoria Station, take a train bound for East Grinstead. At Oxted, change for the train bound for Uckfield. Get off at Hever station. The trip takes one hour. There is no service to Hever on Sundays in winter.

Walk Directions

TIME: 1 1/2 hours

LEVEL: Easy

DISTANCE: 3 miles

ACCESS: By car and train

This walking tour makes a loop that begins and ends at the Hever train station. You walk through fields and woodlands on paved roads, dirt paths, and grass; thorn bushes and thistle at the beginning of the walk pose the only difficulty. Set up a picnic in the fields just beyond Point 7. Buy picnic provisions in London or any village outside of Hever.

TO BEGIN

With your back to the railroad station, walk up the only paved road leading away from the station.

1. At the next intersection, turn right, ignoring the sign pointing to Hever Castle. After about 50 yards, go over a stile that's alongside a wooden gate to your left. A sign will indicate "Public Footpath to Hever;" walk on this path. **Step carefully—a multitude of thorn bushes and thistle crowd the path.** When you have navigat-

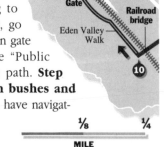

1/8   1/4

MILE

ed past the overgrown plants, continue on through a small patch of woodland.

2. When you emerge in a pasture, turn right. Walk (there will be hedges on your right) toward a black-and-white farmhouse directly ahead. Cross a stile over a hedge, turn left, and follow a foot-

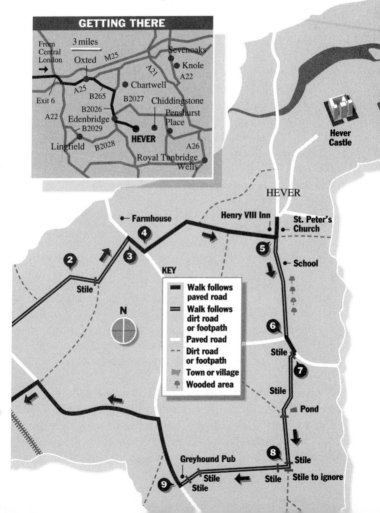

▼

path (with hedges on your left and a barbed-wire fence on your right) toward a road.

3. At the road, you may wish to go several steps to the left to look at a picturesque farmhouse. Otherwise, turn right and walk on the road.

4. When you reach the next junction, turn left onto a paved road, following the direction indicated by a sign for Hever Castle. Follow the road past the *King Henry VIII Inn* (on your left).

5. Just past the inn, at the next intersection, turn left onto a road. On your right is *St. Peter's Church, a 14th-century church that houses the tomb of Sir Thomas Bullen, grandfather of Queen Elizabeth I*. Several yards farther ahead on the right is *Hever Castle*. After exploring the castle, follow the same road back toward King Henry VIII Inn (on your right). Continue on the road straight through the intersection and pass a red post office box on your right. Pass a "No Horse Riding" sign on the right and then a school on your left. Continue straight on a dirt footpath that's to the right of a wooden fence.

6. When the dirt path meets a paved lane, turn left onto the lane. Walk about 40 yards.

7. Just before a telephone pole on your right, turn right. Proceed several steps and cross a stile into a field. Turn left, keeping the hedges and trees to your left, and walk to the left-hand corner of the field, where you cross another stile (a pond will be hidden in the trees to your left). Go straight ahead across the next field and cross a third stile. Two steps in front of you is a fourth stile—**do not cross it.**

8. Instead, turn right onto a path. Follow the path, keeping the barbed-wire fence to your left and hedges to your right. Cross the next stile and walk alongside a barbed-wire fence on your right until you reach yet another stile. Cross the stile and continue on the path (there's a barbed-wire fence to your left, hedges and a barbed-wire fence to

▼

your right). Cross another stile onto the grounds of the *Greyhound Pub, a good place to mingle with the locals.* Proceed toward a paved road that passes in front of the pub.

9. At the paved road, turn right. Go down the paved road. At the next intersection, turn left and go down another paved road. At the next junction, turn left onto another paved road, following the direction indicated by a sign for Cowden and Hartfield. Stay on the road as it crosses a railroad bridge.

10. Just past the bridge, turn right onto a dirt path called *Eden Valley Walk.* Continue on as the dirt path becomes a grass path. Go through a gate and follow a path to the right (a wooden fence stands to the right of the path). This path leads directly to the platform of the Hever train station. If you drove to the parking area next to the station, cross a bridge over the railroad tracks to return to your car.

PLACES ALONG THE WALK
■ **Hever Castle.** *Tel. 0732-865224, fax 0732-866796. Open daily 12-6 (enter by 5) Easter-second week of Nov.; gardens open 11-6. Admission.*

OTHER PLACES NEARBY
■ **Chartwell.** Winston Churchill lived in this Victorian country house from 1922 until his death 43 years later. No architectural wonder, the house was bought by the British leader because of its setting and fine views of the Kent forest. The library contains his book collection, and the study houses the broad mahogany table where Churchill wrote some of his famous books. You may also want to stop at nearby Westerham, where there is a bronze statue of the renowned statesman. *7 mi. north of Hever off B2026, 2 mi. south of Westerham, tel. 0732-866368. Open Tue.-Thu. 12-5:30; Sat., Sun., and bank holidays 11-5:30. Closed the Tue. after bank holidays and Good Friday. Admission.*
■ **Penshurst Place.** This remarkable manor house was built in the 1340s by Sir John de Pulteney, a mayor of London who was attempting to impress the aristocracy. The house's Great Hall rises 60 feet to the

▼

original roof. There's an interesting tapestry collection and a 16th-century minstrels' gallery. Pulteney wasn't able to spend much time enjoying the opulence—he died of the Black Plague in 1349. The manor house has a restaurant and a toy museum. *5 mi. southeast of Hever off B2027, Penshurst, tel. 0892-870307. Gardens open 11-6 and house 12-5:30 Apr.-Sep.; same hours Sat. and Sun. only Mar. and Oct. Admission.*

■ **Chiddingstone.** Picturesque 16th- and 17th-century timber houses stand in a row facing the church in this enchanting hamlet, a favorite setting for the motion picture industry. In the middle of the row, observe the long house with three overhanging gables. Look across the lake at 18th-century Chiddingstone Castle, a manor house designed to resemble a castle. The house displays a collection of Stuart and Jacobite paintings, Egyptian artwork, a Japanese sword collection, and Elizabethan furniture in the Great Hall. The nearby lake, a favorite spot among local anglers, spawned the biggest bream (a freshwater fish) in British history. *3 mi. east of Hever off B2027. Castle tel.: 0892-870347. Open Wed. 2-5:30 and Sun. 11:30-5:30 Apr., May, Oct.; Tue.-Sat. 2-5:30 and Sun. 11:30-5:30 Jun.-Sep. Admission.*

■ **Royal Tunbridge Wells.** During the reign of Charles I (1625-1649), when Queen Henrietta Maria visited this spa after Prince Charles was born, the court slept in tents because very few houses had been constructed. Today, the atmosphere strongly recalls the 18th century, when the spa was at the height of its elegance and popularity. Walk past the many antiques shops on clay-tiled streets in an area called The Pantiles. Edward VII added the word "Royal" to the town's name in 1909, but many English still use the old name. *10 mi. southeast of Hever on A264.*

■ **Knole.** One of England's biggest private houses, this sprawling 15th-century country palace was expanded by Henry VIII and rebuilt from 1603 to 1608 by Thomas Sackville, Earl of Dorset. Much more recently, it was the childhood home of writer Vita Sackville-West, who always loved its fine gardens. The house is so vast that it contains seven courtyards, 52 staircases, and 365 rooms, corresponding to the days of the week, the weeks of the year, and the days of the year. *14 mi. northeast of Hever off A225, Sevenoaks, tel. 0732-450608. Open Wed.-Sat. and bank holidays 11-5, Sun. 2-5 Apr.-Oct. Admission.*

▼

DINING

Hever offers a few pubs with inexpensive bar food, including two below that you pass on the walking tour. For imaginative meals in all price ranges, dine in nearby London.

■ **King Henry VIII Inn** (inexpensive). During the summer, enjoy a beer or a quick lunch in the pub's large garden, well situated next to a pond. The pub offers traditional bar food as well as steak, duck, and various casseroles. Pictures of Henry VIII and Anne Boleyn and copies of the letters they wrote to one another hang on the walls. Look for the Old Henry Castle Bitter, a brew made specially for the pub. *Hever Rd., Hever, tel. 0732-862163. Lunch daily; dinner Tue.-Sat.*

■ **Greyhound Pub** (inexpensive). You only find locals in this 200-year-old oak-beam country pub with a large garden in the back. The kitchen cooks traditional pub food like steak-and-Guinness pie and often supplements the menu with fresh fish, including salmon, plaice (flounder), and oysters. A variety of hand-drawn beers are available, including Harveys Best Bitter and Shepherd Neame Master Brew. *Uckfield Lane, Hever, tel. 0732-862221.*

LODGING

There are few choices in the Hever area; London offers the best and widest range of accommodations.

FOR MORE INFORMATION

Tourist Office:

The Old Brew House, Warwick Park, Royal Tunbridge Wells TN2 5TU, tel. 0892-540766, fax 0892-511008.

For Serious Walkers:

Use Ordnance Survey Pathfinder Map 1228 (TQ 44/54) to extend the walk south from the Greyhound Pub (*see* Point 8, above) to the village of Cowden. You can catch a train back to London from Cowden station, located northeast of the village.

Inside the Royal Hunting Grounds

EXPERIENCE 3: WOODSTOCK

Tourists flock to the old town of Woodstock for one reason: regal **Blenheim Palace,** the grand country mansion where Sir Winston Churchill was born. But they usually miss the magic of another place that's right before their eyes— gigantic **Blenheim Park,** which takes you away from the lines at the palace and lets you unwind at your own pace on thousands of acres of land laced with hidden trails and dotted with grazing sheep.

The Highlights: An ancient town on the edge of the Cotswolds; a large, peaceful park with an old Roman road and one of the country's most beautiful palaces; unique local pubs.

Other Places Nearby: Numerous beautiful Cotswold villages, Sir Winston Churchill's birthplace, a historic home with ornamental gardens, the university city of Oxford.

As you stroll through the landscaped park, you have several excellent views of the palace, the largest home in all of Britain. In 1704, the 2,100 acres on which the palace was built were given by Queen Anne to John Churchill, the Duke of Marlborough, as a reward for defeating the French at the Battle of Blenheim. Construction began the next year and was completed after the duke's death in 1722, at a cost of 300,000 pounds. The palace is now the home of the Eleventh Duke of Marlborough. Sir Winston Churchill, whose father was the younger

▼

brother of an earlier duke, was born in one of the palace bedrooms in 1874. When he died, in 1965, he was buried nearby in a quiet churchyard in **Bladon.**

While Blenheim Palace is an 18th-century creation, the walking tour outlined below will give you a glimpse of many more centuries of history lived on this tract of land. An old **Roman road** still runs through the fields in the park, past an odd group of trees called The Big Clump. Excavations nearby have uncovered the remains of several Roman villas, or country homes, which were burned and pillaged (and their inhabitants massacred) when the Saxons invaded in the 5th century.

Centuries later, this land was known as The Park, or Chase, of Woodstock, and was used by British royalty as a hunting ground. In the early 12th century, Henry I, the third Norman king and youngest son of William the Conqueror, walled off seven square miles of park land, stocking it with exotic animals—camels, lions, leopards, porcupines, and other creatures. He also built a royal home called the Manor House on a site across the lake from where the palace stands today.

His grandson, King Henry II, also an avid hunter, lived at the Manor House as well. Although Henry II went down in history as a great medieval ruler, his home life was madness. His wife, Eleanor of Aquitaine, was 13 years older than he and had previously been divorced from the King of France. Devious and cruel, Queen Eleanor plotted to overthrow Henry, prodding their sons to rebel against their father. He imprisoned her for 16 years and placed his mistress, Rosamond Clifford, in a house he built for her just outside the Manor House walls. After Eleanor was freed, some historians believe she put poison in a cup of wine and killed Rosamond.

In the late 15th century, the somewhat rundown Manor House was extensively rebuilt under the direction of Henry VII, who ruled from 1485 to 1509. One year he spent a colossal sum—845 pounds—on renovations. His son, Henry VIII, benefitted most from the improvements, using the house as a base for all kinds of outdoor sports, including hunting, archery, jousting, and tennis. He also conducted some business

▼

there, issuing an order that the University of Oxford, only a few miles to the southeast, include study of the Bible in Greek in its curriculum. His elder daughter, Mary Tudor, who ruled from 1553 to 1558, imprisoned her sister Elizabeth at the Manor House for plotting to overthrow her.

During the British Civil War in the next century, the Manor House was attacked and suffered severe damage. In 1710, the Duchess of Marlborough ordered it torn down after a disagreement with John Vanbrugh, her architect, who wanted to preserve the historic park-side palace and hunting lodge. Vanbrugh and another architect, Nicholas Hawksmoor, were already building the much grander Blenheim Palace, which would supersede the Manor House.

In the 1760s, renowned landscaper Capability Brown converted a small stream into a lake spreading out before the palace gates and then landscaped the surrounding lands and gardens that you see today. It's a prototypically English landscape design, striving to look like rolling countryside, unlike the formal gardens of French and Italian parks. Dominating the park's landscape is a 134-foot-high statue, the **Column of Victory,** built in 1730 to commemorate the Duke of Marlborough's victorious battles against the French.

The town of Woodstock, which lies right outside the park walls, makes a pleasant place to stroll around. The predominant building material is a soft golden stone similar to that used in many of the charming villages scattered throughout the nearby **Cotswold hills.** Blenheim Palace is also built of this golden stone, though the effect is decidedly different when displayed in a huge Italianate palace.

Woodstock has several interesting shops and pubs, one of them being the **Black Prince Pub.** This unique local hangout began as a malt house in the late 15th century and has been a pub for 350 years; the original fireplace and walls still stand. The pub is named after the Prince of Wales, the eldest son of King Edward I, who was born at Woodstock; he was dubbed "the Black Prince" because of the black armor he wore. The pub had fallen into disrepair until it was bought by an American trumpet player, Larry O'Brian, who played with Frank Sinatra, among other musicians. O'Brian, who owned the pub until 1986, not only sank a lot of money into renovations but also introduced a novel concept for a British pub: Mexican food. The tradition continues today, and the food is actually quite good.

GETTING THERE
By car:
From London (67 miles away), take *M40* west past Beaconsfield and High Wycombe to Exit 8. Connect to *A40* west toward Wheatley. Continue on *A40* through Wheatley to Woodstock. Follow signs for the tourist information office and the public parking lot. They're located on *Hensington Road*.

From Oxford (eight miles away), take *A40* west or *A34* north to *A44* north. *A44* runs into Woodstock; follow signs for the tourist information office and the public parking lot on *Hensington Road*.

Walk Directions

TIME: 1 1/2 to 3 1/2 hours
LEVEL: Easy to moderate
DISTANCE: 2 1/2 to 6 1/2 miles
ACCESS: By car

This walk through Blenheim Park traverses mostly flat land on paved roads and dirt paths. The only challenge is its length and the two low fences you must step or climb over. If you want to shorten the walk to an hour and a half and eliminate the fences, follow the directions below to the paved path just beyond Point 4. Then walk to the body of water adjacent to the path, called the Queen Pool. Walk in either direction completely around the pool—you'll cross over Grand Bridge outside Blenheim Palace—and retrace your steps to your car. Picnic next to the pool or anywhere inside the park. Pick up provisions at the many shops in the heart of Woodstock.

TO BEGIN
From the parking lot, walk to the left of the toilets and past telephones to a paved road, *Hensington Road*. Turn right and walk alongside the road.

▼

1. Make the next right onto *Union Street*. Follow the street until it ends at an intersection and then turn left onto another street. When you reach a fork in the road, take the lower road to the right. Then walk straight toward a main road, *A44*.

2. Turn right onto *A44*. Walk along this road as it passes the *Black Prince Pub* and crosses a bridge over a river. Cross to the other side of the road and continue on for about 50 yards, passing a picket fence on your left in front of house number 7. Pass a driveway and turn left up the stone steps. Turn right and walk on the pavement with the houses on your left and the main road on your right.

Cattle crossing

Wooden gates

6

Roman road

7

The Big Clump

KEY

- ▬▬ Walk follows paved road
- ══ Walk follows dirt road or footpath
- ── Paved road
- --- Dirt road or footpath
- 🏠 Town or village
- 🌲 Wooded area

8

Wooden gate

Fence and signpost

Tree clump

9

10

Tree clump

N

Farm

Wooden fence and stile

11

GETTING THERE

WOODSTOCK

A495

3 miles

Bladon

A44

A40

From London via M40 through Beaconsfield and High Wycombe

A44

A40

Oxford

▼

3. Just after you pass the row of houses, turn left onto a paved driveway. Walk to the right of a garage door and go through a wooden gate. *You are now in Blenheim Park.* Proceed on a dirt path toward another dirt path.

4. At the intersection of the two paths, turn left. Follow the path as it circles downhill and joins a paved path. Make a right onto the paved path. *The body of water to your left is the Queen Pool.* Proceed on the paved path. Ignore a paved driveway heading to a house on your left and ignore the next paved turnoff to the left.

5. At the next intersection of two paved paths, continue straight. Follow this paved path as it curves to the left and then to the right. Head slightly uphill on the path. *Directly behind you is the Column of Victory.* Proceed straight on the path. Walk over a cattle crossing and continue on.

▼

6. Just before the next cattle crossing, turn left onto the grass. Walk toward wooden gates. Go through the gates and continue straight, with trees on your right and a big clump of trees across a field to your left. Continue straight past the big clump of trees.

7. When you reach a wide dirt track a few hundred yards before a tree line, turn left onto the track. Follow the track through another tree line toward a wooden gate. **Don't go through the gate—it's private property.**

8. Instead, turn left at the gate and step carefully over a fence. Take three steps forward and turn right. Climb carefully over another low fence into a field with two clumps of trees. Continue straight across the field, walking to the left of the clump of trees that's on your right.

9. When you reach the clump of trees, turn left. Walk straight toward a monument (the Column of Victory) in the distance. When you reach a fence, step over it at a signpost.

10. On the other side of the fence, turn right. Walk alongside the fence and to the left of another clump of trees. When the fence ends, continue straight to a wood fence just outside a farm. Climb over a stile, bear left, and walk on a paved road.

11. At the next intersection of paved roads, turn left and follow the paved road. Ignore a paved road to the right. Continue on as the road winds to the left. Ahead, in the distance and to your left, is the Column of Victory.

12. Immediately after the paved road passes the Column of Victory (to your left), turn right onto a grass path between the trees (a small white auto-speed marker should be on your right just beyond the turn). Follow dirt tracks through a ditch between two embankments.

13. When you arrive at a dirt path in front of trees that line a bank, turn left onto the dirt path. Follow the path as it winds to the right around a lake. Continue on the path as it winds uphill to the left. *To*

▼

your right, across the water, is Grand Bridge. Farther on, you'll see Blenheim Palace across the water to the right.

14. When you reach a paved path, turn right. Follow the path across the Grand Bridge toward the gates of Blenheim Palace.

15. At the gates, turn left. Follow the paved road that circles to the left of the palace. *This road leads you to the visitors' entrance.*

16. At the next intersection of paved roads, turn left onto the paved road leading away from the palace. At the next intersection of paved roads, turn left onto a paved road that will take you to the Triumphal Arch. Follow the paved road as it bears left around the arch. Proceed on the paved road as it crosses a small bridge. Continue until you reach a dirt path on your right. Make a right onto the dirt path—the same one you walked on in Point 4—and retrace your steps to the car.

PLACES ALONG THE WALK

■ **Blenheim Palace.** *Tel. 0993-811325. Open daily 10:30-4:45 mid-Mar.-Oct. Admission.*

OTHER PLACES NEARBY

■ **Bladon.** Sir Winston Churchill's grave lies in a churchyard southeast of Blenheim Park. *1 mi. south of Woodstock on A4095.*

■ **The Cotswolds.** In this popular region of high treeless hills crisscrossed by stone walls, take your pick from among several charming villages, including Lower Slaughter, Chipping Campden, and Bibury. Experience 6 (Wyck Rissington) is also in the Cotswolds. *West of Woodstock, alongside or off A44, A424, and A429.*

■ **Oxford.** Although it's hardly pastoral—with auto and pedestrian traffic, heavy industry, and too many modern buildings—this university city offers a treasure chest of architectural and historical wonders. *9 mi. southeast of Woodstock on A44.*

■ **Minster Lovell.** A tiny, scenic Cotswolds town on the river Windrush is the site of a ruined moated manor house, Minster Lovell

▼

Hall. In 1487, Lord Francis Lovell hid in the manor house after rebelling against the king. His servant was the only one who knew his hiding place in an underground vault and, in a Hitchcockian twist, the servant died, leaving the lord to starve to death. *12 mi. southwest of Woodstock on A40 or B4047.*

■ **Rousham House.** This historic home with a 20-acre ornamental garden was built in 1635. It was renovated a century later by William Kent, the father of English landscape gardening, who designed the house's magnificent walled garden. *6 mi. northeast of Woodstock off A4260; 1 mi. south of Steeple Aston, Rousham, tel. 0869-47110. Gardens open daily 10-4:30; house open Wed., Sun., and bank holidays 2-4:30 Apr.-Sep. Admission.*

DINING

Excellent food is not far away, at hundreds of top restaurants in London and Oxford (*see* also Experience 6, Wyck Rissington). But if you insist on eating in Woodstock itself, you won't do badly either.

■ **The Feathers Hotel & Restaurant** (expensive). Head chef David Lewis changes the lunch and dinner menus daily at the dining room of this 17th-century Woodstock hotel. Recent appetizers included the warm wild boar and ewe's cheese with pesto and the char-grilled locally smoked salmon with sweet peppers and lime. Entrées were more subdued: loin of Cotswolds lamb with rosemary and olive oil and fillet of Angus beef with roasted shallots and tarragon. If they're on the dessert menu, don't miss the honey marshmallow with apricots and toasted almonds or the crème caramel with summer berries and eau de vie. Try the courtyard bar and garden for a light lunch or a cocktail. *Market St., Woodstock OX20 1SX, tel. 0993-812291, fax 0993-813158.*

■ **Vickers Hotel & Restaurant** (expensive). For centuries, exquisite steel jewelry was made from horseshoe nails in this stone building. Now the finest creations are coming out of a kitchen specializing in flambés and fresh pastries. A picture of Margaret Thatcher, who once ate dinner here, graces one wall. *7 Market Pl., Woodstock OX7 1SY, tel. 0993-811212, fax 0993-811030.*

■ **Black Prince Pub** (inexpensive-moderate). A pub for 350 years, this 15th-century malt house is quite a departure from traditional

English pubs: It serves Mexican food, and it's surprisingly good. The refried beans are nothing to rave about, but the steak in the beef burritos is excellent—and oh, those glorious, wicked jalapenos imported from Mexico! Margaritas are available, but believe it or not, a burrito and a pint of bitters seem to go well together. *Manor Rd., Woodstock, tel. 0993-891530.*

■ **The Punch Bowl Inn** (inexpensive). This 18th-century pub has a varied menu that includes some Mexican food. It also happens to be an excellent place to hear live music—call to inquire who (and what style of music) is playing. *12 Oxford St., Woodstock, tel. 0993-811218.*

LODGING

Numerous hotels for all budgets are available in London and Oxford. You can also stay at one of the lodgings in Experience 6 (Wyck Rissington) or at the two Woodstock hotels below.

■ **The Feathers Hotel & Restaurant** (very expensive). This classy, small 17th-century hotel made of Cotswold stone sits right in the center of Woodstock. (But don't worry about noise—it's a quiet town.) The recently refurbished guest rooms feature fine curtains and marble bathrooms. *Market St., Woodstock OX20 1SX, tel. 0993-812291, fax 0993-813158.*

■ **Vickers Hotel & Restaurant** (moderate). In the heart of town, this 16th-century building is owned by former pro soccer player Keith Vickers. If you're in the mood for something different—and very private—book the modern, spacious treehouse cottage in the courtyard. Freddie, the hotel's tuxedoed jack-of-all trades, provides fabulous service and pours great ales at the bar or for take-out to your room. *7 Market Pl., Woodstock OX7 1SY, tel. 0993-811212, fax 0993-811030.*

FOR MORE INFORMATION

Tourist Office:

Hensington Rd., Woodstock OX7 1TG, tel. 0993-811038.

For Serious Walkers:

The above walk can be found in Ordnance Survey Pathfinder Sheet SP 41/51 (Map 1092).

▼

On the Banks of the Thames

EXPERIENCE 4: RICHMOND

As you exit the Richmond subway station, you hear a lot of noise and encounter throngs of people scurrying from store to store. Hardly your idea of a short escape, you may hastily conclude—but push on a bit farther. This book's only urban experience provides as many rich rewards as any other destination.

Richmond differs from other London suburbs. Its residents feel that they live in a provincial Southeast London town, not a part of the London metropolis. When other suburbanites head for central London, they talk of

The Highlights: A thriving, fashionable London suburb on the Thames river with lively pubs and excellent shopping; the remains of a royal palace; a former royal hunting ground that's now the London area's largest park.

Other Places Nearby: Central London a subway ride away; Twickenham, a village of mansions on the banks of the Thames; the Royal Botanic Gardens at Kew; Hampton Court, an opulent royal palace.

"going to the West End" or "going to Chelsea," but Richmond residents say they're "going up to London."

Several things explain why they act as if the British capital is a distant place. Unlike in other suburbs, there's room to stretch out in Richmond: parks, open spaces, and the shore of the Thames river. And

▼

it's an attractive city that grew up on its own, rather than owing its existence to the London sprawl.

With its attractive waterfront location, Richmond Palace was the favored home of English kings for many centuries, longer than any other royal residence. The first palace here was built by Edward I in the 13th century and was rebuilt by King Edward III in the next century. When it burned down in 1499, Henry VII, founder of the Tudor dynasty, ordered a new palace built. The name of the town had been Shene, a derivative of an Anglo-Saxon word for "bright" or "beautiful," but Henry VII renamed it Richmond. The town swelled with people whose livelihood depended on the palace, including writers, painters, musicians, and actors seeking royal patronage.

As a result, Richmond earned a bohemian reputation that continues to this day. Mick Jagger and many other artists and celebrities now live here. And one of the first sights on the walk outlined below is **Richmond Theatre,** a Victorian-style theater built in 1899 that often presents major plays before they head for the West End.

Signs of royalty begin to emerge as you stroll away from the theater. The **village green** across the street was laid out in the 13th century by King Edward I as a jousting area where his knights could entertain him and his queen, Eleanor of Castille. From the center of the green, you can see **Maids of Honour Row,** a series of town houses built in 1724 for the Princess of Wales's ladies-in-waiting. To the right of the town houses stands the **gate of Richmond Palace,** where three Tudor monarchs lived: Henry VII, Henry VIII, and Elizabeth I. Henry VII's coat of arms is still displayed on the Gate House. You can walk through the **Old Palace Yard,** though the only part of the palace that still remains is the Wardrobe, where the monarchs stored their clothing and furniture (a luxury housing complex now dominates the palace site).

In nice weather, Richmond residents flock to the Thames's shoreline to watch the boats go by, quaff a pint of beer, and eat a pub lunch. To reach the river and its tiny islands, you walk past a restored 18th-century mansion, **Asgill House,** which was built for London's mayor and can be visited by appointment. The house stands between

▼

Richmond Bridge, built in 1773, and **Twickenham Bridge,** constructed in the 1930s. Proceed to the **White Cross Hotel,** a favorite local hangout and former site of a convent built by Henry VII. Walk up an adjacent cobblestone street to the popular **Waterman's Arms** pub, along what was once Richmond's most important street, linking the palace with the river. Alongside the river you follow a towpath where horses plodded during the 19th century, pulling ropes attached to river barges. Although Richmond's official emblem features a white mute swan, that fowl has been chased away by the Canadian geese and mallard ducks you'll see paddling here today.

Past Richmond Bridge, there's a boat-launching area where in summer you can board a river steamer to London or **Hampton Court.** Near the launching area, the **Terrace Gardens** make an ideal spot for a picnic among numerous species of colorful flowers. Your riverside stroll concludes at **Ham House,** built in 1610 and said to be a perfect example of an English Jacobean house, with rooms full of original furniture and paintings by Van Dyck. The gardens are open, but extensive renovation is expected to keep the house closed until spring 1994. There is a chance it may open sooner, so call the house or the local tourist board for an update.

From Ham House, walk through a quiet little village named Petersham to the gate of 2,500-acre **Richmond Park,** the largest park in the London area. Originally walled off as a hunting ground by Charles I in 1637, the park was closed to the public until the last century. The royal family still owns it. Its inhabitants include large red and smaller roe deer, as well as sheep, rabbits, and many species of birds. Atop a hill in Richmond Park, Henry VIII watched for a rocket that signaled the execution of his second wife, Anne Boleyn, the mother of Elizabeth I. The view of the surrounding area from this hill is fabulous.

An even better view awaits after you exit the park and walk part of the way down *Richmond Hill.* From a bench across the street from the **Roebuck** pub, you savor England's most famous view of the Thames, a sight captured by many painters throughout the centuries. William Byrd, a rich Virginian, came here in the early 18th century and was captivated by the view. When he went back to the colonies, he named a city along the James river after this lovely Thameside town—Richmond, Virginia.

GETTING THERE

Go by Underground (subway) to avoid the traffic congestion and the hassles of finding your way in an automobile.

By subway:

From Victoria Station or many other central London Underground locations, take a District Line train to Richmond, the last stop on the line. A train bound for Richmond will display the city's name on the front of the first car. The trip takes about half an hour.

By car and taxi:

From central London (eight miles away), follow *A4* west past Hammersmith. At the traffic circle just before Chiswick, instead of taking *Hogarth Lane* toward the *M4* motorway, follow *A316,* called *Burlington Lane* (in two blocks it changes names to *Alexandra Avenue,* and after another block becomes *Great Chertsey Road*). This road soon crosses the Thames over the Chiswick Bridge. Go straight for about three miles, crossing one main intersection and passing one roundabout (traffic circle). At the next roundabout, turn left onto *Kew Road,* which almost immediately becomes *The Quadrant.* Park in the multistory parking garage in *The Quadrant* next to the Underground station. With no traffic, the drive takes about 20 minutes. A cab ride will cost you about $30 each way. To begin the walk, proceed to the Underground station entrance in *The Quadrant.*

By riverboat:

Riverboats leave from London's Westminster Pier during the summer months. For information, contact Westminster Passenger Services (0719-302062). If you arrive in Richmond by boat (a 2 1/2- to 3-hour journey each way), start the walk below in the middle of Point 5 (heading for the 3 Pigeons Pub).

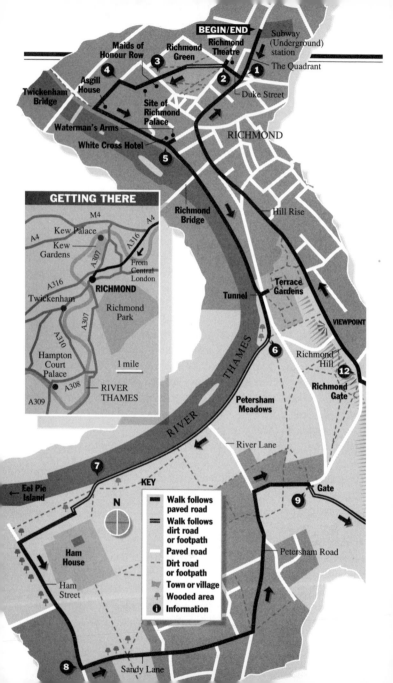

▼

Walk Directions

TIME: 1 to 3 hours

LEVEL: Easy to moderate

DISTANCE: 2 1/2 to 5 miles

ACCESS: By subway, car, taxi, and riverboat

Most of the walk is on sidewalks, paved paths, and level ground. The only challenge is the length of the walk and one hill in Richmond Park. You can shorten this walk to an easy 1- to 1 1/2-hour stroll by walking up through the Terrace Gardens in Point 5 to *Richmond Hill,* a street bordering the gardens. Turn right onto the street and proceed to the benches across from the Roebuck pub for a superb view of the Thames; then, head downhill following directions from Point 12. You can picnic along the Thames, in the gardens, or in Richmond Park. You can pick up picnic provisions at one of the many shops near the Underground station, and there are many pubs and restaurants along the way.

TO BEGIN

Exit the Richmond Underground station and make a left onto *The Quadrant,* a busy commercial street.

1. At the next major intersection, called The Square, make a right onto *Duke Street* (a Jigsaw store is on the corner). At the next street, turn right to visit *Richmond Theatre, a lovely, intimate Victorian theater.* Go back to *Duke Street* and then cross the street at a 45-degree angle to your right to reach Richmond Green.

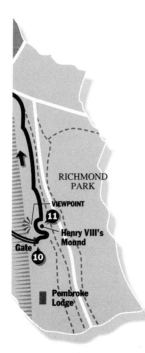

RICHMOND PARK

VIEWPOINT

11

Henry VIII's Mound

Gate

10

Pembroke Lodge

⅛   ¼

MILE

▼

2. Begin walking on the center dirt path that cuts diagonally across the green. Follow a paved path to your left that enables you to exit the green. On your left *across the street is Maids of Honour Row, the town houses built in 1723 to accommodate the Princess of Wales's maidservants*. Cross the street.

3. Walk under the arch of Old Palace Yard. *Richmond Palace was the residence of King Henry VII, King Henry VIII, and Queen Elizabeth I.* Pass the Palace Gate House on your left and then bear to the right down a lane, following a sign for the river.

4. Turn left at a paved road. Proceed to the river. *There's a good view of the Thames and the tiny islands in the middle of the water.* Turn left and immediately pass, on your left, *Asgill House, an 18th-century mansion*. Walk on the paved path along the river (the river is on your right). *Ahead is Richmond Bridge, probably the most frequently painted bridge in England. On your left, you can stop in at the White Cross Hotel and pub.*

5. Make the next left up a historic cobblestoned street, *Water Lane.* Proceed to the *Waterman's Arms, a traditional pub standing on a site that has housed a pub since the 1660s.* Then retrace your steps to the river and turn left at the White Cross Hotel. Go underneath Richmond Bridge and continue on the paved path along the river. Pass the 3 Pigeons Pub and *take a break or picnic on the soft grass to your right just beside the Thames.* About 30 yards past the 3 Pigeons Pub—and a few steps beyond the fat tree on your left—turn left down brick steps and go through a small, grubby tunnel. Walk up the steps on either side and you are now in *Terrace Gardens. The path to your left leads up to the main garden area, a fine picnic spot among the multicolored flowers and the tall trees.* Go back through the tunnel, make a left, and continue along the paved path.

6. When you reach a fence, bear right. Walk on a dirt and gravel road, with the river to your right and Petersham Meadows to your left.

▼

Pass a boat-launching area on your right (ignore a paved road leading away from the river to the left). *Straight ahead across the river is Twickenham, a village known for its mansions.* Continue on, with woodland on your left, until you see a path to the left next to a wooden gate (there will be a green "Ferry Running" sign to the right).

7. Turn left down this path. Bear right through an opening in a wooden fence and follow a grass footpath across a small meadow, ignoring a dirt footpath that runs alongside a fence on your left. Walk up to a paved path and make a right. *Ham House is to your left.* Proceed to a paved road (*Ham Street*) and turn left.

8. At *Sandy Lane* (the Royal Oak Tavern is on the corner), turn left. When you reach a major thoroughfare, *Petersham Road,* make another left. Pass the Fox and Duck pub and the Ham Polo Club. Follow *Petersham Road* as it curves to the right at *River Lane.* Pass the Dysarts pub and cross *Petersham Road.*

9. Walk through an iron gate (just before a stone wall and just before the road goes uphill). *You are now in Richmond Park.* Make a quick left, following a "Pembroke Lodge" signpost, and proceed along a wide, well-worn path up a hill between the trees (ignore a path alongside the red brick wall to your left).

10. Go through a tall metal gate at a "Pembroke Lodge Gardens" sign. Follow a path to your left. Head straight through the trees to the left of a wooden fence (with a sign for Henry VIII's Mound). Bear right up the paved path to the left of the wooden fence. After several yards, make a sharp left (actually a U-turn) onto another paved path. Follow this path several steps toward a sitting area.

11. Atop the peak of the hill, at a sitting area, you will see where *Henry VIII watched for the rocket that announced the execution of Anne Boleyn, his second wife.* Looking down from the sitting area, make a right turn onto the paved path. Follow the path through vine-covered

▼

John Beer Laburnum Walk. Continue straight on the paved path through a metal gate. Continue on this path (the road is on your right) toward Richmond Gate.

12. When you reach the gate, go through it. Cross the road and bear right down the street called *Richmond Hill*. There will be hedges and a fence to your left, houses across the street on your right. *A short distance down the hill, across from the Roebuck pub, is a famous view of the Thames. Grab a pint at the pub and sit on a bench overlooking the river.* Continue down *Richmond Hill,* which turns into *Hill Rise.* Pass a major roundabout (traffic circle) and proceed to *George Street* (a Dickins and Jones store is on the corner). Turn right onto *George Street,* which becomes *The Quadrant.* The Underground station is on your right.

PLACES ALONG THE WALK
■ **Richmond Theatre.** *Open Mon.-Sat. 10-8. Box office tel.: 0819-400088.*
■ **Asgill House.** *Open by appointment only. Contact Mr. F. Hauptfuhrer, Asgill House, Old Palace Lane, Richmond TW9 1PQ.*
■ **Ham House,** *Ham St., Richmond, tel. 0819-401950. Scheduled to reopen spring 1994. Admission; gardens open free of charge during renovation.*

OTHER PLACES NEARBY
■ **Twickenham.** Across the Thames opposite Richmond, this village is known for its many mansions, including 18th-century Marble Hill House, where the mistresses of King George II and King George IV lived. In the summer, Shakespeare's plays are presented on the expansive grounds. *Less than 1 mi. southwest of Richmond across the Richmond Bridge.*
■ **Royal Botanic Gardens.** A feast of floral beauty, more than 60,000 species of plants grow in the gardens and greenhouses. In the Princess of Wales Conservatory, temperatures vary from room to room, allowing plants from jungles, deserts, swamps, and forests to grow. The gardens were founded by Princess Augusta, the widow of Frederick,

▼

Prince of Wales. Opposite the Buckingham Gate, stop at Newins, an inexpensive tearoom offering tasty lunches and tea and scones in a unique setting. *Less than 1 mi. north of Richmond, Kew, tel. 0819-401171. Open daily 9:30-6:30 Apr.-Aug.; 9:30-5:30 in Sep.; 9:30-5 first two weeks of Nov.; 9:30-4 mid-Nov. to Mar. Admission.*

■ **Kew Palace.** The home of King George III, this palace stands on the grounds of the Royal Botanic Gardens. Its formal gardens are a fine example of 17th-century design. *Less than 1 mi. north of Richmond, Kew, tel. 0819-403321. Open daily 11-5:30 Apr.-Sep. Admission.*

■ **Hampton Court Palace.** One of England's most well-known royal homes, this gorgeous 16th-century palace with beautiful gardens is located on rolling parkland alongside the Thames. Built by Cardinal Wolsey, the palace was later the home of King Henry VIII and Anne Boleyn. Elizabeth I supposedly slipped away from Westminster and brought her lovers here. During the summer, you can come here by boat from the launching area next to Richmond Bridge in Richmond. *5 mi. southwest of Richmond, East Molesey, tel. 0819-778441. Royal apartments open Mon. 10:30-6, Tue.-Sun. 9:30-6 Apr.-Sep.; Mon. 10:30-4:30, Tue.-Sun. 9:30-4:30 Oct.-Mar. Grounds open dawn-dusk. Admission.*

DINING

Most travelers will probably eat in London, with its top-notch restaurants, but don't rule out the idea of eating in Richmond—this stylish suburb has a number of fine places to eat.

■ **Petersham Hotel** (very expensive). The hotel's attractive Nightingales Restaurant has a fabulous location, looking out across a bend in the Thames. The imaginative French cuisine served in the large dining room lives up to the elegant setting. *Less than 1 mi. south of Richmond, Nightingale Lane, Petersham, tel. 0819-407471. Closed Christmas Eve, Christmas Day, and Boxing Day.*

■ **Bellini Restaurant** (moderate). Superb Italian food makes this modern bistro a favorite of local resident Mick Jagger and fellow Rolling Stone Ron Wood. Don't miss the homemade gnocci and ravioli or the excellent braciole. It's across the street from the Underground station, a convenient if not scenic location. *12 The Quadrant,*

Richmond, tel. 0819-400138 or 0819-400086.

■ **White Cross Hotel** (inexpensive). In a perfect setting next to the Thames, this old pub offers good buffet lunches and pub dinners. Look for the unusual sight of a fireplace built under a window. Feel free to take a beer outside and sit along the river. In the summer months, there's an outdoor bar as well. Try a Young's Porter or a Beamish Stout. *On the riverside at the corner of Water Lane, Richmond, tel. 0819-406844.*

LODGING

Central London is your best bet for all budgets.

FOR MORE INFORMATION

Tourist Office:

Old Town Hall, Whittaker Ave., Richmond TW9 1TP, tel. 0819-409125, fax 0819-406899.

For Serious Walkers:

The above walk can be found in Ordnance Survey Pathfinder Map 176 or on a much larger scale in A-Z Street Plan Map for Hounslow, Richmond, Feltham, Twickenham (available in Richmond or London shops). The tourist office also sells a Richmond-upon-Thames Official Street Map.

In the Footsteps of Shakespeare

EXPERIENCE 5: WILMCOTE

Each year several hundred thousand tourists invade the beautiful but congested town of Stratford-upon-Avon to see Shakespeare's birthplace and to follow in the footsteps of the great writer. With the next guy's camera clicking and his kids stepping on your toes, it can be difficult to come away with the spirit of the literary giant and his works. This experience lets you escape alone to the lands where Shakespeare himself walked.

The Highlights: Pastureland in which Shakespeare walked, the Tudor farmhouse where his mother was born, a charming village, a hidden canal navigated by pleasure boats.

Other Places Nearby: Stratford-upon-Avon, the birthplace of Shakespeare; Warwick Castle, England's finest medieval castle; Ragley Hall, a stately mansion with lovely gardens; Kenilworth, a fortress that inspired Sir Walter Scott.

You begin a few miles away from Stratford-upon-Avon on the village green at Wilmcote, a pleasant village of timber-framed houses and stone cottages dating to the 1830s. Although Wilmcote sits between two major roads, it's a rural village with few shops and services. It feels very remote, and the only sound you often hear is the wind whistling through the trees.

Near the green, you'll find **Mary Arden's House,** the birthplace and childhood home of Shakespeare's mother, Mary Arden. The picturesque 16th-century Tudor farmhouse in which she lived with her family has been decorated to look as it might have in her day. The large fireplace has one of the biggest ovens in England, and there's a monk's table built in 1480. The house remained a residence until 1930, when it was acquired by the Shakespeare Birthplace Trust. Adjoining the farmhouse is the **Shakespeare Countryside Museum,** which displays rural crafts and, most notably, a 16th-century stone dovecote with nesting places for 650 doves.

From Wilmcote, a short walk will lead you into the former **Forest of Arden,** now a green land of pasture and low-cut meadow with clumps of ancient trees. Sheep and other livestock scurry out of your way as you approach. Shepherds, hunters, and foresters roamed through the Forest of Arden during Shakespeare's youth, and it was incorporated into several of his works—most unforgettably *As You Like It,* in which Orlando and Rosalind find their true love in this pastoral setting. Many trees in the forest disappeared in the 16th century after Queen Elizabeth I ordered them chopped for the building of battleships during Britain's war against Spain.

When you pass through a row of hedges at the end of a field in the former Forest of Arden, the **Stratford-upon-Avon Canal** and the **Draper Bridge** appear like a mirage in front of you. Built between 1802 and 1816, the canal runs for 25 miles between Birmingham and Stratford-upon-Avon. Canal boats carefully negotiate their way on the waterway, so don't be surprised as you walk along the bank if you travel faster than the boats, which must sometimes make several attempts before they can fit snugly under the bridges that cross the narrow canal. Of course, there's no need to hurry. Unlike the tourists who flock to the various Shakespearian properties in the nearby town of Stratford, you can feel the essence of the great writer at your own pace, as you like it.

GETTING THERE
By car:
From Stratford-upon-Avon (3 miles away), take *A3400* north for

▼

about 2 1/2 miles. Turn left onto a minor road signposted to Wilmcote. Park along the main street near the village green.

From Worcester (20 miles away), take *A422* east. Just outside of Alcester, follow *A46* east. Stay on *A46* for about four miles. Make a left on a minor road signposted to Billesley. When you reach the fork in the road at Billesley, take the road to the right, which leads to Wilmcote. Park along the main street near the village green.

By train:

Wilmcote is on the Regional Railways line. From Stratford-upon-Avon, it's a five-minute ride to Wilmcote, one stop away. From Birmingham, the train takes 47 minutes to Wilmcote. From the Wilmcote station, walk to the main road, *Featherbed Lane,* and turn left. Continue on the road to the village green. *For train information, call 0212-002700 or 0216-432711.*

Walk Directions

TIME: 2 hours
LEVEL: Easy to moderate
DISTANCE: 4 miles
ACCESS: By car and train

Beginning and ending near the village green in Wilmcote, this loop winds through the countryside and follows a footpath along a canal. Most of the walk traverses dirt paths and grass fields; there are no inclines. The walk is moderately difficult for inexperienced walkers because there are several stiles to cross, brush conceals ruts in some paths, and there is thistle and an overgrowth of wildflowers for a short stretch. Do not wear shorts because of thorn bushes and thistle.

Enjoy a picnic in the pasturelands or along the Stratford-upon-Avon Canal. Wilmcote has few services, so pick up picnic provisions in one of the many stores in Stratford or another village nearby.

TO BEGIN

Stand on the village green in the middle of Wilmcote and face the Swan House Inn. Turn right, cross the street, and walk along the side-

▼

walk for about 35 yards.

1. Make a right into a driveway across from a post office. Then bear left, keeping a wooden fence to your right.

2. Bear left again through a passageway. Go straight (with a barbed-wire fence to your right and a wooden fence to your left) for about 150 yards.

3. Turn left through a metal gate. Cross over a stile and bear right alongside a wooden fence. Go straight until you reach the driveway of a farm and then proceed straight over a stile. Continue on toward another stile.

4. Cross the stile. Go straight down a long field (with hedges to your left). *You are walking in the former Forest of Arden, where Shakespeare walked as a youth.* Pass a tree line (to your right) and continue through the next field (again with hedges to your left).

5. The next tree line blocks your path, jutting out at a 90-degree angle from the hedges on your left. Go to the left-hand corner, where the tree line and hedges meet, and cross a stile at a yellow trail marker. Continue straight to a row of hedges that blocks your path. Go over another stile at a trail marker. Go straight through high grass (with hedges to your left). **Be sure to step carefully—there are ruts in the path.**

6. At the next row of hedges, cross a stile **watching out for thorn bushes at the stile.** Continue straight through high brush. Cross a stile and go straight toward a metal gate.

7. Pass through the gate, or cross a stile to the right, and immediately turn right onto the dirt tracks. Walk past the houses on your right until you reach an intersection. Make a right and go down a paved road. When the paved road curves sharply to the left, bear right onto a dirt path leading through hedges and a gate (and to the right of a stile).

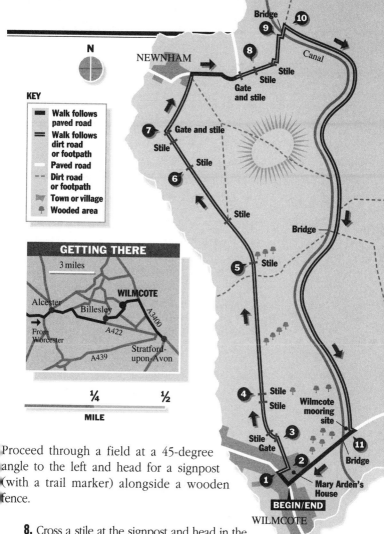

KEY

Walk follows paved road

Walk follows dirt road or footpath

Paved road

Dirt road or footpath

Town or village

Wooded area

NEWNHAM

Bridge

9

10

8

Canal

Stile

Stile

Gate and stile

7 Gate and stile

Stile

Stile

6

Stile

Bridge

5 Stile

GETTING THERE

3 miles

WILMCOTE

Alcester

Billesley

A3400

From Worcester

A422

A439

Stratford-upon-Avon

¼   ½

MILE

4 Stile

Stile

Wilmcote mooring site

3

Stile Gate

2

11

Bridge

1

Proceed through a field at a 45-degree angle to the left and head for a signpost (with a trail marker) alongside a wooden fence.

Mary Arden's House

BEGIN/END

WILMCOTE

8. Cross a stile at the signpost and head in the same direction (diagonally) to the next signpost, which is at the left-hand corner of the next field. Cross another stile and then bear right. Turn right toward a wooden fence and either climb over it or duck under it. Make an immediate left. Continue straight through the next field of high grass (keeping the trees to your left).

9. At the next tree line blocking your path, turn right. Take about 40 steps alongside the tree line. To your left is an opening through hedges. Go through it and proceed a few steps toward the Draper Bridge, which crosses *the Stratford-upon-Avon Canal.*

10. Pass over the bridge and immediately turn right. Head straight along a footpath (with the canal to your right) for 1 3/4 miles. You will pass one bridge; at the next bridge (the Wilmcote mooring site for canal boats), bear left up an embankment toward a paved road.

11. Turn right onto the sidewalk alongside this paved road. Proceed straight on the sidewalk to *Mary Arden's House, the home of Shakespeare's mother.* Visit the house or continue on to the village green, which lies on the left.

PLACES ALONG THE WALK
■ **Mary Arden's House** and **Shakespeare Countryside Museum.** *Open Mon.-Sat. 9:30-5 and Sun. 10:30-5 Mar.-Oct.; Mon.-Sat. 10-4 and Sun. 1:30-4 Nov.-Feb. Closed Dec. 24-26 and in the morning on Good Friday and New Year's. Admission.*
■ **Stratford-upon-Avon Canal.** Canal boats with sleeping quarters and kitchen facilities can be rented from: *Stratford Marina Ltd., The Boatyard, Clopton Bridge, Stratford-upon-Avon CV37 G44, tel. 0789-269669; or Alvechurch Boat Centre, Scarfield Wharf, Alvechurch B48 7SQ, tel. 0214-477120.*

OTHER PLACES NEARBY
■ **St. John Baptist Church.** In 1557, Shakespeare's parents, Mary Arden and John Shakespeare, were married in this church. The chancel dates to the 13th century and some of the glass to the 14th century. Note the old stone sculpture of the Nativity outside the north porch. *Less than 2 mi. northwest of Wilmcote, Aston Cantlow.*
■ **Stratford-upon-Avon.** Tourists swarm this theater town in the summer to visit Shakespeare's birthplace and other attractions related to

the literary giant's life. After you swallow up all the history, head for the beauty of the gardens alongside the river Avon. *4 mi. southeast of Wilmcote on A3400 or A46. Shakespeare's birthplace open Mon.-Sat. 9:30-4 and Sun. 10:30-4 Jan., Feb., Nov., and Dec.; Mon.-Sat. 9:30-5:30 and Sun. 10-5:30 Mar.-Oct. Admission.*

■ **Warwick Castle.** Considered England's finest medieval castle, this fortress built on a small escarpment rises nobly above the river Avon. Most of the exterior, including two extraordinary towers, dates to the 14th century. Step inside the dark dungeon and the grisly torture chamber, and leave enough time to study the large collection of paintings and possessions in the Armoury and State rooms. *9 mi. northeast of Wilmcote, Warwick, tel. 0926-495421. Open 10-5:30 Mar.-Oct. and 10-4:30 Nov.-Feb. Closed Christmas Day. Admission.*

■ **Ragley Hall.** A stately home of the Earl and Countess of Yarmouth, Ragley Hall was built in 1680 on 27 acres of land. Decorated with baroque plasterwork, it contains a huge Great Hall and a modern mural, *The Temptation.* There's a formal rose garden, and the surrounding parkland has a lake. *4 mi. west of Wilmcote, Alcester, tel. 0789-762090 (0839-222007 for recorded information). Open mid-Apr.-last week of Sep. Closed Mon. and Fri. except bank holiday Mondays. Admission.*

■ **Chipping Campden.** With stone houses of various styles lining its curving main street, this may be the most attractive town in the Cotswolds. Notable structures include the 15th-century St. James Church and the 14th-century Woolstaplers Hall, which houses a museum and a 70-year-old movie theater. *15 mi. south of Wilmcote.*

■ **Kenilworth Castle.** The red stone ruins of this 13th-century stronghold stand on a slope away from the center of town. In 1279, some 100 knights of the Round Table met for a three-day tilting tournament outside the castle at a wide lake that has since disappeared. King Edward II signed his abdication here. Sir Walter Scott's novel *Kenilworth* was named after the castle. *15 mi. northeast of Wilmcote, Kenilworth, tel. 0926-52078. Open 10-6 Apr.-Sep. and Tue.-Sun. 10-6 Oct.-Mar. Admission.*

▼

DINING

The likely choice for an excellent meal would appear to be Wilmcote's popular neighbor Stratford-upon-Avon, but that bustling tourist town lacks any really first-class restaurants. Settle for one of the limited number of choices below, or visit a restaurant in a nearby Cotswold town or village (*see* Experience 3, Woodstock, or Experience 6, Wyck Rissington).

■ **Ettington Park** (very expensive). The formal dining room has oak-paneled walls with 19th-century hand-carved family crests and an 18th-century Rococo ceiling. Recent winning appetizers included oak-smoked Scotch salmon and fresh oysters on lightly grilled mushrooms with Hollandaise sauce. The excellent entrée choices were rosette of Scotch beef fillet wrapped in bacon with madeira and truffle sauce, breast of chicken with spinach mousse baked in puff pastry with a light tomato-mustard sauce, and steamed fillet of bream stuffed with vegetables and topped with tarragon cream. Jacket and tie are required. *9 mi. southeast of Wilmcote off A3400, Alderminster CV37 8BS, tel. 0789-450123, fax 0789-450472.*

■ **Charingworth Manor** (very expensive). Four oak-beamed rooms make up the intimate dining room in this beautiful country house hotel. The chef aims for light meals: an appetizer such as pepper and celery soup with croutons and chives or an entrée such as escalope of salmon with cucumber and sour cream. But the desserts can ruin the calorie count: warm chocolate muffins with white chocolate ice cream or lemon meringue pie. Jacket and tie are required. *15 mi. southeast of Wilmcote, near Chipping Campden, Charingworth GL55 6NS, tel. 0386-78555, fax 0386-78353.*

■ **King's Head** (moderate). A friendly pub with good food is located in this 15th-century building where Shakespeare's parents supposedly had their wedding breakfast. The specialty is roast duck, and the recommended brew is Martin's Pedigree Bitter. In summer sit in the garden or outside the front door. *Less than 2 mi. northwest of Wilmcote, Aston Cantlow, tel. 0789-488242.*

■ **The Swan House Hotel** (inexpensive). This 17th-century inn looking out on Wilmcote's village green is a good "free house"—a pub

▼

that isn't owned by a particular commercial brewery. Popular appetizers include garlic mushrooms in cream sauce and pancakes filled with pâté covered with bechamel sauce and cheese. For an entrée, try the steak-and-mushroom pie or the steak on the stone (a steak cooked at table-side on a hot stone). Moderate to expensive rooms are also available, including one that has a four-poster bed and a view of Mary Arden's house. *The Green, Wilmcote CV37 9XJ, tel. 0789-267030.*

LODGING

■ **Ettington Park** (very expensive). An elegant neo-Gothic 48-room country home is situated along the river Stour, offering nice views of the countryside and the hotel's Victorian gardens. For the finest quarters, book the Shirley Suite, with its four-poster bed and fireplace. Other recommended rooms are the Victorian Garden Suite and the double-bedded Room 34. There's an indoor swimming pool and a sauna. *9 mi. southeast of Wilmcote off A3400, Alderminster CV37 8BS, tel. 0789-450123, fax 0789-450472.*

■ **Charingworth Manor** (very expensive). Built in the 14th century, this manor house on 54 acres of land in the Cotswolds countryside offers 24 tasteful guest rooms. Relax in wing chairs before the fireplace in the oak-beamed sitting room. If you're looking for spaciousness and a fine view, ask for the Brismar Suite in the main house. The cottage rooms have been beautifully restored and feature marble bathrooms. Facilities include a sauna, steam room, and tennis court. *15 mi. southeast of Wilmcote, near Chipping Campden, Charingworth GL55 6NS, tel. 0386-78555, fax 0386-78353.*

■ **Folly Farm Cottage** (inexpensive-moderate). This attractive three-bedroom country cottage—part of which was originally a stable—is situated at the foot of the Campden Hills. All rooms are elegant and overlook a wonderful garden. The moderately priced Rose Suite has a king-size four-poster canopy bed, and the inexpensive Honeysuckle Suite has a kingsize half tester bed and antique pine furnishings. Breakfast is served in your room at a lace-covered table overlooking orchards and the garden. It's a short walk to two country pubs. *10 mi. southeast of Wilmcote, Ilmington CV36 4LJ, tel. 0608-82425.*

▼

■ **Gravelside Barn** (inexpensive). Set on a hill in the middle of open countryside in the lovely village of Binton, this four-bedroom bed and breakfast was once a thatcher's barn. It's now equipped with a central heating system, refrigerators, and color TV. The bedrooms have fabulous views of the Malvern Hills and the Cotswolds. Lunch and dinner are served on request. *3 mi. south of Wilmcote, Binton, tel. 0789-750502 and 0789-297000, fax 0789-298056.*

FOR MORE INFORMATION
Tourist Office:
  Bridgefoot, Stratford-upon-Avon CV37 6GW, tel. 0789-293127, fax 0789-295262.

For Serious Walkers:
  The above walk can be found on Ordnance Survey Pathfinder Sheets 975 and 997. These sheets can also guide you to the St. John Baptist Church in Aston Cantlow, where Shakespeare's parents were married.

A Cotswolds Hideaway

EXPERIENCE 6: WYCK RISSINGTON

O rdinary tourists never get to see the hidden lands of Wyck Rissington, though it sits next to the popular Cotswold village of Bourton-on-the-Water. Only a short drive from the bustling university town of Oxford, the tiny hamlet could be the quietest place in England. As you pass through it, the noise of an infrequent automobile is startling, and you may be hard-pressed to find any locals or tourists around.

> **The Highlights:** Two scenic Cotswold villages, rushing rivers, captivating valley views, a pre-Roman camp, a church where composer Gustav Holst worked.
> **Other Places Nearby:** Four unique Cotswold villages, including one called the most beautiful in all of England.

That's what makes Wyck Rissington so unique. Certainly there are Cotswold villages more beautiful, and almost all of them are more exciting. But how many can boast of not a single shop, pub, or restaurant? When you visit, be sure to bring your own food and drink for a picnic, and settle in to listen to the silence of old England.

To pick up provisions, stop first in Bourton-on-the-Water, a picture-perfect village that has been dubbed the Venice of the Cotswolds. It sits on the green banks of the gentle **Windrush river,** which is so shallow here, as it murmurs over its gravelly bed, that even the ducks

▼

find it easier to walk than to paddle. In the 8th century, the river's name was spelled "Wenrisc," a combination of two Anglo-Saxon words meaning "to wind" and "reed"—an appropriate name for a river that winds among the rushes and under graceful low-arched bridges. The town's gray and yellow buildings are reflected in the shallow water—but unfortunately, in summertime, you'll also see the reflections of many tourists.

The walk outlined below leads you out of crowded Bourton, away from the Windrush river, and into the valley shared by the Windrush tributaries Eye and Dickler, rich with trout and crayfish. Here are the earthworks of pre-Roman Salmonsbury Camp, perceived as a threat and partly destroyed by the Romans.

There are three Rissingtons—Wyck, Little, and Great—sitting secluded in the Dickler valley; Wyck Rissington is the most northerly. This small farming community lies on a road alongside a wide green of rough grasses with a Victorian drinking fountain. Idly clumped houses, mellow beneath their roofs of Cotswold stone, are scattered haphazardly throughout the hamlet. Gracious horse chestnut trees grow, and colorful gardens bloom.

There are no really notable buildings in Wyck Rissington, apart from **St. Laurence Church,** with its squat and solid Norman tower. (The tower's walls measure about nine feet thick at the base.) Famous composer Gustav Holst was 17 years old when he spent a year here as the organist in 1892, his first professional appointment. Inside the church, 12 Elizabethan-era wooden plaques, believed to be of Flemish origin, portray scenes of Christ's life. You may also want to look in the church for a mosaic illustrating the maze that until recently stood in the vicarage garden, part of a quaint chapter in the hamlet's history. The vicar, Harry Cheales, had a dream showing him how to construct the maze; remembering the plan upon awakening, he set about building the maze and unveiled it on Elizabeth II's Coronation Day in 1953. Just before the vicarage was sold in 1980, Cheales had the maze demolished because he didn't want it ever to fall into secular hands. A wall tablet memorializing Cheales now rests above the mosaic of the maze.

In the well-groomed churchyard you pass through, look for the

▼

grave of James Loveridge, an itinerant Gypsy who died while passing through Wyck Rissington. Behind the church, the 812-foot-high hill known as **Wyck Beacon** hovers above the hamlet. From the hill, there are magnificent views of steep wooded slopes, open farmland, and broad river valleys where cattle graze in wide, lush meadows. Cotswold villages lie hidden from sight, camouflaged in the nooks and crannies of the land. And, just as stimulating as the view, complete silence rings in the ears—a welcome change of pace from the clamor of the tour buses that regularly invade the rest of the Cotswolds.

GETTING THERE

By car:

From Oxford (30 miles away), take *A40* west to *A429* north. Take *A429* north to Bourton-on-the-Water. Park near the main street next to the village green (wherever there isn't a double yellow line) or in the public parking lot on *Station Road.*

Walk Directions

TIME: 2 to 3 hours

LEVEL: Easy to moderate

DISTANCE: 3 1/2 to 5 1/2 miles

ACCESS: By car

This walk through the Cotswold countryside is rated moderate only because of its length. You ascend one hill, but it's an easy climb. There are some paved roads, but most of the walk is on level dirt and grass paths. To return to Bourton, follow the same route in reverse from the main street of Wyck Rissington. If you want to shorten the walk by about two miles, take a taxi back from Wyck Rissington (to call a cab, *see* Point 12, below). Set up a picnic near the Eye or Dickler rivers or on the slopes of Wyck Beacon. There are no services in Wyck Rissington, so buy provisions in Bourton-on-the-Water at The Bread Basket on *High Street* or David Betteridge Greengrocery & Whole Food on *Moore Road.* You can also buy lunch supplies in nearby Stow-on-the-Wold, from Campden Bakery or Hamptons delicatessen on the main square.

▼

TO BEGIN

From the Bourton village green, walk along the main street, keeping the river Windrush on your right.

1. At the post office, turn left. Go up *Station Road* past a parking lot and toward an intersection.

2. When you reach the intersection (there will be a sign for Roman Way), bear right. Walk along the street to the next junction, where you bear right and proceed on *Moor Lane.*

3. At the first house on your right, go up a set of steps built along a stone wall. Cross a stile into a field. *You are now on the Oxfordshire Way, one of Britain's long-distance footpaths.* Go straight and then cross another stile. Follow the path as it veers to the right over a footbridge. Continue straight toward a metal gate. *You are now on the ramparts of Salmonsbury Camp.*

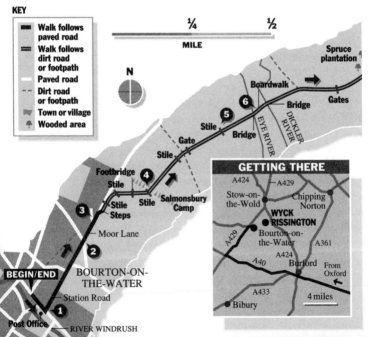

KEY

▬	**Walk follows paved road**
=	**Walk follows dirt road or footpath**
	Paved road
- -	**Dirt road or footpath**
⌂	**Town or village**
♣	**Wooded area**

¼   ½
MILE

N

Spruce plantation

Boardwalk
6
5
Stile
Gate
Stile
Bridge
Bridge
EYE RIVER
DICKLER RIVER
Gates

Footbridge 4
Stile
3
Stile
Steps
Stile
Salmonsbury Camp
Moor Lane
2

GETTING THERE

A424 — A429
Stow-on-the-Wold   Chipping Norton
WYCK RISSINGTON
A429
Bourton-on-the-Water   A361
A424
A40   Burford   From Oxford
Bibury
A433
4 miles

BEGIN/END
BOURTON-ON-THE-WATER
Station Road
Post Office
RIVER WINDRUSH

▼

4. Cross a stile next to the gate. Follow the path—with the high hedges to your left—through a field. At a metal gate in the lefthand corner of the field, cross a stile and continue through another gate into the next field. Proceed, keeping the hedges on your left, toward a stile—**beware of the electric coil blocking your path.**

5. Cross the stile next to the electric coil. Continue straight with the hedges still on your left. Cross a wooden bridge over the river Eye and continue straight; there will be a barbed-wire fence on your left.

6. At a metal gate, step across a boardwalk to the right. Then cross a wooden bridge over the rapidly moving river Dickler. Go straight up a grass path, walking away from the river. Cross a field on the path and go through two metal gates. Continue on the path as it bears to the left; there will be a barbed-wire fence to your right. On your left is a spruce plantation. Continue on through a gate.

7. Go through another gate and turn right onto a paved road.

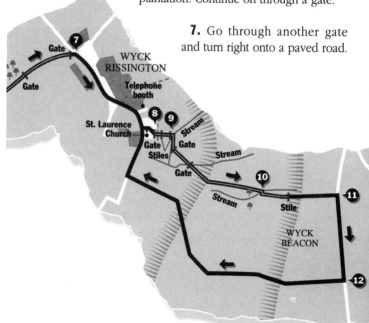

▼

Walk on the road into Wyck Rissington until you arrive at a little church on your left with a squat tower. *This is St. Laurence Church, where Gustav Holst first worked as a musician.* Go through a wooden gate into the churchyard and follow a pebble path to the church door. Go inside the church *and see the numerous Elizabethan plaques and the mosaic commemorating the former maze garden.* Exit the church from the same door and make a right. Walk alongside the church. After you reach the corner of the church, turn at a 45-degree angle to the right and walk across the churchyard toward a stone wall.

8. Go through a metal gate in the stone wall. Cross a dirt track and then climb over a stile into a pasture. Veer slightly to the right and walk on the grass toward a wooden fence. Step over the fence at a yellow marker alongside hedges. Immediately after the fence, cross a footbridge and walk forward toward a stile.

9. Cross the stile and immediately turn right. Head for a gap in the trees across the field. There you encounter a metal gate; go through it and head diagonally across the field toward a pole with electric wires. Continue past the pole to a metal gate. Go through the gate and proceed straight uphill. Follow a grass path as it bears left, to the left of the trees.

10. At a treeline about halfway up the field, turn right. Follow a dirt path and pass a yellow marker. Cross a stream and turn left onto a grass path, which you follow uphill, with trees and the stream on your left. Go over a stile and continue uphill on the path, with trees to your left.

11. When you come to a paved road, turn right. Proceed on the road 1/4 mile.

12. At the next intersection of paved roads, turn right, following the road indicated with a sign for Wyck Rissington. The road winds its way to the main street of Wyck Rissington. Turn right and proceed to the church. Once you reach the church, retrace your steps through Point 7 back to Bourton-on-the-Water. *If you're tired or in a hurry, you*

▼

can call a cab and ride back to Bourton-on-the-Water. To find the phone booth, keep walking on the paved road past the church and then past a pond on your right. Make a right onto the next paved road. There's a red phone booth on the left, behind a hedge. Call Nelson's Taxi Service (tel. 0451-20329) or Wilson's Taxis (tel. 0451-21165). The fare should be about five or six pounds.

OTHER PLACES NEARBY

■ **Stow-on-the-Wold.** The highest town in the Cotswolds (elevation 800 ft.) used to host a sheep market on the broad square in the middle of town. Today, the numerous old stone buildings that line the square house antiques dealers and other shops. About one mile north, in tiny Donnington, the last battle of the English Civil War was fought in 1646. *4 mi. north of Wyck Rissington on A424 or A429.*

■ **Burford.** Full of 14th- to 18th-century buildings, this former wool center is now considered the gateway to the Cotswolds, and it's a popular place for antiquing. Its long main street, *High Street,* runs steeply downhill to the river Windrush and a Norman church that was restored in the 1870s. Some of the tombs in the churchyard are shaped like bales of wool. The town's history can be explored in the Tolsey Museum on *High Street. 8 mi. southeast of Wyck Rissington on A40 and A361. Museum open daily 2:30-5:30 Easter-Oct.*

■ **Chipping Norton.** The tall chimney of a former tweed mill and old buildings, including a series of gabled stone almshouses, stand throughout this town, known to locals as "Chippy." On Wednesday—market day—it buzzes with activity. Henry VIII gave the village unwelcome notoriety when he hanged its vicar from the church steeple for refusing to use a particular prayer book. *12 mi. northeast of Wyck Rissington on A44.*

■ **Bibury.** This enchanting, picture-perfect village with miniature stone houses and a tiny medieval bridge across the river Coln was a horse-racing center in the 17th century. Writer William Morris once called it England's most beautiful village. Stop at the Arlington Mill Museum, a 17th-century corn mill with adjacent cottages. There are 17 exhibit rooms, including a reconstructed blacksmith's and wheelwright's

▼

shop, various agricultural displays, and a Morris exhibition. *15 mi. southwest of Wyck Rissington. Open daily 10:30-7 mid-Mar. to mid-Nov.; weekends 10:30-7 mid-Nov. to mid-Mar. Admission.*

DINING

These restaurants are in the immediate vicinity; *see* also Experience 3 (Woodstock) and Experience 5 (Wilmcote) for several other good spots less than 25 miles away.

■ **Wyck Hill House** (very expensive). Chef Ian Smith often succeeds with such creative dishes as glazed young vegetables and stuffed spring cabbage. Vegetarians choose between three entrées—look for the fresh spinach and nutmeg soufflé accompanied by a casserole of wild mushrooms. Leave room for a dessert soufflé, such as hot toasted fresh coconut with a warm pineapple coulis. *4 mi. north of Wyck Rissington on A424, Burford Rd., Stow-on-the-Wold GL54 1HY, tel. 0451-31936, fax 0451-43611.*

■ **King's Head Inn & Restaurant** (moderate). The locals rave about this 1530 inn, which sits in full Cotswold splendor on a village green looking out at a brook. Seated by a nice fireplace, you can devour traditional steak-and-wine pies, rack of lamb, stuffed lamb cutlets, and fresh fish. *6 mi. east of Wyck Rissington on B4077, Bledington OX7 6HD, tel. 0608-658365.*

■ **The Lamb Inn** (moderate). A country inn with home-cooked food is tucked away in this charming Cotswold village unknown to tourists. Specialties include steak with Stilton cheese and bacon, fresh trout with lemon stuffing, and plaice (flounder) with prawn sauce. Try the cask-conditioned Hook Norton, a hand-drawn local ale. *4 mi. south of Wyck Rissington, Great Rissington GL54 2LP, tel. 0451-820388.*

LODGING

Besides the following accommodations in the immediate area, the hotels, inns, and bed and breakfasts in Experience 3 (Woodstock) and Experience 5 (Wilmcote) are less than 25 miles away.

■ **Wyck Hill House** (expensive-very expensive). It's on 100 acres,

▼

and there are 16 bedrooms inside the 18th-century mansion and 14 additional bedrooms in nearby cottages. Each antique-filled room has its own character. Rooms 1 and 8 have king-size beds, and the latter has a nice view of the Windrush valley. Twin-bedded Room 7 is bright and very attractive. If you're looking for more space, ask for Suite 1. Request that a meal be served in the sunny conservatory, with its fine valley view, and have a before-dinner drink in the elegant library. *4 mi. north of Wyck Rissington on A424, Burford Rd., Stow-on-the-Wold GL54 1HY, tel. 0451-31936, fax 0451-43611.*

■ **King's Head Inn** (moderate). A few rooms are available above the popular restaurant in this 16th-century inn on Bledington's village green. Rooms 1 and 6 have double beds. *6 mi. east of Wyck Rissington on B4077, Bledington OX7 6HD, tel. 0608-658365.*

■ **The Lamb Inn** (moderate). This 350-year-old inn stands on the village green of a pretty, unspoiled Cotswold village on a hill alongside the Windrush valley. The innkeepers have decorated the 12 bedrooms with Laura Ashley fabrics. Room 7 has a hand-carved four-poster bed and looks out on the village green. There's one suite, Room 10, with a king-size four-poster and its own sitting room. *4 mi. south of Wyck Rissington, Great Rissington GL54 2LP, tel. 0451-820388.*

■ **Bretton House** (inexpensive). This bed and breakfast, handsomely decorated with Laura Ashley fabrics and wallpaper, is run by a former chef who will serve his guests dinner on request. Originally a late-Victorian vicarage, the house sits on two acres of land atop a hill and provides lovely views over the Bourton Vale. All three guest rooms have good views, but two are corner rooms, each with a four-poster bed and two different views. The twin-bedded room has a bay window. *4 mi. north of Wyck Rissington, Fosse Way, Stow-on-the-Wold GL54 1JU, tel. 0451-830388.*

■ **Orchard House** (inexpensive). This friendly bed and breakfast used to be the cottage for the head gardener of Wyck Hill House. The master bedroom is the most spacious and has two windows with different exposures. *4 mi. north of Wyck Rissington on A424, Wyck Hill, Stow-on-the-Wold GL54 1HX, tel. 0451-31456.*

▼

FOR MORE INFORMATION

Tourist Offices:

Hollis House, The Square, Stow-on-the-Wold GL54 1AF, tel. 0451-31082.

The Old Brewery, Sheep St., Burford OX18 4LP, tel. 0993-823558.

For Serious Walkers:

The above walk can be found in Ordnance Survey Pathfinder map 1067. For more information on the Oxfordshire Way, one of Britain's longest footpaths, inquire at the tourist office in Stow-on-the-Wold, above, or write to the *British Tourist Authority, Thames Tower, Black's Rd., Hammersmith, London W6 9EL.*

Land of the Unknown

EXPERIENCE 7: AVEBURY

Great mysteries of ancient civilization converge at **Windmill Hill** and the ghostly **stone circles of Avebury.** This fertile grass plain is oddly spectacular, dotted with towering burial mounds, prehistoric avenues, and huge white sandstone rocks standing on end in vast rings.

Stonehenge, about 20 miles to the south, may be more famous than Avebury, but it is so encircled by bar-

The Highlights: Wondrous stone circles that predate Stonehenge; panoramic hilltop views of mysterious Silbury Hill; Windmill Hill, site of a Neolithic trade center and burial ground.

Other Places Nearby: Ancient man-made ditches, hills, and burial grounds; a museum with artifacts from the Iron and Bronze ages.

riers and overrun by tourists that a visit there is often disappointing. A walk in Avebury, however, still has a haunting sort of solitude about it. There's no admission charge, and the modern world impinges quietly upon these awesome relics. Sheep graze freely all around you, and the tiny village's quaint thatched cottages and houses have actually been constructed with some of the circles' original stones.

The standing stones of Avebury predate Stonehenge by about 200 years, and its outer stone circle, which encompasses nearly 29 acres of land, is the largest such alignment in Europe. The circle was originally

▼

built with about 100 "sarsen" stones, each weighing up to 40 tons. The term sarsen probably derives from "saracen," or heathen, because the stones were considered non-Christian monuments. Geologists believe the rocks were fragments of an enormous sheet of sandstone formed at least 25 million years ago. Four of the largest still stand, marking entrances through the deep ditch and the wide grass bank that ring the circle. Today you can walk or drive for half a mile down **West Kennet Avenue,** where numerous sarsen stones were excavated and restored—with a touch of concrete—to their positions.

Why 4,000 years ago a prehistoric race equipped with few tools hauled 40-ton stones from the nearby downs is anybody's guess. And what was the purpose of a design that consists of an outer ring, two smaller rings within, and two avenues leading away, one of them 1 1/2 miles long? Some say the circles served astronomical purposes; others believe they marked a huge burial ground. A few people even insist that flying saucers used the stones as landing bases. But evidence indicates that the stones may have served as a temple for magical ceremonies and strange rituals. Imagine ancient priests, perhaps wearing antlers on their heads, leading mystical ceremonies that may have even involved human sacrifices. People probably danced around the stones and participated in a sexual ritual aimed at restoring fertility to the soil.

Long before the erection of Avebury's stones, a thriving prehistoric farming community with its own unique customs and bizarre rituals lived nearby on a hill you'll walk to, Windmill Hill. Unlike other similar Neolithic monuments, which are usually encircled by a single ditch and bank, Windmill Hill has three concentric rings of man-made banks and ditches. During the Neolithic period, the first farmers migrated to the British Isles from continental Europe; from about 3400 B.C. to 2000 B.C., farmers used this 21-acre hilltop site as a trade center, a defensive earthwork fortification, and a massive burial ground.

Excavations of Windmill Hill's ditches revealed human bones scattered about, a few of them complete skeletons, suggesting that corpses may have been put on scaffolds or placed outside their relatives' earth-

▼

en homes. Some of these bones, as well as numerous chalk carvings of male genitalia (discovered by modern archaeologists), apparently were part of religious ceremonies and fertility rites. The farmers here also made their own flint pottery and traded for pots from as far away as Cornwall, the Thames river valley, the Cotswolds, and Yorkshire. Since they imported both pottery and stone tools, we can gather that they were fairly prosperous and that they owned many herds and flocks. The credit for much of the early excavation work around Avebury goes to a wealthy Scot, Alexander Keiller, heir to a thriving marmalade business. In 1924 Keiller purchased Windmill Hill, mainly to stop a wireless company from placing an antenna there, but he became fascinated by the hill. After excavating it, Keiller bought more and more land around it, including all the land on which the stone circles of Avebury stood. He excavated about half the circles and much of West Kennet Avenue, finding many buried sarsen stones and restoring them to their upright positions. In the village, the **Alexander Keiller Museum** displays many objects removed in the excavations during the 1920s and '30s, including the skeleton of a Neolithic child found on Windmill Hill.

Although excavations have revealed much about the secrets of Windmill Hill and Avebury, little is known about its gigantic neighbor, **Silbury Hill,** which you can see from atop Windmill. Shaped like a truncated cone, Silbury is 120 feet tall and 410 feet in diameter—the largest mound built by human hands in prehistoric Europe. It was constructed around 2750 B.C. (roughly 650 years after Windmill Hill was built) from tightly rammed chalk that workers quarried from adjacent land; the land surrounding the hill still bears the scars of the chalk extractions. Clay, gravel, and soil form the hill's core.

It's unlikely that Silbury Hill was a burial spot—excavations have not uncovered any bones or, indeed, any significant clues hinting at its purpose. (A highly publicized dig broadcast on British television became a major embarrassment when nothing was found.) But the ancient builders undoubtedly were dedicated to their mission: It is believed that it took far more time to build Silbury Hill than it did Avebury or Stonehenge.

Many centuries later, Roman engineers used the massive hill as a

▼

marker while aligning a road from Bath to Cunetio, an ancient town near Marlborough. And every Palm Sunday in the 18th and 19th centuries Silbury Hill came alive with townspeople from Avebury, Kennerton, and Overton, who shared cakes and desserts in a festival to celebrate the holy day.

Although no one knows why the ancient people built Silbury Hill, local folklore provides numerous explanations. One tale says that the hill holds the remains of ancient King Zel, who gallops on his horse over the downs on moonlit evenings. Another tale claims that it marks the spot where priests triumphed over the Devil. As the story goes, the Devil planned to smother the people of Marlborough with a huge sack of earth and chalk. Before he reached the town, however, the priests forced him to drop the sack, thus creating Silbury Hill.

Circular barbed-wire fence

Stile

Tall hump

Gate to ignore

Windmill Hill

Today, many people still believe that spiritual forces meet in Avebury and the surrounding countryside. In search of answers to life's fundamental questions, mystics and psychics come here to touch the stones, expecting a jolt of otherworldly energy. There's definitely a countercultural aura about the village, from its vegetarian cafeteria to the local gift shop, where you can buy all kinds of crystals and soak up the subtle powers of piped-in New Age music. Whether or not the stones provide any sort of spiritual rush, it's hard not to be stirred by a walk through this landscape, where the very distant past is so tangibly present.

▼

GETTING THERE

By car:

From Bath (20 miles away), take *A4* east toward Chippenham. *A4* leads into Avebury. Park across the street from the post office.

From London (80 miles away), take *M4* west to exit 15 outside of Swindon. Connect with *A345* south (an old Roman road) to Marlborough. In Marlborough, get on *A4* west toward Chippenham and Bath. Take *A4* west to Avebury and park across the street from the post office.

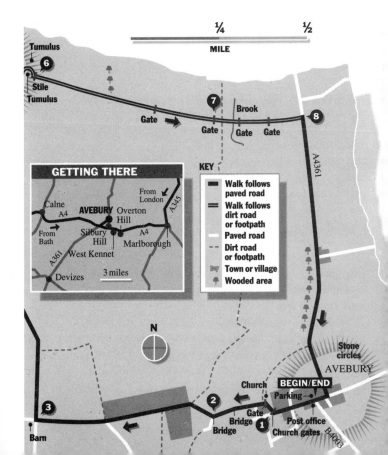

▼

Walk Directions

TIME: 2 1/4 hours
LEVEL: Easy
DISTANCE: 4 miles
ACCESS: By car

Much of the walk is on paved paths and roads through Avebury and surrounding farmland. There's one easy-to-ascend grass hill, and you step over two stiles. During the final several hundred yards, be careful of cars driving into Avebury. The best place to picnic is atop Windmill Hill, looking out at mysterious Silbury Hill. It's probably wise to pick up picnic provisions before you come into Avebury; otherwise, you can grab something at a cafeteria-style natural-foods restaurant next to the gift shop.

TO BEGIN:

From the parking lot across the street from the Avebury post office, walk toward the post office and make a right onto a paved road.

1. When you reach a church on your right, go through the church gates. Follow a paved path to the left. At the next intersection of paths, go straight and through a metal gate. Walk straight down the paved path, ignoring a path on your left, alongside a house. Continue on the paved path (with a high wooden fence to your right). Bear right at the next junction of paved paths, and follow the path, keeping a chain-link fence to your right. *To your left, in the distance, is a view of Silbury Hill.*

2. At the next junction, turn right onto a paved path. The path turns into a wider paved road. At the next intersection of paved roads, continue straight. There are hedges on your right and a barbed-wire fence on your left.

3. At the barn, make a right. Follow a paved road between fields. Go straight for about one mile to the crest of a hill, ignoring gates and turnoffs into the fields. At the "National Trust Windmill Hill" sign on your right, continue straight (don't go through a gate to your right) and follow a path that curves downhill to the right. You are circling behind

▼

Windmill Hill, which is to your right.

4. At the next "National Trust Windmill Hill" sign (at a metal gate to your right), go right across a stile. Head straight up the hill, with the line of trees to your right. Continue straight until you reach the barbed-wire fence surrounding the highest hump atop the hill. Proceed several steps to your right.

5. Go left through a wooden gate. Ascend the hump. *You are now on Windmill Hill. All around you are ditches, banks, and burial grounds of Neolithic farmers. Straight ahead in the distance is Silbury Hill.* To descend Windmill Hill, go out of the wooden gate and make a left (with a barbed-wire fence to your left). Follow alongside the fence as it veers to the left for a distance of four fenceposts. The fence continues to curve to the left, but head instead straight across the grass toward the trees and the hump that's farthest to the right in the distance. You are walking across the hill parallel to Silbury Hill, which is on your right. Go to the left of the hump and circle around it toward a stile.

6. Cross the stile. Proceed to the left down the hill (a barbed-wire fence is to your left). Pass a line of trees to your left. Go several hundred yards to a gate in the left-hand corner of a field and proceed through it. Continue straight down a path with hedges to your left.

7. Go through a wide metal gate. Follow the path across a brook. Go through two more metal gates and proceed toward a main road.

8. Make a right turn onto the road—**be careful of automobiles.** Follow the road back into Avebury. Pass the prehistoric stone circles and make the next right turn to the parking lot.

PLACES ALONG THE WALK

■ **Alexander Keiller Museum,** *Avebury, tel. 0672-3250. Open daily 10-6 Easter-Sep., 10-4 Oct.-Easter. Closed Dec. 24-26, Jan. 1. Admission.*

▼

■ **Silbury Hill.** This ancient hill can be seen in the distance throughout the walk. *Less than 1 mi. south of Avebury on A4.*

OTHER PLACES NEARBY

■ **West Kennet Long Barrow.** Built around 2500 B.C. and used for more than 1,000 years as a burial chamber for ancient chiefs, this is the largest chambered burial ground in England. *1 mi. east of Avebury off A4, West Kennet.*

■ **Overton Hill.** Probably used as a religious shrine, this hill was crowned with two stone rings and five rings of wooden posts in 3000 B.C. A double circle of megaliths known as the Sanctuary later replaced the seven rings. *West Kennet Avenue,* with its procession of stones, linked the megaliths to Avebury's circles. *1 mi. east of Avebury off A4.*

■ **Wiltshire Archaeological and Natural History Society.** The society preserves a collection of rare artifacts from the Neolithic, Bronze, and Iron ages. Objects from the West Kennet Long Barrow, Salisbury Plain, and Marlborough Downs are on display. *7 mi. southwest of Avebury, Long St., Devizes, tel. 0380-727369. Open Mon.-Sat. 10-5. Closed bank holidays.*

DINING & LODGING

With Bath less than 20 miles away, don't bother looking for a fine restaurant or a place to stay in the Avebury area, which has little of note to offer. But if you're looking for a quick bite to eat or a thirst-quencher after your walk, there are a few good pubs nearby.

■ **The Waggon and Horses** (inexpensive). Under a thatched roof in a 16th-century stone building, this pub serves vegetarian and traditional English meals, including beef-and-ale and steak-and-kidney pies baked on the premises. A "Crop Circle," when locals discuss the mysterious circles that appear in the fields, meets here every Friday evening. *Less than 1/2 mile southwest of Avebury, Beckhampton, tel. 0672-3418. Closed Christmas Day.*

■ **The New Inn** (inexpensive). A pretty garden and a nice view of the countryside are the highlights of this small brick pub, part of which is 300 years old. The menu is basically good pub fare; there's a roast for

▼

lunch on Sunday. Inexpensive rooms are available in the barn house or above the pub. *2 mi. northeast of Avebury on A4361, Winterbourne Monkton SN4 9NW, tel. 0672-3240. Closed Christmas night.*

■ **George & Dragon** (moderate). Unlike so many of England's pubs, this one serves fresh food and cooks creatively. Specialties are homemade pasta and an assortment of fish dishes that are regularly listed on a blackboard above the bar. A recommended appetizer is Provençal fish soup, which is so filling you may not want an entrée. Look for the salmon cakes with hollandaise sauce, and for dessert try the sinful brown sugar meringue accompanied by unpasteurized Jersey cream from the farm down the road. *9 mi. southwest of Avebury on A342, High St., Rowde, tel. 0380-723053. Open for lunch Tues.-Sun., dinner Tues.-Sat.*

FOR MORE INFORMATION
Tourist Offices:
The Great Barn Museum, Avebury SN8 1RF, tel. 067-234-25.
The Crown Centre, 39 St. John's St., Devizes SN10 1BL, tel. 0380-729-408.

For Serious Walkers:
The above walk can be followed in two Ordnance Survey maps: Pathfinder 1185 and Sheet SU 07/17 (formerly Pathfinder 1169). The maps can also direct you on walks from Avebury to the West Kennet Long Barrow and Silbury Hill as well as to scores of other Neolithic mounds (tumuli) and earthworks in the area.

Beauty Above the Mines

EXPERIENCE 8: LUXBOROUGH

Beginning with the Romans 2,000 years ago and lasting until the 19th century, a multitude of miners tore various metals from the depths of the **Brendon Hills**. But today, as you ascend these tall green hills in southwestern England, the scars have disappeared, leaving only the beautiful vistas of **Exmoor National Park.**

Near the border between the counties of Somerset and Devon, this 267-square-mile reserve contains heather-carpeted woodland, sparkling trout-

The Highlights: Panoramic views atop high, fertile hills in a national park; an ancient village with an award-winning 14th-century pub in a Roman mining area.

Other Places Nearby: A medieval town with a 13th-century castle, the harbor where Coleridge envisaged his *Rime of the Ancient Mariner,* fabulous Bristol Channel views of southern Wales.

filled rivers, picturesque harbors, and ancient villages with thatched cottages. Exmoor's hogback mountains tower above the Bristol Channel coastline and provide magnificent views of southern Wales and its distant mountains.

Our starting point for exploring this landscape is tiny Luxborough, the most remote village in the Brendon Hills, about five miles south of the coast. Various narrow country lanes provide the only access, and no

▼

public transportation serves the village. The population has shrunk from 180 in 1961 to 153 in 1990; nearly all residents of the village, which sits within the national park, work in agriculture or forestry.

For most of its history, Luxborough has been a poor place, solitary in a wild valley. Set on the south slope of massive Croydon Hill, the village centers around **St. Mary's Church,** a late 13th-century building with a 14th-century tower extensively restored between 1870 and 1900. The base of a medieval cross—a stump in red sandstone—is in the churchyard. To get a taste of the 14th century, step inside the **Royal Oak,** a small inn with low oak ceilings, known for its award-winning pub. The pub believes in natural ales, using no pressurized gases, and the bartender draws the ales directly out of aged casks.

A countryside path rises from Luxborough to the tops of the Brendon Hills. To the east, about ten miles away, stand the Quantock Hills, where the Romantic poets William Wordsworth and Samuel Taylor Coleridge once lived. To the west, less than a mile away, rises 1,388-foot Lype Hill, the tallest in the Brendon Hills. The steep-sided hills were once topped by heath-clad open fields, most of which have now been planted with coniferous trees or fenced to form a checkerboard pattern of grazing lands. At Lype Hill, however, open moorland still prevails, dotted with stunted trees.

The **Brendon Forest** that surrounds Luxborough was part of the ancient Royal Forest of Exmoor. To medieval society, "forest" meant a place of deer, not of trees, and this forest was renowned for the sport of stag hunting. The wild red deer that you may catch a glimpse of today are descendants of the deer hunted by the Saxon kings of England long before William the Conqueror claimed the crown in 1066.

But the Brendon Hills are best known for their mining history: The Romans came first, and much later, in the 17th century, the Germans arrived. At their peak in the 19th century, this area's mines were valuable for their iron ore (a rare feature in British deposits), suitable for making Bessemer steel. Railway lines were built to transport the ore from the mines to the small port of **Watchet,** where it was shipped to the steelworks of south Wales. One railway led from outside

▼

Roadwater, about three miles east of Luxborough, to Watchet. During the 1860s the railway lines carried about 30,000 tons of ore each year—a figure that jumped to 52,000 tons in 1877. When an influx of less expensive ore from abroad made the price of iron drop rapidly in the early 1880s, the Brendon mines suffered great losses and the miners left. By 1883 the area was deserted. The mines reopened briefly in 1907 but were quickly shut once more. During World War I, the railway track was lifted and taken to France.

Today the old pits are silent, and grass and scrub have grown over the rubble. But there's no need to worry about falling into a hidden shaft during your walk—all the shafts on Exmoor National Park land have been sealed.

One of England's smallest national parks, Exmoor offers about 600 miles of footpaths to explore. As you wander along them, keep an eye out for two unique species that roam the Exmoor Hills: the red deer, Britain's largest wild animal, and the shaggy Exmoor pony. Red deer gather in herds of up to 100, and there are at least four herds of pure-bred shaggy ponies, descendants of wild horses that survived the Ice Age.

These lands inspired Romantic poet and avid walker Samuel Taylor Coleridge. His haunting poem *Kubla Khan* supposedly resulted from a dream he had inside his farmhouse at Culbone on the Bristol Channel coast, and his *Rime of the Ancient Mariner* was set in the nearby port of Watchet, from which the Mariner supposedly set forth on his fateful journey. Another famous Romantic poet, Percy Bysshe Shelley, rented a cottage in the coastal village of Lynmouth in 1812, accompanied by his young bride, Harriet. He wrote a few sonnets there and behaved bizarrely, ordering servants to attach messages to trees, tossing bottles containing messages into the channel, and making small hot-air balloons.

GETTING THERE
By car:
From Bridgwater (27 miles away), follow the coastal road, *A39* west, past Williton to Washford. Make a left turn at the Luxborough sign

▼

and stay on the country road until it winds into Luxborough. Park along the road in the center of Luxborough.

From Bristol (65 miles away), take *M5* south to Exit 23. Follow *A38* south to Bridgwater. Connect to *A39* west and follow it past Williton to Washford. Follow the directions above.

Walk Directions

TIME: 3 hours
LEVEL: Moderate
DISTANCE: 5 miles
ACCESS: By car

This walk takes you on a loop from Luxborough through the surrounding countryside. You'll travel on some paved roads and numerous dirt and grass paths. A dirt track winds uphill, but there are no major inclines. Some attention to navigation may be required in Point 7. Set up a picnic anywhere in Exmoor National Park after you pass through the wooden gate in Point 3. Luxborough lacks facilities, so buy lunch provisions before you arrive.

TO BEGIN

From where you parked on the main road in the center of the village, proceed to the Royal Oak Inn. *Stop inside the historic 14th-century pub for one of its special cask-drawn beers or a quick lunch.* Walk out of the Royal Oak, turn left, and proceed toward the main road.

1. At the next intersection, turn right onto the paved main road. Walk 350 yards and then follow the road as it turns to the right and crosses a stone bridge. After the bridge, ignore the public footpath to the right that goes into the woods. Take the right-hand fork of the paved road and head uphill, following the direction indicated by a sign to Dunster (ignore the sign to Wheddon Cross). Continue on this road for another 400 yards.

2. Turn left onto dirt tracks, following the sign toward Wheddon Cross via Colley Hill. Pass a pond on your right and then a cottage on your left. Follow the dirt road as it bears right.

3. Turn right at the signpost for Wheddon Cross. Continue along the dirt tracks and follow them uphill. Follow the tracks through a wooden gate (a red trail marker is at the gate). Continue straight on the dirt tracks toward a footpath marker on your right.

4. At the marker, bear right. Follow a grass path (ignore the dirt tracks on the left, which go down to a house). Go through a metal gate and bear left alongside a barbed-wire fence. Go through a wooden gate into a coniferous forest. Follow a track as it bears left through the trees.

5. At the next junction of dirt paths, turn left. Go uphill through the trees following a red trail marker. Follow the dirt path as it heads uphill to the right.

6. At the next junction of paths, bear right, following red markers. Continue straight on this path, with the wire-mesh fence of a *pheasant game reserve* to your right. Go through a wooden gate, ignoring a dirt path to your left. Go straight (with a barbed-wire fence on the left) and proceed through a field toward a wooden gate (a stream is on your right).

▼

7. Go through the wooden gate and step over the stream. Step up onto a narrow path leading away from the stream and proceed to the right of a tree with a red mark. Follow a grass path uphill and bear right to another tree with a red mark. Continue up the path toward a wooden gate.

8. Proceed through the wooden gate. Go right around the bushes to a barbed-wire fence. Turn left at the barbed-wire fence and walk along it, keeping the fence on your right. Go through a wooden gate and walk toward a metal gate, with the fence still to your right.

9. Proceed through the metal gate. Walk straight ahead, with the

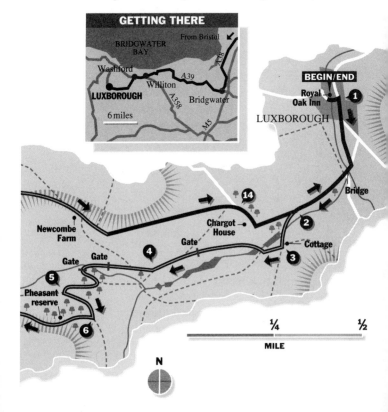

fence to your right. Ignore a black metal gate to your right. Continue alongside the barbed-wire fence toward another metal gate.

10. Turn left just before the metal gate. Proceed forward with the barbed-wire fence and the red markers to your right. Continue straight toward a metal gate, ignoring another metal gate on your right.

11. Go through the metal gate and immediately turn right. Follow a path alongside a barbed-wire fence and hedges, keeping the fence and hedges to your right. Continue past the metal gate that's on your right and head down toward another metal gate with a yellow trail marker. You'll pass a signpost (with a yellow marker) directing you to Luxborough.

12. Go through the metal gate with the yellow marker. Proceed downhill on dirt tracks. Go through a wooden gate and then bear right down a dirt road, ignoring a metal gate to the right.

13. Pass the junked vehicles on your right. Then bear left down the hill, following yellow markers. Continue on the dirt road, keeping the barbed-wire fence to your left. Pass metal storage barns on your right, then exit the farm through a metal gate. Head straight, ignoring a path to the right. Pass a metal storage barn on your right. Continue straight on a paved path with a barbed-wire fence to your right.

14. At the next junction, turn right onto a paved road. Pass a sign for Hall Farm on your left and pass the Chargot House on your right. Continue on the road as it bends to the left. Go past a sign for Wheddon Cross and Langham Hill and continue straight on the road.

15. At the next junction of paved roads, turn left, following signs to Roadwater and Washford. Follow the paved road to the next junction (at the red phone booth). Turn left and you will soon be back at the Royal Oak Inn.

▼

PLACES ALONG THE WALK

■ **Exmoor National Park.** *Information Centre, 4 mi. northeast of Luxborough at Dunster Steep, Dunster TA24 6SG, tel. 0643-821835.*

OTHER PLACES NEARBY

■ **St. Mary's Church.** This late-13th-century house of worship was extensively restored between 1870 and 1900. The tower was built in the 14th century and the base of a medieval cross—a stump in red sandstone—is in the churchyard. *Alongside the minor paved road that leads uphill from the Royal Oak Inn. Luxborough.*

■ **Riding stables.** To many English vacationers, Exmoor means horse country. You can saddle up at various stables. *Porlock Vale House (see* Lodging, below*); The West Somerset Riding Centre, Moor Rd., North Hill, Minehead, tel. 0643-705406; Knowle Riding Centre, Timberscombe near Minehead, tel. 0643-841342, fax 0643-841644.*

■ **Dunster.** There's a medieval feel throughout this pleasant town, with stone houses crowding against a road that in some places is not wide enough to accommodate two cars traveling in opposite directions. The road winds to a main square lined with graceful Elizabethan houses. A 13th-century castle sits above the town in a nice setting—on a wooded escarpment surrounded by trees. Notice the lemon trees at the south wall—a type of vegetation seen at no other British castle. *4 mi. northeast of Luxborough on A396 or A39. Castle tel.: 0643-821314. Open Sun.-Thu. 11-5 Apr.-Sep. Admission. Gardens open Sun.-Thu. 11-5 Apr.-May and Sep.; daily 11-5 Jun.-Aug.; Sun.-Thu. 2-4 Oct.*

■ **Watchet.** This busy 19th-century harbor town saw many ships carrying iron ore from the Brendon mines to south Wales. The quayside is still lively and there's a quiet seaside resort with a sandy beach. *8 mi. northeast of Luxborough off A39.*

■ **Porlock.** A close-knit friendly village located in a fertile dale, Porlock has lovely views of southern Wales across the Bristol Channel. There are crafts shops, a 13th-century church, and a 13th-century pub. Visit the scenic harbor of Porlock Weir, less than two miles west. *13 mi. northwest of Luxborough on A39.*

▼

DINING

■ **Carnarvon Arms Hotel** (expensive). The dinner menu at this Victorian sporting lodge regularly features three meat entrées and a seafood dish. A typical menu may include roast loin of pork with sage-and-onion stuffing, escalope of veal, carbonade of beef, and king scallops poached in white wine with a mushroom cream sauce. Look for the fresh-caught trout and the home-made desserts. The vegetables are locally grown. *15 mi. southwest of Luxborough off A396, Brushford near Dulverton TA22 9AE, tel. 0398-23302, fax 0398-24022.*

■ **Karslake House** (moderate). Step into another era inside this 15th-century malt house in one of England's most picturesque villages. House specialties frequently on the limited menu are baked crab, roast leg of Exmoor lamb, and fillet steak with port and peaches. If it's available for dessert, try the raspberry-and-almond flan. *8 mi. southwest of Luxborough off A396, Winsford, tel. 0643-85242.*

■ **The Dragon House Hotel** (moderate). Traditional English food with fresh ingredients is served in a refurbished 15th-century house covered with creeper and climbing roses. Don't go if you're in a hurry at dinnertime—this is a place to relax over a fine bottle of wine in a romantic setting. The menu often features venison, charcoal-grilled meats, game birds, and lobster. *8 mi. northeast of Luxborough on A39, Bilbrook, tel. 0984-40215.*

■ **The Royal Oak** (inexpensive). This small 14th-century inn has an award-winning pub and a quaint backyard for eating and drinking. The beer flows directly out of a cask—no preservatives are used in the brewing process. You won't find a jukebox or a video game in this unspoiled pub. *Luxborough, tel. 0984-40319.*

■ **Raleghs Cross Inn** (inexpensive). You'll find good food in this pub, along with relics of the area's history: Pictures of the old mining railway and other remembrances of yesteryear are on the wall, and two original fireplaces remain. Fresh meats (roast beef, lamb, turkey, and pork) are carved for lunch and dinner on Wednesday, and on Friday and Saturday evenings. There's a traditional roast at lunch on Sunday. Local Exmoor ale is on draft. Inexpensive chalet rooms with bath are available. *3 mi. west of Luxborough on B3124, Raleghs Cross, tel. 0984-40343.*

■ **The Notley Arms** (inexpensive). This 250-year-old Georgian pub has a fireplace and a wood-burning stove. All beers are hand-drawn: Wadworth 6X, Theakstons Best Bitter, Ruddles, and Ushers Best. Sit in the garden next to the stream in the summertime. A tasty, eclectic menu features Indian, Chinese, vegetarian, and pasta dishes. Bed-and-breakfast accommodations are available. *10 mi. east of Luxborough on B3188, Monksilver, tel. 0984-56217. Closed first two weeks in Feb.*

LODGING

■ **Carnarvon Arms Hotel** (expensive). Built in 1884 on the bank of the river Barle by the Fourth Earl of Carnarvon, this 25-room hotel overlooks the Barle and Exe valleys. Room 32 is modern but has the best views of the surrounding hills. Facilities include a billiard room, heated pool, croquet on the lawn, and a patio overlooking the hills and the pool. For a fee, guests can fish for salmon and trout at a 5 1/2-mile area reserved exclusively for the hotel's guests. *15 mi. southwest of Luxborough off A396, Brushford near Dulverton TA22 9AE, tel. 0398-23302, fax 0398-24022.*

■ **The Wyndcott Hotel** (moderate). This small 11-room mansion was built on a hillside in 1882 for the powerful Luttrell family. Many rooms have four-poster beds. Room 4 overlooks the village and the harbor and also has a view of a lovely garden. The dining room contains a fireplace and provides a sea view. *6 mi. north of Luxborough, Martlet Rd., Minehead TA24 5QE, tel. 0643-704522.*

■ **Little Quarme** (inexpensive-moderate). You'll get a fantastic view down the Exe valley from this 16th-century farmhouse bed and breakfast or the six self-catering stone cottages nearby. The well-furnished cottages, set on 18 acres, are modern but have character, with open staircases and wood-burning stoves. Cottages must be rented for the week except in November, December, and March, when they can be rented for three-day periods. *6 mi. west of Luxborough, Wheddon Cross TA24 7EA, tel. 0643-841249. Closed Jan.-Feb.*

■ **Porlock Vale House** (inexpensive). This seaside country house is on 25 acres with fabulous views of Porlock Bay and the Wales coastline across the Bristol Channel. For a spacious room with a double

▼

bed and a great view, book Room 4. The house is also a horseback-rid
ing center for beginners or experts. Traditional English meals are served
in a dining room with a wood-beam ceiling and a carved fireplace. The
menu always includes game meats and birds, as well as two seafood
dishes. *14 mi. northwest of Luxborough, Porlock Weir TA24 8NY, tel.
0643-862338.*

■ **Wood Advent Farm** (inexpensive). When you stay at this 250-
year-old farmhouse with six rooms on 360 acres of land, ask for the
Tennis Court Room, which has a large double bed and a view of the
Exmoor Hills over the sunken tennis court. The working farm has a
swimming pool and offers moderately priced dinners emphasizing
pheasant, teal, and other game. *3 mi. east of Luxborough, Roadwater,
tel. 0984-40920.*

FOR MORE INFORMATION
Tourist Offices:
17 Friday St., Minehead TA24 5UB, tel. 0643-702624.
The Guild Hall, Dulverton TA22 9NH, tel. 0398-23665.
For a guide to the region, call or write: *West Somerset Tourism, 2
Fore St., Williton TA4 4QA, tel. 0984-632766 (anytime).*

For Serious Walkers:
The walk above is contained in Ordnance Survey Sheet SS 83/9
(Pathfinder map 1235). If you're interested in other nearby walks in the
Brendon Hills, pick up Ordnance Survey Sheet ST 03/13 (Pathfinder
map 1236).

The Rugged Devon Coast

EXPERIENCE 9:
EAST PORTLEMOUTH

The Highlights: Magnificent estuary and English Channel views, sandy beach, ruined castle, great picnic spots, memorable bed and breakfasts.

Other Places Nearby: A resort town with nice beaches, excellent walking trails, and nightlife; the town from which U.S. forces departed during the D day invasion.

Some of the greatest explorers and seafarers sailed from the South Devon coast: Sir Francis Drake, Sir Walter Raleigh, and the Pilgrims on the Mayflower. You can easily picture them setting off to discover new worlds as you walk along this spectacular, rugged coastline on the edge of the English Channel.

Your starting point is East Portlemouth, a village tucked away alongside the **Kingsbridge estuary.** To reach East Portlemouth by car, you must drive up and down on a twisting maze of narrow, hilly country lanes crowded on both sides by hedges; you can also get there by driving to the resort town of **Salcombe,** on the opposite side of the estuary, and taking a passenger ferry across (no automobiles allowed). The drive on the narrow lanes may be slow, but it's worth the time—an unbelievable, fairy-tale way to approach the sea.

There's not much to see in East Portlemouth itself, apart from an

▼

old church and a mill, but the hills and cliffs around the village provide an amazing series of views of this beautiful but treacherous coast. Looking north, there's a relatively peaceful view of the Kingsbridge estuary, lively with sailboats. The estuary's tidal inlets head back inland, fingering their way along the green valleys between rounded hills. At high tide, the inlets form broad silvery ribbons, but at low tide they become an expanse of mud and rocks.

At **Mill Bay,** you can relax on a beach where children build sand castles and families lounge in the sun. During the Middle Ages, ocean vessels were built here, and during World War II the sandy cove was a safe haven for landing craft preparing for the D day invasion.

O n the cliffs above Mill Bay, you see the wide-open waters of the English Channel to the south and, to the west, lying at the mouth of the estuary, the town of Salcombe and its harbor. On the harbor's edge are the minimal remains of **Salcombe Castle**, built in the Tudor era and hotly fought over in the mid-17th century, during the English Civil War. Sir Edmund Fortescue, a supporter of King Charles I, held the castle until an attack by Parliamentarian gunners forced him to surrender; the gun pits dug by the Parliamentarians can be seen on the edge of the cliff you walk on.

Salcombe's narrow streets bear witness to its history as a thriving ship-building port in the 16th and 17th centuries; today it's a seaside resort town loved by yachtsmen, with its sandy beaches and the mildest climate in Britain. Except for the tip of Cornwall, this is the southernmost part of the British mainland—brace yourself for the shock of lemons, oranges, palm trees, and tropical plants growing here. Even in December, wildflowers bloom.

The most spectacular part of the walk is on the cliffs above England's jagged southern coast, once home to many smugglers. The cliffside **Gara Rock Hotel** was originally a Coast Guard lookout station, built in 1847 to protect local citizens from smugglers and wreckers. A sort of ragged staircase descends to the sea—a series of former beaches cut by the waves within the past two million years, when the water level was higher than it is today.

▼

The rugged coastline often poses its own threats. In 1936 the four-masted steel bark *Herzogin Cecilie,* one of the last tall ships, struck a rock and broke apart in a storm, spilling its cargo of grain overboard into **Starehole Bay,** just south of Salcombe. The most notable tragedy took place in 1760 when the 90-gun frigate *Ramillies* wrecked on the coast and 700 lives were lost. A little farther west, one of the Spanish Armada ships, *St. Peter the Great,* was destroyed in 1588.

As ships sail into **Salcombe Harbour** from the English Channel, they must contend with one other menace: a notorious sandbar that has claimed many victims. In the spring, when the water level drops, the sandbar is just five feet below the surface during low tide. While visiting the Salcombe home of historian J. A. Froude, Carlyle's biographer, in May 1889, Alfred Lord Tennyson was sailing in a yacht on the estuary and noticed that the waves gave out a hollow moan as the boat crossed over the sandbar. This was the germ of one of Tennyson's most famous poems, "Crossing the Bar," a moving meditation on fate, faith, and death. Such immense thoughts are easily inspired by this stretch of coast, where the meeting of land and sea is so dramatic.

GETTING THERE

By car:

From Plymouth (25 miles away), take *A379* east to Kingsbridge. Go through Kingsbridge, cross the finger of the estuary and continue on *A379* to Frogmore. At the sign for South Pool, turn right. Follow signs to East Portlemouth. Stay on the road as it descends into East Portlemouth and pass a red telephone booth on your right. Just before the roads bends down to the right, go straight across the road and into a public parking lot.

From Exeter (45 miles away), take *A38* south to *A382.* Follow *A382* south to Newton Abbot. From Newton Abbot, take *A381* south to the Kingsbridge exit. Follow *A379* east through Kingsbridge. Cross the finger of the estuary and continue on *A379* to Frogmore. At the sign for South Pool, turn right and follow signs to East Portlemouth. Stay on the road as it descends into East Portlemouth and pass a red telephone booth on your right. Just before the road bends down to the right, go straight across the road and into a public parking lot.

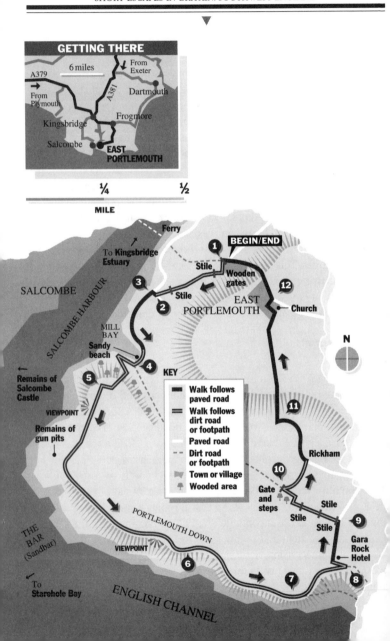

GETTING THERE

6 miles

From Exeter

A379

From Plymouth

A381

Dartmouth

Frogmore

Kingsbridge

Salcombe

EAST PORTLEMOUTH

¼   ½

MILE

Ferry

To Kingsbridge Estuary

BEGIN/END ①

Stile

Wooden gates

SALCOMBE

③

② Stile

⑫

EAST PORTLEMOUTH

Church

SALCOMBE HARBOUR

MILL BAY

Sandy beach

④

KEY

⑤

Remains of Salcombe Castle

VIEWPOINT

Remains of gun pits

KEY

▬▬ Walk follows paved road

══ Walk follows dirt road or footpath

── Paved road

--- Dirt road or footpath

🏠 Town or village

🌲 Wooded area

N

⑪

Rickham

⑩

Gate and steps

Stile

Stile

Stile

⑨

Gara Rock Hotel

PORTLEMOUTH DOWN

VIEWPOINT

⑥

THE BAR (Sandbar)

To Starehole Bay

PORTLEMOUTH DOWN

ENGLISH CHANNEL

⑦

⑧

▼

Walk Directions

TIME: 2 1/2 hours
LEVEL: Easy to moderate
DISTANCE: 3 1/2 miles
ACCESS: By car

The walk follows some paved roads but is mostly on dirt paths that rise and fall along the English Channel coastline. There's one relatively steep (but very safe) hillside path that zigzags through the woods, and you must cross a few stiles. On the cliffs above the English Channel, there are numerous places to stop for a picnic and enjoy the unforgettable views, including the benches mentioned in Points 6 and 7. Pick up supplies before you arrive in East Portlemouth. In Kingsbridge, the Kingsbridge Creamery, *28A Fore St.,* sells inexpensive sandwiches, pastries, home-baked pies, and Devonshire clotted cream. In Salcombe, the Upper Crust Bakery, *3 Fore St.,* has fresh bread, rolls, sweets, and drinks.

TO BEGIN:

From the parking lot on the ridge overlooking the estuary, walk downhill past the wooden benches.

1. Go through the wooden gates and immediately turn left following a sign marking the public footpath to Mill Bay. Cross a stile into a green pastoral valley. Go down the path, with a barbed-wire fence to your right. Cross another stile and continue on the path.

2. When you reach a junction of paved roads, turn right.

3. Turn left at the next road, following the sign to Mill Bay. Walk on the paved road ignoring a paved driveway on your left. Follow the paved road as it curves to the left and then to the right. Continue on the road, following the sign for the parking lot, until you reach the beach. Go past the rocks on the right and continue walking on the dirt path into the woods. Pass the "National Trust" sign on your right.

4. Turn right onto the upper cliff path, following the "Coast Path

▼

Gara Rock" sign. About 50 yards ahead, take the path to your left, following the sign for "Upper Cliff Path." Continue on the path as it zigzags up through the woods.

5. When you reach a clearing, follow the path as it curves to the left. *At this point, you should be able to see the remains of Salcombe Castle across the estuary.* Continue on the path, following it downhill to a clearing and then back uphill. You emerge next to some fields, where you can look across the mouth of the harbor. (If you'd like, take a detour on the trail to your right to sit on the bench overlooking the water and set up a picnic. Then return to the path.) Continue on the path around a headland and follow the path for several thousand yards along the cliff, with the sea on your right.

6. When the path eventually turns to the left, stay on it—**don't go straight or you may go over the side of the cliff.** Follow the path as it heads away from the water and runs uphill. Ignore the gap in the hedges to the right. Continue on the path, which returns to the cliffside along the water.

7. When you reach a wooden bench on your left—**proceed slowly because the cliff ends straight ahead**—turn left and follow the path inland. *Atop the hill is Gara Rock Hotel, a former Coast Guard lookout station.* At an intersection of two paths, bear left and proceed uphill on the path. Pass a bench on your left and then follow the path to the left.

8. At a stone wall outside the hotel, turn left. Then turn right into the hotel's parking lot. Walk up a paved road that leads away from the hotel and between hedges.

9. About 250 yards past the hotel, turn left and cross over a stile, where you see a "Public Footpath Mill Bay" sign. Go straight and follow the path across the fields over Portlemouth Down. Cross one stile and continue on the path toward a clump of trees. Cross another stile and follow the path through the trees. Go through a wooden gate and down some steps.

▼

10. Make an immediate right turn onto a dirt path, ignoring the blue markers and the "Public Footpath" sign. Continue on the path as it winds to the left between houses in the town of Rickham. At a junction of two paved paths, take the path to your left.

11. After about 30 yards, bear right and follow the paved road that forks uphill. Continue on this road as it goes uphill and then between hedges. The road curves to the right and goes straight between hedges. Pass a church on your right and follow the road past the old mill on your left and toward the main road.

12. Turn left onto the road and follow it back to your car.

OTHER PLACES NEARBY

■ **Salcombe.** Situated on a hill, this resort town next to the English Channel has charming streets, fine beaches, fabulous walking trails, and some nightlife. *By ferry, less than 1/2 mi. west of East Portlemouth; by car, 10 mi. from East Portlemouth.*

■ **Overbecks Museum and Garden.** Covering six acres, this National Trust garden overlooking Salcombe Harbour contains rare and exotic plants and shrubs. The elegant Edwardian house displays 18th- and 19th-century curios and memorabilia. *By ferry, less than 2 mi. from East Portlemouth; by car, 11 mi. from East Portlemouth or 1 mi. southwest of Salcombe; Sharpitor, tel. 0548-842893. Garden open daily 10-8; museum open Mon.-Fri. and Sun. 11-5 Apr.-Oct. Admission.*

■ **Kingsbridge.** An old commercial center at the head of Kingsbridge estuary, Kingsbridge has a 16th-century market arcade and plenty of shops. It's a popular town for sailing; it's also the birthplace of William Cookworthy, the first person in England to make porcelain. *5 mi. north of East Portlemouth on A379.*

■ **Dartmouth.** This pretty beach resort was once an important medieval port, with two castles standing on opposite banks of an estuary. U.S. forces left from here to invade Normandy on D day. *13 mi. northeast of East Portlemouth on A379.*

▼

DINING

■ **The Galley** (moderate). Watch the boats dock outside this seafood restaurant in the heart of town. Recent specials included 3/4-pound local lobster and baked bass with spring onions and ginger. *By ferry, less than 1/2 mi. west of East Portlemouth; by car, 10 mi. from East Portlemouth; 5 Fore St., Salcombe, tel. 0548-842828. Closed Jan.-Mar. and Mon.-Tues. Nov.-Dec.*

■ **Crabshell Inn** (moderate). Before you set out on the narrow, twisting lanes leading to East Portlemouth, you may want to stop for lunch at this pub, which was built as a watering hole for sailors. If the weather's fine, grab a waterside table. Try the smoked trout sandwich, one of the seafood specials on the blackboard, and the Death by Chocolate cake. *5 mi. north of East Portlemouth; Quay, Embankment Rd., Kingsbridge, tel. 0548-852345.*

■ **The Fortescue Inn** (inexpensive). Come here for a beer, a deep-fried fish sandwich, and good live music—rhythm and blues, jazz, and rock—without a cover charge. *By ferry, less than 1/2 mi. west of East Portlemouth; by car, 10 mi. from East Portlemouth; Union St., Salcombe, tel. 0548-852868.*

LODGING

■ **The Wood** (moderate). Perched on the edge of a wooded hill, this turn-of-the-century house offers a magnificent view over Salcombe Harbour and the English Channel. Room 2 has a balcony, a queen-size bed, and a whirlpool bath. Room 5 has a balcony and a four-poster. Enjoy an excellent five-course dinner by candlelight. *By ferry, less than 1/2 mi. west of East Portlemouth; by car, 10 mi. from East Portlemouth; De Courcy Rd., South Sands, Salcombe TQ8 8LQ, tel. 0548-842778.*

■ **Hines Hill** (inexpensive). Could this be Big Sur or a rugged Hawaiian shoreline? No, it's a mind-blowing view of the English Channel from this modern hilltop four-room bed and breakfast. It's owned by a former commercial airline pilot and his wife, a professional cook specializing in Provençal cooking—the dinners here are recommended. Ask for the blue-and-white room, and be sure you allow enough time to just sit and gawk. *Less than 3 mi. southeast of East*

▼

Portlemouth; East Prawle TQ7 2BZ, tel. 0548-51263. Closed Christmas-New Year's.

■ **Court Barton Farmhouse** (inexpensive). This 16th-century farmhouse stands adjacent to an ancient Norman church. There's little to see in the nearby village, Aveton Gifford (pronounced "Orton Jifford"), but this 35-acre farm, which grows wheat, barley, peas, and oilseed rape, is a good place to unwind and get acquainted with the land as it once was. *10 mi. northwest of East Portlemouth; 5 mi. northwest of Kingsbridge; Aveton Gifford, TQ7 4LE, tel. 0548-550312. Closed Christmas.*

FOR MORE INFORMATION

Tourist Offices:

> *The Quay, Kingsbridge TQ7 1HS, tel. 0548-853195.*
> *Council Hall, Market St., Salcombe TQ8 8QL, tel. 0548-843927.*

For Serious Walkers:

The walk above can be found in Ordnance Survey Outdoor Leisure Sheet 20. If you're looking for an additional challenge, take the ferry from East Portlemouth to Salcombe and head south along the coast to Bolt Head at the mouth of Salcombe Harbour. From Bolt Head, you can retrace your steps to the ferry or continue west along the shoreline for as long as you like.

An Ancient Harbor on the Wild Atlantic

EXPERIENCE 10: BOSCASTLE

As you look down at the Atlantic Ocean pounding against the rugged black slate cliffs, you may be surprised that only a century ago, many large ships sailed up the treacherous, winding inlet that leads into the inland port of Boscastle. Carrying supplies of coal, timber, wine, and other goods that the county of Cornwall depended upon, the ships had to avoid razor-sharp rocks protruding from the water and maneuver around **Meachard,** the rocky island at the mouth of the estuary. Men in rowboats teamed with horses on the shore to pull the ships to safety.

Once rail service reached the area in 1893, it was no longer necessary to bring goods in by sea, and **Boscastle Harbour** quickly

The Highlights: A tiny port village with an unusual harbor, local shops, and a witchcraft museum; an unparalleled view of the Atlantic Ocean; a peaceful river valley where the writer Thomas Hardy lived.

Other Places Nearby: A charming harbor town known for its lobster fishing; the spectacular clifftop castle Tintagel, where King Arthur was supposedly born; some of the country's best pubs.

▼

declined. Today, only small fishing boats remain and the village depends on tourism. Sea birds still circle overhead, finding roosting places on the rock walls that drop 300 feet to the sea. If you're in Boscastle an hour before low tide, you'll still hear a sound familiar to sailors from years gone by: a booming noise coming from the **Devil's Bellows Blowhole,** followed by a spurt of water shooting halfway across the harbor. European tourists come in summer to watch the Blowhole performance, as well as to see the imposing coastline and browse the shops.

Y ou can avoid the tourists by ducking into the **Cobweb Inn** (across the street from the big public parking lot) and mingling with the hearty bunch of locals at either of the two bars. The pub offers old-fashioned atmosphere, good food, and great ales and lagers. The building dates to the 17th century, though it has only been a pub since the 1940s. Look for the assortment of interesting relics: a goat bell, a wooden rattle to scare away crows, and a delicately carved figurehead from a Swedish ship that was destroyed by strong winds toward the end of the last century.

You can also get away from some of the tourists—particularly the easily frightened ones—by stepping into the **Museum of Witchcraft,** which houses an eerie but interesting collection of objects pertaining to the occult. The museum is geared to items native to southwestern England, including a skeleton of a witch who was hanged in the region.

But to get completely away from the tourists, you must head for the coastal vantage point atop Penally Hill, where you can get a good view of the Atlantic Ocean and Boscastle Harbour. The harbor was a haven for smugglers in early times and was later a port for exporting slate from a huge pit at nearby Delabole. In 1584, amid growing fears of an imminent attack by Spain, the Elizabethan seafaring hero Sir Richard Grenville rebuilt the inner breakwater. The outer breakwater, constructed in 1820, was blown up by a floating mine during World War II. The National Trust rebuilt it in 1962 with stone from an old bridge in Plymouth.

A safe, easy walk from clifftop to clifftop on the 520-mile **South-West Peninsula Coast Path,** Britain's longest footpath, takes you to an overlook with a fabulous view of the **cliffs of Pentargon.** A landslide destroyed Pentargon's clifftop path 70 years ago and created a thin waterfall that spills 120 feet to the beach. On the north cliff, there's a 200-foot cave called Double Doors.

Along the walking tour outlined below, you can also escape to the solitude of the **Valency valley.** This wooded valley and its soft-flowing river remain virtually unchanged since Thomas Hardy walked through it, often with his girlfriend, Emma Gifford, who later became his wife. As a young architect, Hardy first came to the Valency valley in 1872 to help restore the **Church of St. Juliot.** Wearing a dirty raincoat with one of his poems sticking out of a pocket, he was welcomed by the minister's sister-in-law, Emma. A romance blossomed and four years later they married. The marriage lasted 30 years, but it was far from blissful—Emma frequently belittled her husband and his work, and she lived apart from him in an attic for years. At one point, she publicly announced that his novel *Jude the Obscure* was obscene and sought to have it banned. Despite their difficulties, after her death in 1912 Hardy returned to the Boscastle area and wrote some of his best love poems in her honor. Hardy had already immortalized Boscastle in his 1873 novel *A Pair of Blue Eyes;* its hero is a young architect who comes to Cornwall to rebuild a church and, naturally, falls in love.

Your walk through the valley, now National Trust property, will take you to old **Minster Church,** seemingly a mirage in the middle of the woods. No houses stand nearby—just daffodils and trees covered with ivy. Sixteenth-century glass remains in one window, and the grave of a 17th-century knight is in the churchyard. And don't miss a pair of scissors carved, for unknown reasons, on the church tower.

Returning to Boscastle through the Jordan valley, you'll pass the site of Bottreaux Castle, from which Boscastle derived its name. The 11th-century castle, which disappeared long ago, was once the residence of the Bottreaux family, descendants of the Earl of Brittany, who was given land by William the Conqueror for his actions during the Battle of Hastings.

GETTING THERE

By car:

From Plymouth (45 miles away) take *A38* west to Bodmin. Go through central Bodmin and follow the road to Wadebridge. About two miles outside of Bodmin, turn right onto *B3266* toward Camelford. Cross *A39* just south of Camelford and stay on *B3266* until you reach Boscastle. Follow the sign to Boscastle Harbour. Descend a hill and make a right at the Diverside Hotel. A parking lot is ahead on the right.

Walk Directions

TIME: 1 to 2 1/2 hours

LEVEL: Moderate

DISTANCE: 1 1/2 to 4 1/2 miles

ACCESS: By car

Most of the walk is on dirt paths on hilltops next to the ocean and in a river valley. There are two steep inclines: one up a rocky hill, the other up a dirt path in the river valley. No special navigational skills are needed. If you want to abbreviate the walk to an hour or so, head back to your car and pass Point 8, instead of proceeding into the Valency valley. Incredible picnic spots can be found on any of the hilltops on the coastline or at a more subdued site near the river in the valley. Stop for supplies at P. Smith & Son, a 30-year-old family grocery store in the center of town, opposite the Olde Manor House and across the street from the Cobweb Inn.

TO BEGIN

From the parking lot, face the Cobweb Inn and make a left. Proceed through the village. Go to the right of a telephone booth, pass a bridge on your left, and walk on the paved path (the river is on your left) past the next bridge.

1. Bear right up a hill to the right of the Pixie Shop, following signs for the Coastal Footpath. Bear to the left of the white cottages and follow a dirt path as it winds alongside an embankment. Pass two benches.

▼

2. About 100 yards past the second bench, walk past rocks that stick out onto the path and then veer right, leaving the path. Step over the rocks and head along a hillside toward a gap in the rocky cliff (the path is on your left).

3. Just before the gap, as you get your first glimpse of the Atlantic Ocean, make a right. Climb uphill to a path.

4. Turn right and follow the path uphill as it winds toward a fish-shaped weather vane on the top of Penally Hill.

5. Walk to the right of the weather vane. Follow a clifftop path

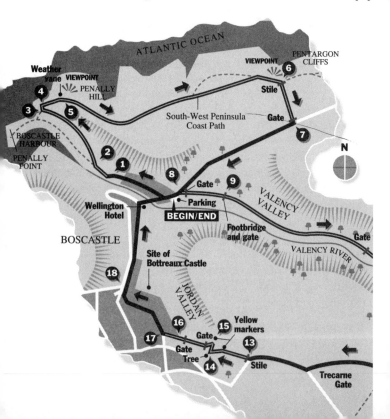

▼

downhill. Continue uphill on this path, *a part of the 520-mile South-West Peninsula Coast Path,* with the Atlantic Ocean on your left and a stone fence on your right. Atop the next hill, pass a bench on your left. Follow the path to the top of the next hill and continue on downhill. *On the opposite side of the cove is a small waterfall caused by a massive coastal landslide about 70 years ago.*

6. Turn right at a wooden fence above the *400-foot-high Pentargon cliffs.* Cross a stone stile. Go along the edge of a field, with the embankment to your left. Ignore the next two stiles on your left and continue along the edge of the field. Go through a wooden gate (next to a metal gate).

7. Turn right onto a paved road that leads back toward Boscastle. Follow this road all the way downhill to the parking lot where you left your car or, about 80 yards before you reach the parking lot, turn left into a driveway just before the Lower Meadows House (the driveway is across the road from the old garages on your right).

KEY

▬	**Walk follows paved road**
▬	**Walk follows dirt road or footpath**
▬	**Paved road**
─ ─	**Dirt road or footpath**
🏘	**Town or village**
🌲	**Wooded area**

8. Go through a wooden gate. Turn left and head into the Valency valley. Go straight, keeping the edge of a field to your left.

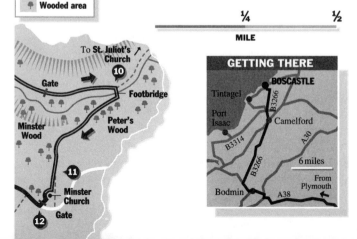

¼   ½

MILE

To St. Juliot's Church
10
Gate
Footbridge
Peter's Wood
Minster Wood
11
Minster Church
Gate
12

GETTING THERE

BOSCASTLE
Tintagel   B3266
Port Isaac   Camelford
B3314   A30
B3266   6 miles
From Plymouth
Bodmin   A38

▼

9. At the left-hand corner of the field, follow a dirt path over a foot-bridge. Go through a gate. Continue on the path, keeping the river on your right. Walk through a wooden gate and continue on the path through the woods alongside the river. Go through another wooden gate and continue on the path to a wooden footbridge. (*If you want to visit the Church of St. Juliot, where Thomas Hardy met his wife, ignore the footbridge and continue east along the footpath. The church is about one mile away in St. Juliot. Then retrace your steps another mile to this point.*)

10. If you opt not to visit St. Juliot's, turn right and cross the footbridge, following a sign to Minster Church. Bear right and go uphill on a dirt path through Peter's Wood. Near the top of the hill, pass a green bench on your left.

11. At a signpost, take the path to the right and continue to the Minster Church wall. Make a right and proceed up stone steps into the churchyard. Turn left before the gravestones and follow a paved path. At the next junction of paved paths, turn right and proceed uphill on a paved path. Atop the hill, turn left and go through a gate to a paved road.

12. Make a right onto the road. Follow the road to a junction at Trecarne Gate (there's a sign for Trecarne Gate on a white house to your left). Follow the road as it winds to the right.

13. Just before the road winds to the left, turn right, following the "Public Footpath" sign. Climb over a stone stile. Walk straight to a marker in the middle of a field—you're now in the Jordan valley—and continue on downhill in the same direction to a big tree.

14. Turn right at the tree. Walk along a grass path through a gap in two clumps of bushes. Proceed to a yellow marker on your left along-side some bushes.

15. Make a left at the yellow marker. Follow a dirt path to the right and immediately through a wooden gate. Follow the path alongside a duck pond on your left and a house on your right. Continue on the path uphill and through a wooden gate.

16. At a junction of two paths, bear left. Continue uphill. Pass houses on the right and left, and proceed to a paved road (*Fore Street*).

17. Turn right onto the street and head downhill. *On your left is a girl's school built in 1879. On your right is the site of Bottreaux Castle. There are no remains.* Pass the post office on your left and continue on the road as it winds to the right.

18. At the next junction of two paved roads, bear right. Proceed downhill on a paved road. Pass the Wellington Hotel on your right. At the next intersection, turn right and proceed to the parking lot.

PLACES ALONG THE WALK
■ **The Museum of Witchcraft.** *On Boscastle's main street. Open 10-6 Good Friday-Jun.; 10-9 Jul.-Aug.; 10-6 Sep.-Oct. Admission.*

OTHER PLACES NEARBY
■ **Port Isaac.** In this charming little port village on the Atlantic Coast, you'll find winding streets and good pubs. Visit the lobster storage area by the harbor. *13 mi. southwest of Boscastle, off B3314.*

■ **Tintagel.** Since the town has been ruined by tourist shops, come in the off season to see its spectacular clifftop castle on the coast. King Arthur was supposedly born here, though archaeological evidence suggests otherwise. *3 mi. southwest of Boscastle, on B3263. Castle information: Tel. 0840-770328. Open daily 11-6 Apr.-Sep.; daily 1-5 in Oct. Admission.*

DINING
You can find decent pub food in Boscastle itself, but you must go outside the town to find fine dining or an artful chef.

■ **Port Gaverne Hotel** (expensive). Some locals consider this early 17th-century coastal inn the best restaurant in the area. Favorite appetizers include duck breast sautéed on a bed of salad greens with poppyseed dressing. The cold seafood platter entrée costs a fortune, but it's a feast: lobster from local waters, crab, crevettes, and langoustines. *12 mi. southwest of Boscastle, off B3314, Portgaverne, tel. 0208-880244. Closed mid-Jan. to mid-Feb.*

■ **Bottreaux House Hotel and Restaurant** (moderate). The chef emphasizes Italian cooking without pasta on the menu. Recent selections included an appetizer of mussels baked with olive oil, garlic, and bread crumbs; entrées included duck breast with mango and pork with apricots, lemon juice, Worcestershire sauce, and white wine. *On B3266, Boscastle, tel. 0840-250231. Closed Nov.-Jan.*

■ **Cobweb Inn** (inexpensive). Come here for good pub food, a wide selection of beers, and a taste of the local atmosphere. *Bridge Walk, Boscastle, tel. 0840-250278.*

■ **Min Pin Inn** (inexpensive). This modern pub-restaurant brews its own bitters and serves good food for lunch or a quick dinner. Try home-brewed Brown Willy or Legend beers as accompaniments to the local trout, homemade lasagna, or a daily special. Outdoor garden seating is available. *4 mi. southwest of Boscastle, on B3263, Tregatta Corner, tel. 0840-77024. Open daily Easter-Oct. and weekends in winter.*

■ **Port William Pub** (inexpensive). Could this be a remote corner of a tropical island? Surfers race to shore outside one of Britain's best pubs, located next to the swirling Atlantic Ocean at the end of a remote valley. The fare includes good pub food and fresh fish and lobster. It's located two miles southwest of Tintagel; take B3263 toward Camelford, turn right and drive through Treknow to Trebarwith Strand. *5 mi. southwest of Boscastle, Trebarwith Strand, tel. 0840-770230.*

LODGING

You won't find top accommodations in Boscastle; stick with a bed and breakfast if you decide to stay overnight in the area.

■ **Tolcarne Hotel** (inexpensive). There's a nice, comfortable living room with a working fireplace, a piano, and a valley view in this 1887 house. Book Room 2 for its sea view and double bed. There's also a nice sea view in the family room, Room 1, which includes a bunk bed. A three-course dinner is served daily. *Tintagel Rd., Boscastle PL35 OAS, tel. 0840-250654.*

■ **Melbourne House** (inexpensive). Although the building itself is Georgian, it's been refurbished into a Victorian home, where you'll have good views of the old village and the Jordan valley. Some areas of the house may appear a bit tired, but it's a good value, and the owners are very warm and friendly. Three-course dinners are available. *New Rd., Boscastle PL35 0DH, tel. 0840-250650.*

■ **Failand House** (inexpensive). You don't come to this modern house for character—you come for great value, a great ocean view, and a large bedroom. Ask for the sea-view room. *Tintagel Rd., Boscastle PL35 0AR, tel. 0840-250302.*

■ **The Mill House Inn** (inexpensive). Voted England's best inn in 1985, this former corn mill has seen better times and was, at press time, in receivership. But it's still a good value and a convenient place near Boscastle to escape into remote Trebarwith valley. Rooms 6 and 9 offer views of the hills, glimpses of the Atlantic Ocean, and comfortable double beds. A new, inexpensive restaurant featuring steak and seafood recently opened. *5 mi. southwest of Boscastle, Trebarwith Strand PL34 0HD, tel. 0840-770932.*

FOR MORE INFORMATION

Tourist Offices:

The Crescent Car Park, Bude EX23 8LE, tel. 0288-354240.

Cornwall Tourist Board, *59 Lemon St., Truro TR1 2SY, tel. 0872-74057 (from the U.S., your best source for obtaining information).*

Books:

About Boscastle, *by Michael Williams, Bossiney Books, Great Britain (available in local shops).*

For Serious Walkers:

The above walk is contained in Ordnance Survey Pathfinder Sheet 1325. This region also offers one of the world's greatest long-distance walks, the 520-mile South-West Peninsula Coast Path. Running from Minehead to Poole Harbour, it is Britain's longest footpath.

The Merry Men of Robin Hood

EXPERIENCE 11: HATHERSAGE

Hathersage sits between two huge industrial centers—sprawling Manchester and the steel-manufacturing city of Sheffield—but it seems as remote today as it did centuries ago when it was one of the stamping grounds of Robin Hood and his Merry Men.

The village lies within the **Peak District,** Britain's first national park, an area of two completely different landscapes. The central and southern region is called the White Peak: rolling limestone country with steep wooded dales and green pastures crisscrossed by stone walls. To the north, the dramatic Dark Peak is full of 2,000-foot-high wild peat moorlands and precipitous dark stone crags that rise above lush valleys.

This experience takes you through the Dark Peak's beautiful **Hope valley.** This Derbyshire valley follows the river Derwent from just outside Hathersage to the village of **Hope,** four miles to the west. Robin Hood and his band often ventured this far from their famous Sherwood

The Highlights: A lively village surrounded by moors; the grave of Little John, friend of Robin Hood; a peaceful river in the countryside.

Other Places Nearby: A national park that's a favorite of walkers, a boat ride through a mine, a deep cavern containing a rare stone, an old castle, a regal mansion.

▼

Forest base, about 35 miles to the east, wandering through this valley and others nearby.

Hathersage itself was the home village of Robin Hood's stalwart lieutenant, seven-foot-tall Little John. In old tales, Little John was sometimes referred to as John the Nailer, because he was brought up to be a nail maker. Not much is known about his career until 1265, when he fought along with Robin Hood in the Battle of Evesham, under the rebel banner of Simon de Montfort. When Simon was defeated, his followers were outlawed.

Robin Hood retreated into Sherwood Forest and organized a band of so-called Merry Men, who aimed to live there carefree, defending the righteous and stealing from the rich to give to the poor. Their sworn enemies were those in authority, and the Sheriff of Nottingham in particular. One night Little John entered the Sheriff of Nottingham's house disguised as a servant and stole his valuable silver plate. Little John was also a champion archer who used a gigantic bow with deadly precision. The bow supposedly required a force of 160 pounds to draw it back to its fullest.

Some say that Robin Hood and his Merry Men never existed, that he was merely the personification of a forest elf or the wind god. Undoubtedly, many of the stories and customs associated with the 13th-century outlaw band were made up at a later date, but there does appear to be a sound historical basis for the band's existence. Robin Hood is mentioned in historical accounts from as early as 1377, and he was the subject of many ballads in the 15th century.

When Robin Hood died, Little John returned broken-hearted to Hathersage and later died in a cottage to the east of **St. Michael's Church.** The cottage no longer remains, but for many years Little John's enormous longbow of spliced yew, a few of his arrows, his chain mail, and his Lincoln green cap were displayed in St. Michael's Church. Set on a hill behind Hathersage's main streets, the church dates mainly to the 14th and 15th centuries. It has a fine tower and battlements and remarkable gargoyles: a tiger's head, a Turk's head, and a muzzled bear.

In St. Michael's churchyard, you can stop to see **Little John's**

▼

grave, a site that he personally selected. With his huge bow, he supposedly shot an arrow up into the air, saying he wished to be buried
wherever it landed. The arrow fell to the earth opposite the south door
of the church. When the grave was opened in 1780, it contained an
enormous 32-inch thigh bone that one onlooker said looked more like
a mammoth's than a man's. The thigh bone was displayed in town as a
curiosity, but its owners were dogged by a mysterious run of bad luck.
Once they reinterred the bone, the bad luck immediately stopped.

At St. Michael's Church you can also see, emblazoned over the
porch, the arms of the Eyre family, who were the inspiration for
Charlotte Brontë's *Jane Eyre*. The Eyres lived in many different houses
in Hathersage; a family member donated the church font and the
Sanctus bell that has hung in St. Michael's belfry for almost 550 years.
Though the tales of Little John may be half legend, the Eyre family's
deeds were an indisputable part of history. In the time of Queen
Elizabeth I, they were persecuted for remaining Roman Catholic—several members died for their beliefs in the 1590s. A century later, during
the reign of William of Orange, the Eyres were forced to flee their
home at **North Lees Hall,** and the chapel below the house was
destroyed by a Protestant mob. North Lees Hall is now privately
owned, but you can drive by to see the exterior—it's located about two
miles north of Hathersage, on the right-hand side of a minor road
toward Stanage Edge. Look for the house that resembles a miniature
castle with a battlement tower.

In 1845, Charlotte Brontë came down from her home in Haworth
(*see* Experience 13) to Hathersage to stay at the vicarage with her friend
Ellen Nussey and prepare the house for Ellen's brother and his bride.
The visit clearly made an impression on her, for in her famous novel
Jane Eyre, written a year or so later, she took the Eyre family name for
her heroine and used North Lees Hall as a model for Rosamond Oliver's
house. Hathersage—called Morton in the novel—and its environs are
described in several passages of *Jane Eyre*. As you walk along the river
Derwent today and sheep scurry out of your way, you see much of the
same beauty that Charlotte Brontë and Little John saw in Hathersage so
many years ago.

▼

GETTING THERE

By car:

From Sheffield (10 miles away), follow *A625* west to Hathersage. Park at the public parking lot on *Oddfellows Street,* which intersects *Station Road (B6001).*

From Manchester (30 miles away), take *A6* south to Chapel-en-le-Frith. Follow *A625* east to Hathersage. Park at the public lot on *Oddfellows Street,* which intersects *Station Road (B6001).*

By train:

From Sheffield or Manchester, take Britrail's Hope Valley line to Hathersage Station. The journey will take 18 minutes from Sheffield or 64 minutes from Manchester. To reach the starting point of the walk, exit the Hathersage Station and proceed to *Station Road (B6001),* the paved road adjacent to the station. Turn right onto it and proceed straight (past the Little John Pub) until you reach *Main Road,* Hathersage's major street. Pick up the walk at Point 2, below.

Walk Directions

TIME: 2 hours

LEVEL: Easy

DISTANCE: 4 miles

ACCESS: By car and train

This walk through Hathersage and the Hope Valley has two short uphill stretches, on a sidewalk and a paved lane. Most of the route is on sidewalks, paved roads, and dirt paths; there are several stiles to cross. When you come to the river Derwent in Point 11, you cross it on huge stepping stones. (If the river is particularly high and the stones are submerged, you must retrace your steps to Hathersage.) Set up a picnic on a bank on either side of the river. Pick up provisions at one of the shops on *Main Road* in Hathersage.

TO BEGIN

With your back to the public parking lot, make a right (at a swimming pool sign) onto *Oddfellows Street.*

▼

1. Make the next right, onto *Station Road*. Proceed past the Little John Pub (across the street on your left) toward *Main Road,* Hathersage's main street.

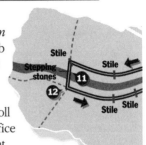

2. Turn right onto *Main Road*. Stroll along the sidewalk, passing a post office and the Hathersage Inn. Continue straight.

3. When you reach an intersection at *School Lane,* turn left. Proceed on the sidewalk toward St. Michael's Church. Follow a road uphill to the left (there's an iron railing on your left). When you reach an intersection, bear left and proceed up the paved road.

4. When you reach St. Michael's Church, turn left through the wooden gates and enter the churchyard, filled with gravestones. Proceed straight, then turn left just before a bench. *Several steps ahead lies Little John's grave. The headstone says: "The friend and lieutenant of Robin Hood."* Go back to the paved path, turn left, and follow the path to the left (with a stone wall to your right).

5. Go through a wooden gate and turn left, then make a quick right through another gate. Proceed down a footpath that leads you through three wooden gates. After the last gate, turn left.

6. When you reach a paved footpath on your right, *Besom Lane,* make a right onto it. Follow this path toward *Main Road.*

7. At *Main Road,* turn right. Continue on past the George Hotel.

8. At *Jaggers Lane,* bear right, follow the lane uphill, and continue on it.

9. When you reach an open field on your left, turn left onto a footpath that crosses the field at a 45-degree angle. Cross a ladder stile and go over the railroad tracks—**beware of trains.** Just past the tracks

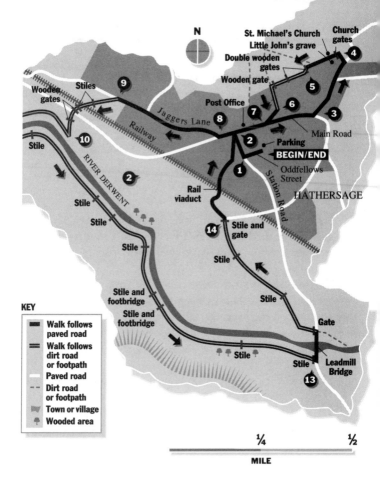

N

St. Michael's Church
Little John's grave
Church gates
Double wooden gates
Wooden gate
Post Office
Jaggers Lane
Railway
Wooden gates
Stiles
Main Road
Parking
BEGIN/END
Oddfellows Street
Station Road
HATHERSAGE
Stile
RIVER DERWENT
Rail viaduct
Stile
Stile
Stile
Stile
Stile and gate
Stile
Stile and footbridge
Stile and footbridge
Stile
Gate
Leadmill Bridge
Stile

KEY

- ▬ Walk follows paved road
- ═ Walk follows dirt road or footpath
- Paved road
- - - - Dirt road or footpath
- Town or village
- Wooded area

¼   ½
MILE

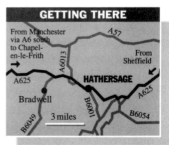

GETTING THERE

From Manchester via A6 south to Chapel-en-le-Frith
A57
A6013
From Sheffield
A625
HATHERSAGE
Bradwell
B6049
B6001
A625
B6054
3 miles

▼

cross another stile. After the stile, bear right and go over the planks alongside a wooden gate. Cross the main road and go through a wooden gate across the street. Go straight across a field.

10. At a footpath on the far side of the field, alongside the river Derwent, turn right. *You are walking in the Hope valley.* Continue along the bank for about 1/4 mile (you'll cross a stile). At the next stile, cross over and follow some steps down toward the river.

11. Use the large stepping stones to cross the river. **If the stones are submerged, do not try to cross the river—go back to Hathersage.** After you cross, continue up a dirt path to the river bank.

12. Turn left onto a riverside path, which you follow with the river on your left. *There are many great picnic spots on the soft grass along the way.* Proceed on the riverside path for about 1 1/2 miles, crossing eight stiles and two footbridges. After the second footbridge, continue to your left along the river. Cross the next stile and continue on the path.

13. Cross a stile just before a main road, and turn left onto the road. Cross Leadmill Bridge. Just past the bridge, there will be a stone wall on your left—go through an opening in the wall and through a gate adjacent to it. Follow a grass footpath (a barbed-wire fence is to your left) and cross a stile. Continue straight and cross another stile. Proceed straight and exit the field by either going over a stile or walking through an adjacent gate.

14. Make an immediate left onto a paved road. Go under a railroad viaduct and continue straight into the village. When you reach *Station Road,* stop at the Little John Pub (to your right) for refreshment or turn right and proceed to *Oddfellows Street.* Turn left onto *Oddfellows Street* and return to your car. If you took the train to Hathersage, continue on *Station Road* past *Oddfellows Street* to the rail station.

▼

OTHER PLACES NEARBY

■ **Peak District National Park.** This 542-square-mile park encompasses a variety of terrain: moorland, dales, grassy hills, huge craggy rocks, and green fields crossed with stone walls. *Information is available at Aldern House, Baslow Rd., Bakewell DE45 1AE, tel. 0629-814321.*

■ **Speedwell Cavern.** A 40-minute boat ride in an old lead mine takes you from one illuminated cave to another. The final goal is a point 840 feet below ground where the water rushes headlong into a "bottomless pit." During the height of summer, this attraction can be overwhelmed by tourists, but it's a fun ride in the only English cavern you can tour by boat. *5 mi. west of Hathersage, Castleton, tel. 0433-620512. Open 9:45-5:15 Easter-Sep.; 9:45-4:15 Oct.-Easter. Admission.*

■ **Treak Cliff Cavern.** During a 40-minute guided walking tour of the cavern, you can see lots of Blue John, an amethystine spar prized for the manufacture of ornaments and jewelry since Roman times. This may be the only region in the world where Blue John is found. *5 mi. west of Hathersage on A625, Castleton, tel. 0433-620571. Open 9-5 Apr.-Oct.; 10-4 Nov.-Mar. Admission.*

■ **Peveril Castle.** This restored ruin atop a limestone crag behind the town of Castleton was one of the first Norman castles to be built of stone rather than of wood with earthen ramparts. Some parts of the fortress date to the 11th century. *5 mi. west of Hathersage, Castleton, tel. 0433-620613. Open daily 10-6 Apr.-Sep.; Tue.-Sun. 10-4 Oct.-Mar. Admission.*

■ **Chatsworth House.** Set in the Peak District National Park on the banks of the river Derwent, this mansion was constructed between 1687 and 1707 for the First Duke of Devonshire. The gardens were designed by two famous landscapers, Capability Brown and Joseph Paxton. *3 mi. south of Baslow off B6012; 10 mi. south of Hathersage, tel. 0246-582204. Open 11-4:30 the third week of Mar.-Oct. Admission.*

DINING

Top restaurants are scarce in the Hathersage area. If you insist on fine dining, you may have to visit a major city such as Manchester, Sheffield, or York.

■ **Hassop Hall Hotel** (very expensive). This stately stone country house has a history that dates back 900 years. Recent entrées included grilled venison steak with béarnaise sauce, rainbow trout meunière with almonds, and roast turkey with cranberry sauce. *8 mi. south of Hathersage, Hassop DE45 1NS, tel. 0629-640488, fax 0629-640577.*

■ **George Hotel** (inexpensive). Mingle with the locals at the pub in this 18th-century hotel in the heart of town. Yorkshire pudding and other traditional bar meals are served. *Main Rd., Hathersage, tel. 0433-650436.*

LODGING

■ **Hassop Hall Hotel** (very expensive). Marble hallways and spacious individually decorated rooms are the hallmark of this historic, though somewhat dark, country house. Room 14 overlooks green fields and has a four-poster double bed and a working fireplace. *8 mi. south of Hathersage, Hassop DE45 1NS, tel. 0629-640488, fax 0629-640577.*

■ **Underleigh House** (moderate). Built in 1870, this former barn near the end of a cul-de-sac has been renovated into a long stone house with seven guest rooms. Book the double-bedded Derwent Room for two different exposures—one of the garden and one of the hillside. Creative, moderately priced four-course dinners are available. *4 mi. west of Hathersage, off Edale Rd., Hope S30 2RG, tel. 0433-621372.*

■ **Highlow Hall** (inexpensive). This unique manor house gives you a taste of what life was like in the 16th century. The house was built by a farmer named Eyre, a member of the local family for whom Charlotte Brontë named her heroine Jane Eyre. Dinner is available. *Hathersage S30 1AX, tel. 0433-650393.*

FOR MORE INFORMATION
Tourist Offices:
Old Market Hall, Market Hall, Bridge St., Bakewell DE4 1DS, tel. 0629-813227.

Castle St., Castleton S30 2WG, tel. 0433-620679.

For Serious Walkers:
The above walk can be found in Ordnance Survey Pathfinder Sheet SK 28/38 (map 743).

▼

A Canal Through the Plains

EXPERIENCE 12: WAVERTON

Sitting on the Cheshire Plain, Waverton lacks dramatic vistas, and there's a lazy feel in the air. It's a landscape of fertile clay soils, lush grass, and buttercup meadows open to the sky—beautiful, but in a much more subtle way than many of the experiences in this book. Rather than marvel at your surroundings, you are free to gently unwind, sitting at an undisturbed picnic spot alongside a narrow canal, while boats pass by and fishermen cast their lines.

The Highlights: Quiet places to picnic on the plains at the edge of an 18th-century canal, an old red-sandstone church.

Other Places Nearby: An 18th-century countryside castle where a king's treasure is supposedly buried; a working watermill; Chester, a small city full of medieval architecture.

The peace belies the area's past. Waverton lies a few miles east of the Welsh border and four miles southeast of **Chester,** the site of a major Roman camp established in A.D. 79. Many bloody battles were fought on these lands, first between Romans and Britons and later between the English and the Welsh.

In addition, the last major battle of the English Civil War was fought on **Rowton Moor,** about a mile from Waverton. There, on September 24, 1645, King Charles I watched as his troops were annihi-

▼

lated on a bare stretch of scrubby, gravelly heath. It signaled the beginning of the end for the king, who was executed four years later. Today, Rowton Moor is a patchwork of fields and houses, and a large hotel stands on the battleground. Bordering the moor on one side, the 66-mile-long **Shropshire Union Canal**—formerly called the Ellesmere and Chester Canal—cuts through Waverton.

On the walk described below, you'll travel for a few miles alongside this 18th-century canal, crossing two of the many old bridges that span it. Until a few years after World War II, the canal was an important commercial waterway used by boats to carry oil products, metal, and other cargo. Today, pleasure boats ply the waters and there's a major boat yard at Rowton Bridge. From the path alongside the canal, you can gaze eastward to a wooded ridge crowned by Beeston Castle and to the dark folds of the Welsh hills. Many of the small patches of woodland you pass were recorded in the Domesday Book, a survey of all English taxpayers conducted in 1086.

The walk also takes you to the heart of Waverton, which isn't much more than a collection of houses and **St. Peter's Church.** Since the red-sandstone church lacks a foundation stone, no one is sure when it was built, but inside there's an original timber-framed chancel. The 15th-century perpendicular tower was topped with a little pyramid roof a century ago; the nave roof dates to 1635.

Waverton was once a farming community with 14 working farms. Today the private Eaton estate dominates much of the old village, and only five farms are still operating.

Although it's small, Waverton has a long-standing tradition of community charity. In 1662, a gentleman named Jonathan Barker bequeathed a few pounds, the interest of which was "to be paid to the poor of Waverton on New Year's Day forever;" Elizabeth Dutton added 30 pounds to this in 1702. Then in 1706, Richard Ralphson donated five pounds, "the interest to be paid out in bread to be distributed at Easter and Christmas yearly forever." Today, the needy of Waverton continue to benefit from these legacies.

▼

GETTING THERE

By car:

From Chester (four miles away), take *A41* south toward Whitchurch. When you spot a sign reading "Waverton Business" on your right, make the next left. Then make the first right and go through Waverton, passing the church on your left. Follow the road straight and go over Golden Nook Bridge. Park near the bridge, on the left at the intersection of two paved roads (at a sign for Huxley and Tattenhall).

Walk Directions

TIME: 2 to 2 1/2 hours
LEVEL: Easy
DISTANCE: 5 miles
ACCESS: By car

Normally, we'd classify a five-mile walk as moderately difficult because of its length, but this walk on the Cheshire Plain, a loop around the Shropshire Union Canal and back, traverses flat land and has no inclines to negotiate. You walk on paved roads and dirt paths and don't have to worry about mud unless a storm has just hit. An optional extension just beyond Point 4 takes you to Rowton Moor and back, a distance of almost 2 1/2 additional miles round-trip. The extension goes through suburban streets and is recommended only for people who want to walk more.

Picnic anywhere along the canal. There are no places to buy picnic supplies near the beginning of the walk, and there are few shops in Waverton, so pick up lunch provisions somewhere else en route.

TO BEGIN

Walking away from the Golden Nook Bridge, follow the direction indicated by the sign to Hargrave. Proceed down the paved road for 700 yards. Pass a telephone booth on your right.

1. At *Cow Lane,* turn left, heading toward Waverton.

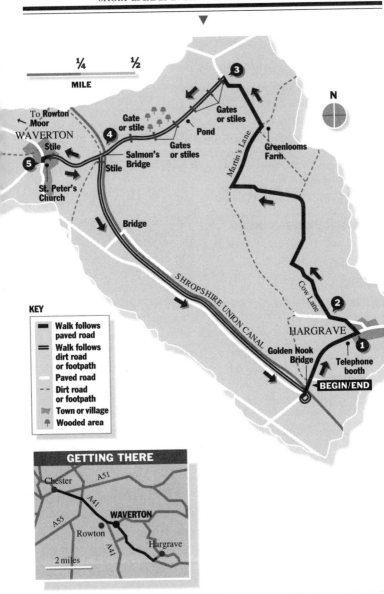

KEY

- ▬ Walk follows paved road
- ═ Walk follows dirt road or footpath
- ▭ Paved road
- - - Dirt road or footpath
- ▮ Town or village
- ♣ Wooded area

GETTING THERE

▼

2. At the next intersection, bear right, remaining on *Cow Lane.* Proceed about a mile, around several sharp bends, to *Martin's Lane* and turn right onto it (ignore a public footpath to the left). About 550 yards along *Martin's Lane,* you come to Greenlooms Farm, where you stay on the road as it circles sharply to the left. Go straight and then follow the road as it curves around to the left once again. Proceed on the road as it curves to the right.

3. Just after the curve to the right, turn left at a Waverton signpost (on your left). You can either cross a stile at the signpost or go through a metal gate (just before the signpost) if it's open. Go straight and proceed over another stile or through another gate. Walk straight across a field. Continue walking straight over four more stiles (or through four more gates). Then proceed toward Salmon's Bridge, a red-brick arch over the Shropshire Union Canal.

4. When you reach the bridge, cross over it. Go straight and follow a path as it bears to the right, into Waverton. Cross a stile and turn left onto a paved road. Walk on the road to a main road, where you turn left. Follow the main road a short distance toward *15th-century St. Peter's Church. If you'd like a longer walk, go back to that last intersection and turn right—instead of left. Proceed on the main road for a little over a mile to Rowton Moor, the site of the last major battle of the English Civil War, in 1645. Unfortunately, a modern hotel sits on the grounds of the battlefield, and there are no commemorative landmarks. Then retrace your steps to the intersection near the church.*

5. From St. Peter's Church, retrace your steps toward Salmon's Bridge, Point 4. Just before the bridge, turn right and cross a stile. Follow a footpath alongside the canal (the canal will be to your left). It's a straight 1 1/2-mile walk back to Golden Nook Bridge—you'll pass underneath one bridge, and then the next bridge is Golden Nook. Go underneath Golden Nook Bridge, turn right onto a path, and then make a quick right onto the main road. Cross over the bridge and return to your car.

PLACES ALONG THE WALK

■ **Shropshire Union Canal.** *Canal boats can be rented from Bithells Boats, The Groves, Chester, tel. 0244-325394, or Chester Packet Horse & Boat Co., Canal Warehouse, Whipcord Lane, Chester, tel. 0244-390059.*

OTHER PLACES NEARBY

■ **Chester.** This city has a lot of charm, with medieval architecture and few modern buildings, but stay away during the height of the day in the tourist season—it's a favorite stop for tour buses and can often be congested. *4 mi. northwest of Waverton.*

■ **Beeston Castle.** King Richard II supposedly buried his treasure in this 18th-century castle with a lovely view of the countryside. *7 mi. southeast of Waverton off A49, Beeston, tel. 0829-260464. Open daily 10-6 Apr. 1-Sep. 30; 10-4 Oct. 1-Mar. 31. Admission.*

■ **Stretton Watermill.** At this small working watermill in the pretty countryside, the miller demonstrates flourmaking. There's also a nice picnic area. *10 mi. south of Waverton off A534, Stretton, tel. 0606-41331. Open Tue.-Sun. 1-5 Apr.-Sep.; Sat. and Sun. 1-5 Mar. and Oct.*

DINING

Top countryside restaurants are scarce in the Waverton area, so we've included an innovative one in an elegant hotel in Chester, a small city nearby.

■ **Arkle** (very expensive). At this Chester hotel, the creations coming out of the kitchen include such appetizers as the parcel of steamed cabbage filled with lobster, smoked salmon, and salmon mousse with champagne butter sauce and topped with Beluga caviar. For entrées, you feast on dishes like grilled lamb cutlet on a purée of black olives with strips of sweet peppers. *4 mi. northwest of Waverton, Grosvenor Hotel, Eastgate St., Chester, tel. 0244-324024. Closed Sun. and Mon. lunch.*

■ **Crabwall Manor** (very expensive). Chef Mike Truelove successfully combines classic French and English cuisines at this 19th-century brick manor house. The menu has featured such dishes as grilled red mullet with garlic roast potatoes, olives, sun-dried tomatoes, and anchovies, and roast pheasant with chestnuts on root vegetables.

▼

Delectable desserts have included a winning warm frangipane of apples with cinnamon cream. *6 mi. northwest of Waverton and 2 mi. north of Chester on A540, Parkgate Rd., Mollington CH1 6NE, tel. 0244-851666, fax 0244-851400.*

■ **Nunsmere Hall** (very expensive). The recipes are creative, but the execution is sometimes lacking at this house in a lovely wooded setting. Entrées recently included roast loin of Cumbrian lamb with sautéed Brixham scallops and a coriander-saffron cream sauce. Try the individual baked Alaska with stewed apples and honey ice cream topped with a honeycomb-flavored meringue. More than 140 different wines are offered, including rarities from Lebanon, Chile, and Australia. *13 mi. northeast of Waverton on A49, Tarporley Rd., Sandiway CW8 2ES, tel. 0606-889100, fax 0606-889055.*

■ **Old Trooper** (inexpensive). This odd canal-side pub contains miniature fairy-tale houses with small windows and red tile roofs. There's a large fireplace in the bar room. *Less than 1 mi. north of Waverton, Whitchurch Rd., Christleton, tel. 0244-335784.*

■ **Plough** (inexpensive). Built in 1750, this timber-walled pub with an old window seat is on the site of the last battle of the British Civil War. The pub's newer addition has tapestry-covered seats and a patio. *Less than 1 mi. north of Waverton, Plough Lane, Christleton, tel. 0244-335784.*

LODGING

■ **Nunsmere Hall** (very expensive). An early-20th-century red-sandstone house built for shipping magnate Sir Aubrey Brocklebank stands on a wooded finger of land surrounded by a six-acre lake. The interior of the 32-room hotel was tastefully refurbished recently. Ask for a room overlooking the lake. *13 mi. northeast of Waverton on A49, Tarporley Rd., Sandiway CW8 2ES, tel. 0606-889100, fax 0606-889055.*

■ **Crabwall Manor** (very expensive). Although it is two miles outside of the small city of Chester, this 1850 red-brick manor house sits in relative seclusion on 11 acres of land. The 48 bedrooms (including many in a new wing) are individually decorated and contain couches, tables, and armchairs. *6 mi. northwest of Waverton and 2 mi. north of*

Chester on A540, Parkgate Rd., Mollington CH1 6NE, tel. 0244-851666, fax 0244-851400.

■ **Hatton Hall** (inexpensive). Surrounded by a moat dug by Normans, this large 18th-century house has four well-decorated bedrooms with garden and countryside views. *1 mi. south of Waverton, Hatton Hall Lane, Hatton Heath CH3 9AP, tel. 0829-70601.*

■ **Newton Hall** (inexpensive). This 300-year-old house on a dairy farm offers its guests views of two nearby castles: Beeston and Peckforton. Ask for the blue bedroom. *5 mi. southeast of Waverton, Tattenhall, tel. 0829-70153.*

FOR MORE INFORMATION
Tourist Office:
Town Hall, Northgate St., Chester CH1 2HJ, tel. 0244-313126, fax 0244-324338.

Vicars Lane, Chester CH1 1XQ, tel. 0244-351609.

For Serious Walkers:
The above walk can be found on Ordnance Survey Pathfinder Map 774.

Brontë Country

EXPERIENCE 13: HAWORTH

As you approach Haworth for the first time, it's hard to fathom how it could ever be considered a short escape. The village sits just west of two industrial cities—Leeds and Bradford—and signs of urbanization are everywhere. But once you head up a hill and reach the narrow streets and old buildings of compact Haworth, you suddenly feel remote, looking out on desolate moorland.

The Highlights: A quaint hillside village that was the home of the Brontë sisters, narrow cobblestone streets with an active nighttime pub scene, lonely moorlands that were the setting for *Wuthering Heights*.

Other Places Nearby: A historic country park with ruins, a restored five-mile steam railway, boat trips on a canal surrounded by steep hills.

The rugged stone buildings and the narrow streets carry you back to the 1800s, when this was home to Charlotte, Emily, and Anne Brontë. These three sisters wove the rough-and-tumble textile town into the plot of several novels, including two classics, *Wuthering Heights* and *Jane Eyre.*

Main Street is still paved with cobblestones as it was when Reverend Patrick Brontë moved into town in 1820 with his wife, six children, and seven cartloads of furniture. Along the walking tour outlined below, you pass **St. Michael's Church,** where he served as minister, and **The Parsonage,** a Georgian house built in 1779 where the family lived from 1820 to 1861. Charlotte, Emily, and other family mem-

▼

bers (not Anne, however) are buried inside the church. Reverend Brontë's successor, Reverend John Wade, made extensive modifications, so the church's appearance has changed greatly since the Brontës' era.

The Victorian rooms in The Parsonage, though, look very much as they did when the Brontës lived there. Many items used by the family are on display, and the house is now a museum exhibiting the famous Bonnell Collection, which includes letters, documents, original manuscripts, and the miniature books the Brontës made when they were children.

Stalked by tragedy, the Brontës found life in Haworth far from peaceful. Within 18 months of their arrival, Reverend Brontë's wife died and his sister-in-law came from Cornwall to help raise the children. The two eldest girls, Maria and Elizabeth, died in 1825, and the younger ones also fell ill. The reverend became a melancholy recluse, shutting himself in his room. Branwell, his only son, who seemed destined to be a great artist, began drinking heavily, became addicted to opium, and died in 1848 at the age of 31. The Druggist Store (now called **The Old Apothecary**), where Branwell bought his opium, is still open for business on *Main Street*, as is **The Black Bull** pub (*see* Dining, below), where he did his drinking. His sister Emily died three months later, at age 30, and Anne followed the next year at age 29. Charlotte lived for another six years, dying at age 39 in 1855, a year after she married her father's curate, Arthur Bell Nichols.

Although the sisters' lives were short, their literary masterpieces made a lasting impression on the world. Haworth's tall-chimneyed mill buildings and surrounding workers' houses influenced the Brontës, who submitted their manuscripts under the masculine pen names of Acton, Currer, and Ellis Bell. But their primary inspiration was the lonely moorland nearby. This walk takes you on the same path to the moors used by the sisters, past the spooky **graveyard** that the Brontës saw when they gazed out of The Parsonage windows, and past a **school** where Charlotte taught for a brief time.

You walk out of town and go through farmlands before you reach **Haworth Moor,** a vast waste of cloud-swept upland littered with rocks and brown grass. Emily in particular saw the beauty of this forbidding land, and it set her wild imagination running free. In one of her poems,

▼

she wrote: "A heaven so clear, an earth so calm, so sweet, so soft, so hushed an air. And deepening still the dream-like charm, wild moor-sheep feeding everywhere." She later used the moor as the setting of her great novel, *Wuthering Heights*.

In the final years of her life, Charlotte walked the moors and wrote: "When I go out there alone everything reminds me of the times when others were with me, and then the moors seem a wilderness, featureless, solitary, saddening. My sister Emily had a particular love for them...The distant prospects were Anne's delight, and when I look 'round she is in the blue tints, the pale mists, the waves and shadows of the horizon. In the hill country their poetry comes by lines and stanzas into my mind: once I loved it; now I dare not read it."

GETTING THERE

By car:

From Bradford (12 miles away), take *A650* to Keighley. Follow *A629* south a few miles toward Halifax. Get on *A6033* west and drive for less than half a mile, where you turn off onto *B6412* and go less than a mile into Haworth. Park in the private parking lot at the bottom of the hill on the road to Stanbury. Don't overstay the number of hours you pay for—your car may get booted.

Walk Directions

TIME: 3 hours
LEVEL: Moderate
DISTANCE: 5 miles
ACCESS: By car

This walk begins on paved streets in the town of Haworth and proceeds through farmland and moorland on dirt paths and grass fields. There are several stiles to cross and a few tiring uphill stretches, so take your time. Picnic in the grass fields or next to a stream in Points 8 or 9, below, or use the picnic tables in the moorland at Point 12. Pick up provisions in the shops on *Main Street*.

TO BEGIN

From the parking lot, head uphill on *Changegate Street* to the center

▼

of the old town of Haworth. Walk straight toward a gray stone church. *This is St. Michael's Church, where Patrick Brontë served as minister. Only the tower of the original structure remains. Patrick's successor, Reverend John Wade, knocked down the old church and built a new one.*

1. Turn right to go through the church gates. Walk to the right of the church and proceed through an opening in a wall to your right.

2. Turn left up a cobblestone street *with an eerie old graveyard that's supposed to be haunted to your left. On the right is a school at which Charlotte Brontë taught. Just ahead on the left is the Brontë Parsonage Museum, where you may want to stop in to see Brontë family artifacts.* Continue along the cobblestoned street (there will be houses on your right) as it turns into a path. Go through a small opening in a stone wall and continue straight.

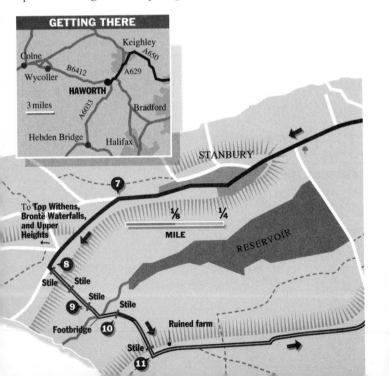

▼

3. When you arrive at a main road, turn left. Follow this main road a very short distance until you come to a fork, where you bear left. Then head straight, ignoring a paved road that branches off to the left. At an automobile parking area on your right, *you can enjoy lovely views of the Worth valley.* Just past the parking area, bear right down a footpath for 200 yards.

4. Just before a wooden gate, make a sharp right down the footpath. Follow the footpath to a road, keeping a wall on your left. Turn left onto the road and walk to a bus stop, which is on your left.

5. Avoid a steep hill on the road by turning right at the bus stop. Proceed on a dirt-and-rock driveway; there will be houses to your left. At a gate, turn left and climb over a stile. **There are two stiles here— be sure to take the one farthest to the left.** Go straight uphill through

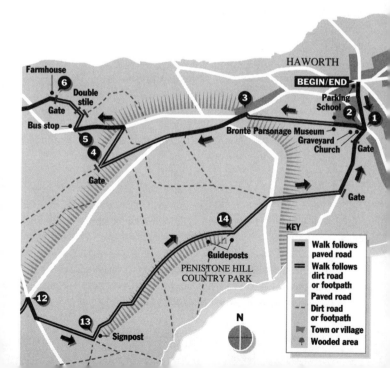

▼

a field (with a stone wall to your left) toward a wooden gate.

6. Pass through the gate. Go through the courtyard of a farmhouse (it's okay to walk through the farm property) and then bear left to a paved road. Walk up the road (with stone walls to your left and right). When you rejoin the main road you walked on in Point 5, continue uphill on it, ignoring a paved minor road to the right. Continue through the village of Stanbury. *You may want to stop for a refreshing hand-pulled pint of ale at the Wuthering Heights Inn, a pub dating to 1835.*

7. When you reach a sign for Top Withens, Brontë Waterfalls, and Upper Heights just outside the village, take the fork to the left (the direction indicated by the sign). Head uphill on a paved road (you pass a house on your right). You will soon reach an intersection with a sign-post. *If you are in the mood for an extra 4 1/2-mile walk, follow the road to the right, to the trail to Brontë Waterfalls and Top Withens, the site of Wuthering Heights. It is suggested that you use Ordnance Survey Outdoor Leisure Map 21 to guide you. The trail loops back to this intersection, where you can rejoin this shorter walk.* If you do not take the longer walk, continue straight on the paved road.

8. About 70 yards past the intersection, turn left at a stile that's opposite a farmhouse. Go over the stile (over a stone wall) and walk straight downhill on a grass field. Continue straight over a stile and down some stone steps toward a stone wall near a stream.

9. At the stone wall, climb over a stile to your left. Cross a footbridge over the stream, make an immediate left, and proceed uphill (a stone wall will be on your left). Continue straight up the hill with your back to the stream.

10. When you reach a barbed-wire fence, cross a ladder stile. Go on uphill, cross a pile of stones, and head for another ladder stile (to the left) at a stone wall. Cross the ladder stile and go straight.

▼

11. When you reach a footpath, turn left. Pass a ruined farm on your left and continue on a paved footpath.

12. When you reach a paved road, turn right (to your left is a rock inscribed "Penistone Hill Country Park"). Walk along the road for about 75 yards. Turn left onto a guideposted path (the sign reads: "No Horses No Motor Vehicles") into Penistone Park. Follow the path for about 350 yards over the moor until you reach a signpost.

13. Turn left onto a dirt road. *For a special picnic in the moor, sit at the picnic tables to your left.* Continue straight across a parking lot and onto a dirt footpath (to the left of a "No Horses, No Motor Vehicles" sign). Go straight across the moor, sticking to the widest, most well-worn path and ignoring other paths that intersect it.

14. When you reach a guidepost that says "Brontë Falls Top Withens," turn left and proceed down a path headed for Haworth. Stay on this footpath as it crosses a road and leads between two stone walls. Turn left at a gate. Follow a stone path between stone walls. Go through a metal gate (to the left is the graveyard that's supposedly haunted) and follow a path as it veers right and into the churchyard alongside St. Michael's Church. Go through the church gates and retrace your steps to your car.

PLACES ALONG THE WALK

■ **The Parsonage.** *Open 10-5 Apr.-Sep. and 11-4:30 Oct.-Mar. Admission.*

OTHER PLACES NEARBY

■ **Wycoller Country Park.** Wycoller was a thriving hand-loom weaving community that was made obsolete by the power loom. The community was abandoned in the 19th century and remained that way until the 1970s. It's now the center of a country park containing the ruins of a 16th-century country house, a 1,000-year-old bridge, and walking paths through pastures, hidden valleys, and moorland. *6 mi. west of Haworth, from Haworth take the signposted road to Colne.*

▼

■ **Haworth Museum of Childhood.** The museum contains a nostalgic collection of toys, dolls, trains, and games from Victorian times to the present. You can purchase items in a collector's shop. *117 Main St., Haworth, tel. 0535-643593. Open 10:30-5:30 Apr.-Oct.; Sat.-Sun. 1-4:30 Nov.-Mar. Admission.*

■ **Keighley & Worth Valley Railway.** Restored steam trains chug along a five-mile stretch of track to Haworth and five other stops. Rail enthusiasts have also restored the charming stations, a remembrance of rail service that operated here from 1867 to 1961. The railway line has been used as a location in several films, including *The Railway Children* and *Yanks. Haworth, tel. 0535-645214. Admission. Operates daily in summer, weekends only the rest of the year.*

■ **Hebden Bridge.** This old cobblestone mill town surrounded by steep hills at the bottom of narrow Calder valley used to be dubbed "Little Switzerland." Take a boat ride on the scenic Rochdale canal or follow the canalside footpath. *7 mi. southwest of Haworth. For boat ride information, contact: Shire Cruises, tel. 0422-832712 ,or Calder Valley Cruising, tel. 0422-844833.*

DINING

■ **Holdsworth House** (expensive-very expensive). This manor house's oak-paneled dining room provides an exquisite setting for a candlelight dinner. Feast on appetizers like the terrine of pheasant, grouse, and partridge with tomato-chutney and Cumberland sauce or the pan-fried queen scallops in a warm coriander dressing garnished with prawns and avocado. For entrées, choose among such dishes as the chicken with a prune-and-almond stuffing and the roast sirloin of beef with horseradish sauce and Yorkshire pudding. You can keep costs down by ordering from a set-price dinner menu. *9 mi. southeast of Haworth off A629, Holdsworth HX2 9TG, tel. 0422-240024, fax 0422-245174.*

■ **Weavers** (expensive). Old weavers' cottages have been converted here into a restaurant with a lot of character. The menu features fresh fish daily and such specialties as crispy roast breast of Gressingham duck with rhubarb sauce. The kitchen does traditional dishes best: Yorkshire pudding with onion gravy or Yorkshire game pie with rabbit, hare, veni-

▼

son, grouse, smoked bacon, and port wine. For dessert, choose a pudding, maybe sticky toffee or traditional bread and butter. *15 West Lane, Haworth, tel. 0535-643822. Open Tue.-Sat. 7-9 and Sun. 12-1:30. Closed for two weeks in July or August and two weeks at Christmas.*

■ **The Black Bull** (inexpensive). A friendly pub opposite the Brontë church, this was where Patrick Branwell Brontë, son of the Reverend Patrick Brontë, drank to excess. Whenever the landlord had an important guest, he sent for Branwell—an expert on many topics—to stimulate the conversation. Some bartenders say they've encountered ghosts at the bar, and the upstairs rooms for overnight guests have incredibly spooky views over a dark, ancient graveyard. The fare includes hand-drawn cask-conditioned beers and decent pub food. *Main St., Haworth, tel. 0535-642249. Mon.-Sat. 11-11 and Sun. noon-10:30.*

■ **Old White Lion Hotel** (inexpensive). This 300-year-old stone inn in the center of town was another of Patrick Brontë's drinking places. It now serves tasty pub meals and vegetarian dishes in the cozy dining room or the intimate barroom. Try the chicken-and-mushroom pie and a hand-pulled beer. *Main St., Haworth, tel. 0535-642313, fax 0535-646222.*

■ **Wuthering Heights Inn** (inexpensive). Offering hand-pulled beers and homemade steak-and-mushroom pie, this pub in a small moorland village outside Haworth makes a convenient rest stop next to the walking path. *1 1/2 mi. west of Haworth, Stanbury, tel. 0535-43332.*

LODGING

■ **Holdsworth House** (very expensive). Built in 1633, this 40-room country house with friendly management and staff strives for elegance, with antique furniture, individually decorated rooms, four-poster beds, and a wine cellar. The nicest and most spacious room is the Adam Brigg Suite, which has a half tester bed. Otherwise, book one of the hotel's other three split-level suites. The Beatles stayed here in the early 1960s; ask the management for a look at the related photographs. Enjoy the lovely gardens and the many trees that hide the house from the town. *9 mi. southeast of Haworth off A629, Holdsworth HX2 9TG, tel. 0422-240024, fax 0422-245174.*

■ **Kildwick Hall Hotel** (expensive). This 16th-century Jacobean

▼

manor house frequently visited by Charlotte Brontë has been turned into a 14-bedroom hotel where oak-beamed ceilings and oak-paneled walls predominate. Sir Laurence Olivier stayed here while filming *Wuthering Heights*. Request the Jacobean Room—spacious quarters with a four-poster double bed. *8 mi. north of Haworth, Kildwick BD20 9AE, tel. 0535-32244.*

■ **Eshton Grange** (inexpensive). This comfortable 18th-century house filled with antiques and paintings is part of a 200-acre farm with a lovely garden and excellent views. The most spacious room is the twin-bedded Brown Room; for a double-bedded room, try the Green Room. At dinner, treat yourself to as many helpings of good home-cooked food as you wish. *16 mi. northwest of Haworth, Eshton Rd., Gargrave BD23 3QE, tel. 0756-749383.*

■ **The Old Apothecary Guest House** (inexpensive). Friendly owners try to keep the peace in this haunted house, located in the heart of Haworth. There have been unexplained footsteps up and down the stairs; the ghosts—usually female—supposedly reach out and touch people and make possessions disappear. Rooms 6 and 7 have had the most reported sightings by guests and owners. A vicar and his assistant recently performed an exorcism to drive out the spirits. The refurbished Victorian rooms all have private bath and television; afternoon tea is served. Branwell Brontë regularly obtained opium from the druggist's shop next door. *86 Main St., Haworth BD22 8DA, tel. 0535-643642.*

FOR MORE INFORMATION

Tourist Office:
2-4 West Lane, Haworth BD22 8EF, tel. 0535-642329.

Books:
You can find the various books written by the Brontë sisters in a public library.

For Serious Walkers:
The above walk can be found in Ordnance Survey Outdoor Leisure Map 21. To extend the walk, *see* Point 7, above. For publications on other walks in the South Pennines, send a large self-addressed envelope to the tourist office in Haworth.

An Inspiration to the Romantics

EXPERIENCE 14: HAWKSHEAD

Travelers throughout the world praise the beauties of England's renowned Lake District, with its rugged mountains, peaceful lakes, dramatic vistas, and alpine scenery that varies in every valley. Encompassing 880 square miles, the Lake District is England's largest national park and contains its highest peak, 3,210-foot Scafell Pike. Not only is the geography unique but the region even has its own wonderfully poetic names for natural features—mountains are called fells, valleys are dales, streams are becks, hills are hows, and lakes have several names: waters, tarns, or meres.

The Highlights: Landscapes that inspired the poets Wordsworth and Coleridge and children's writer Beatrix Potter, spectacular views of England's longest lake, private lakeside picnic spots.

Other Places Nearby: The homes of William Wordsworth and Beatrix Potter, a castle with a 14th-century tower, fine shops and unforgettable pubs.

This experience takes you through forest land owned by the National Trust to the Lake District's most famous mere, 10 1/2-mile-long **Lake Windermere.** While masses of tourists head for the two popular modern towns on the water's eastern edge—Windermere and Bowness-on-Windermere—you begin from the quieter old village of **Hawkshead**

▼

on the opposite side of the lake. Cars and other vehicles are banned from Hawkshead's main streets, so it's a joy to walk through the village's wide squares and along its cobblestone streets, past flower boxes protruding from houses. On a small patch of grassy land jutting out into the lake, you can enjoy a secluded picnic away from the crowds.

Hawkshead was the childhood home of the famous Romantic poet William Wordsworth. You can step inside the **grammar school** he attended in the late 18th century and see the desk on which he carved his name. Wordsworth was so taken by this village and the surrounding region that he took time out from his brilliant poetry to write a guidebook, published anonymously in 1810: *Guide Through the District of the Lakes in the North of England*. An avid walker, Wordsworth supposedly covered more than 150,000 miles during a lifetime of walking. He often hiked to visit two friends who lived nearby, Samuel Taylor Coleridge and Robert Southey, both of whom also became major literary figures (Coleridge wrote *Kublai Khan* and *The Rime of the Ancient Mariner;* Southey became England's Poet Laureate in 1813). As you walk amid the solitude of the same forest Wordsworth passed through en route to Lake Windermere, you can understand why he once wrote:

"I wandered lonely as a cloud
That floats on high o'er vales and hills,
When all at once I saw a crowd,
A host, of golden daffodils;
Beside the lake, beneath the trees,
Fluttering and dancing in the breeze."

Something about this region always beckons writers and poets. John Keats, Alfred, Lord Tennyson, Charlotte Brontë, and Sir Walter Scott made frequent visits; Matthew Arnold and John Ruskin moved here. But no one put their stamp on this region as indelibly as Beatrix Potter.

Born in London in 1866, Potter first came to the Lake District with her parents at the age of 20. They rented a house called Lakeland (now

▼

a country house bed and breakfast called Ees Wyke) on the shores of **Esthwaite Water** at Near Sawrey, about two miles southeast of Hawkshead. In 1902, with the royalties from *The Tale of Peter Rabbit,* she bought the nearby **Hill Top** farm and moved there three years later. She married a local lawyer, William Heelis, and became a respected sheep farmer. Several of her children's stories were written at Hill Top, and nearby lakes, fields, and villages were used in her writings and illustrations. Potter left Hill Top to the National Trust after she died in 1943, and it is now a museum you can visit.

The woods outside of Lake Windermere also used to be the stamping grounds of the Claife Crier, a ghost that haunted the Claife Heights, just south of the path you are walking on. Legend has it that many centuries ago, when the only way to hail the lake ferry was by shouting across the lake to Bowness-on-Windermere, the ghost was constantly calling for a ride. One stormy night a ferry captain rowed over, answering urgent, pleading cries from the Claife Crier. He returned horrified and dumb, remained speechless for days, and died. Travelers began to avoid the ferry, worried about encountering the ghost. The monks from nearby Furness Abbey supposedly came and laid the ghost in a quarry on Claife Heights, and ever since, the haunting has ceased.

GETTING THERE
By car:

From Kendal, which is just a few miles west of the *M6* motorway, it's 12 miles to Hawkshead. Take *B5284* west from Kendal to Bowness-on-Windermere, where you drive your car onto the ferry for the trip across Lake Windermere. (The ferry operates every few minutes during the day and takes less than ten minutes to cross the lake.) Take *B5285* north to Hawkshead. Park in the public parking lot adjacent to the modern shops.

From Windermere (five miles from Hawkshead), follow *A592* south to Bowness-on-Windermere, where you get onto the ferry and follow the same directions as above. If you don't want to take the ferry, you can drive eight miles around the lake from Windermere: Take *A591* north to Ambleside, follow *A593* about one mile west to Clappersgate,

▼

Walk Directions

TIME: 1 to 3 hours
LEVEL: Easy to moderate
DISTANCE: 2 1/2 to 6 miles
ACCESS: By car

The walk follows mainly dirt paths through national park land. You will have to sidestep a few muddy spots and ascend a tiring uphill path for a few minutes on the return to Hawkshead from Lake Windermere. If you wish to shorten the walk to about 2 1/2 miles round-trip, follow the directions out of Hawkshead into the National Trust land, catch the excellent views from the first hill, set up a picnic, and retrace your steps back to the village. For those who do the entire walk, a fabulous picnic spot awaits at lakeside.

Butterworths, located at *50 Quarry Rigg* in Bowness-on-

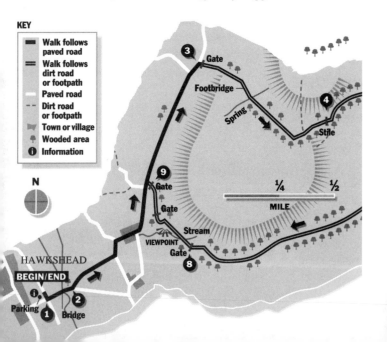

KEY

- Walk follows paved road
- Walk follows dirt road or footpath
- Paved road
- Dirt road or footpath
- Town or village
- Wooded area
- Information

▼

Windermere, is the perfect place for such picnic rations as cheese, onion, and potato pies; home-made scones; excellent sandwiches; and deep-dish apple and rhubarb pies.

TO BEGIN

Walk toward the parking lot entrance that you entered through, heading away from the shops and the church on the hill. Turn right (at the Windermere sign) and follow a paved road.

1. Make the first left onto another paved road. Continue on the paved road, crossing a small bridge over a stream.

2. Turn left onto a paved road, following a sign pointing to Wray Castle. Continue on the road as it curves to the left and then winds to the right. Walk alongside houses and follow the paved road uphill as it curves to the left. You reach a clearing, with lovely mountains straight ahead. When you reach a paved road on the left, ignore it and proceed about 35 yards toward a gate on your right.

GETTING THERE

Grasmere
A591 — A592
LAKE WINDERMERE
HAWKSHEAD Windermere
B5285 — B5284
Near Sawrey
FERRY Bowness-
on-Windermere
4 miles
A592 Sizergh
Castle
A6
A685
Kendal
A591
A65 M6

Stone wall 6
LAKE WINDERMERE
Gate
Gate
VIEWPOINT
Gate
7
Guideposts
5

▼

3. Go through the gate into National Trust land. Follow a trail uphill through an opening in a stone wall. At the next trail intersection, bear right over rocks and immediately cross a wooden footbridge. Continue on the trail (there will be a barbed-wire fence and then a stone wall to your right). Step across a tiny spring and continue on the path, which runs next to a stone wall. When the path fades, continue straight toward a wire fence.

4. Cross a stile at a fence signpost and a white trail marker, and make an immediate left. Follow a well-trodden path through the trees and then through an opening in a stone wall. (The path is blazed with white trail markers.) Head downhill and then immediately uphill.

5. When you reach a guidepost at a junction of trails, follow the trail to the left until you emerge from the woods into a clearing. You can see houses on the bank of Lake Windermere in the distance. Cross a dirt road and head toward a wooden gate. Go through the gate. Follow the path through a field littered with rocks and uprooted trees. Go through a wooden gate, cross over a dirt road, and follow the trail to the left through the woodland. Pass a sign reading "National Trust's Claife Estate" and then one reading "National Trust's Bridleway to Belle Grange." Follow a rock-paved trail downhill until you reach a stone wall. Turn right at the wall and continue on a rock-paved trail.

6. Turn right onto a dirt road. Continue straight on it a few hundred yards.

7. Make a left into a grass patch on your left that juts out into the lake. *There are many large rocks here to sit on and relax—it's one of the best picnic spots you'll find in England.* (If you are looking for a longer walk, continue on the dirt road alongside the lake for as long as you desire, then retrace your steps to this point.) To head back to Hawkshead, retrace your steps back to the guidepost in Point 5. Instead of going right down the trail you came up on, go straight ahead through a wood gate and follow another trail.

▼

8. After a while, you go through a wooden gate, which is in the middle of a wire fence. Step over a stream. Continue on the trail down a hill. *To your left in the clearing is Esthwaite Water, a mountain lake.* Follow the trail alongside (and to the right of) a stone wall. Stay on the trail as it winds to the right and downhill to a gate alongside a stone wall. Go through the gate (with the stone wall on your left) and follow the trail. Step across a spring. Follow the trail downhill alongside a barbed-wire fence that's on your left.

9. Go through a gate. Proceed to the paved road (the one you walked on in Point 2) and turn left. Go straight on the paved road, ignoring another paved road on the right. When you come to a group of houses, follow the paved road as it curves to the right. Continue on the road as it curves left. At an intersection, turn right and follow a paved road. Turn right at the next intersection and go over a bridge. At the next intersection, turn right and proceed to the parking lot.

OTHER PLACES NEARBY

■ **Hawkshead Old Grammar School.** Wordsworth went to school here from 1779 to 1787. There's a library and an exhibition room, as well as the desk on which he carved his name. *Main St., Hawkshead. Open Mon.-Sat. 10-5 Easter-Oct.*

■ **Beatrix Potter Gallery.** The original drawings and illustrations of the author's children's books are on display inside a building that was formerly her husband's office. *Main St., Hawkshead, tel. 0539-436355. Open Mon.-Fri. 10:30-4:30 Apr.-Oct. Admission.*

■ **Bowness-on-Windermere.** An active lakeside resort, it has a steamboat museum, a 15th-century church, and plenty of shops. *4 mi. east of Hawkshead (using car and ferry).*

■ **Hill Top.** This 17th-century farmhouse that was Beatrix Potter's home is now owned by the National Trust and houses a museum containing her furniture, china, books, letters, and other belongings. *2 mi. southeast of Hawkshead, Near Sawrey, tel. 0539-436269. Open Sat.-Wed. 11-4:30 Apr.-Oct. Admission.*

■ **Dove Cottage.** Wordsworth lived at this well-preserved home

▼

near the shores of Lake Grasmere from 1799 to 1808, when he wrote *The Prelude, Sonnet Upon Westminster Bridge,* and other works. Another building on the grounds houses the Wordsworth Museum, which displays manuscripts, paintings, and memorabilia. *8 mi. north of Hawkshead on A591, Grasmere, tel. 0539-435544. Open daily 9:30-5:30. Closed mid-Jan. to mid-Feb. and Dec. 24-26. Admission.*

■ **Sizergh Castle.** A private home for 700 years, this castle sports a 14th-century tower and an interior with extensive early-Elizabethan wood carving. There's a large rock garden with waterfalls and pools. *10 mi. southeast of Hawkshead (using car and ferry); 3 mi. southwest of Kendal, tel. 0539-560070. Open Sun.-Thu. 1:30-5:30 Apr. 1-last Thu. in Oct. Gardens open at 12:30. Admission.*

DINING

■ **Linthwaite House Hotel** (expensive). Hearty, traditional four-course dinners are served by candlelight on mahogany tables at this lovely country house hotel. Specialties include the loin of lamb with rosemary and garlic accompanied by mint-flavored gravy and the pan-fried breast of duckling with honey-and-sherry-vinegar sauce. For dessert, don't miss the hot puddings. *4 mi. east of Hawkshead (using car and ferry), Crook Rd., Bowness-on-Windermere LA23 3JA, tel. 0539-488600, fax 0539-488601.*

■ **The Porthole Eating-House** (moderate-expensive). Excellent steaks and pastas top the menu at this intimate 17th-century cottage, situated on one of the oldest streets in Bowness-on-Windermere. The aim is traditional Italian, French, and English cooking combined with nouvelle cuisine. A frequent special dessert, hot sticky toffee pudding with cream, will catapult you to heaven. *4 mi. east of Hawkshead (using car and ferry), 3 Ash St., Bowness-on-Windermere, tel. 0539-442793, fax 0539-488675. Dinner only. Closed Tue. and mid-Dec. to end of Feb.*

■ **Queen's Head Hotel** (inexpensive-moderate). Vault back to the 16th century inside this hotel/pub with low oak-beamed ceilings and a fireplace. You can order hand-pulled beers at the bar, good traditional English pub food, and restaurant meals. *Main St., Hawkshead LA23 0N5, tel. 0539-436271.*

▼

■ **Masons Arms** (inexpensive). You tend to forget about the fine food in this unbelievable pub, because it stocks more than 200 beers, including many rarities on tap. This place is so serious about its beers that it insists on serving many beers only in the glasses designed for them by their breweries. Tables outside the pub let you throw back a few pints while looking at a magnificent countryside of high green hills. *10 mi. southeast of Hawkshead (using car and ferry), Strawberry Bank, Cartmell Fell, tel. 0539-568486.*

■ **The Drunken Duck Inn** (inexpensive). A centuries-old pub loaded with character, the Drunken Duck serves good pub meals and excellent beer in a very attractive setting. Favorites frequently offered include Cumberland sausage casserole, deep-fried duckling, and, for the vegetarian set, fennel orange and butterbean bake. All beers are hand-pulled or pumped directly from the barrel. *2 mi. north of Hawkshead, Barngates LA22 0NG, tel. 0539-436347.*

LODGING

■ **Linthwaite House Hotel** (expensive). There are fabulous lake and mountain views from this 18-room country house built in 1900 and enlarged in 1910. Set on 15 acres of woodland, the hotel is known for its first-rate service. Request Room 14 for its outstanding view and king-size bed; Rooms 15 and 16 also have excellent views and similarly sized beds. In-room satellite television is available. *4 mi. east of Hawkshead (using car and ferry), Crook Rd., Bowness-on-Windermere LA23 3JA, tel. 0539-488600, fax 0539-488601.*

■ **The Drunken Duck Inn** (expensive). This 400-year-old ten-room inn sits on 60 acres in the countryside. From the front there's a view of Lake Windermere, while from the back there's a view of valley and woodland. Room 2 has a double bed and a lake view; Room 5 has a half tester bed with a patchwork quilt and antique furniture; twin-bedded Room 9 is the brightest and has the largest bathroom. *2 mi. north of Hawkshead, Barngates LA22 0NG, tel. 0539-436347.*

■ **Fayrer Holme** (moderate). Perfectly situated on five acres of land on the eastern bank of Lake Windermere, this modern country home is a reasonably priced alternative. The bright and spacious breakfast room faces the front gardens. Request Room 5 for a superb view of the lake—as well as a four-poster bed and a small Jacuzzi. *4 mi. east of Hawkshead (using car and ferry), Upper Storrs Rd., Bowness-on-Windermere LA23 3JP, tel. and fax 0539-488195.*

■ **Sawrey House Country Hotel** (moderate). This Victorian country house overlooks three acres of gardens that lead down to Esthwaite Water. The hotel stands a short distance away from Beatrix Potter's Hill Top farmhouse. The hotel dining room serves dinner. *2 mi. southeast of Hawkshead, Near Sawrey LA22 0LF, tel. 0539-436387.*

■ **Lindeth Howe** (moderate). Built in 1879 for a wealthy mill owner, this 14-room country house hotel was later bought by famous author Beatrix Potter for her mother. The hallways, lounge, and grounds are lovely, but the guest rooms lack charm. *4 mi. east of Hawkshead (using car and ferry), Storrs Park, Bowness-on-Windermere LA23 3JF, tel. 0539-445759.*

■ **Silverholme** (inexpensive). You approach this small Georgian mansion from a long azalea- and rhododendron-lined driveway and immediately feel secluded on the western bank of Lake Windermere. Ask for the corner room for excellent lake views. Dinner is available for guests. *Graythwaite, Hawkshead LA12 8AZ, tel. 0539-531332.*

FOR MORE INFORMATION
Tourist Office:
Victoria St., Windermere LA23 1AD, tel. 05394-46499.

For Serious Walkers:
The walk in this experience is contained in Ordnance Survey Outdoor Leisure Sheet 7. For 95 pence, the Masons Arms pub (*see* Dining, above) sells a packet containing detailed directions for five walks from its front door. For the same price, you can buy a booklet of 14 walks in the Cumbria region from the tourist board.

▼

Land of Ruins

EXPERIENCE 15: BARNARD CASTLE

Everywhere you roam in Barnard Castle there are reminders of the old market town's glorious past. From the ruined castle at the junction of the town's two major streets to the idyllic remains of a late-12th-century abbey across the riverbank, Barnard Castle's long history beckons as strongly as its plethora of shops, cafés, and pubs.

> **The Highlights:** The ruins of an old castle, an ancient abbey, a historic market town with interesting shops and cafés where Charles Dickens researched *Nicholas Nickleby*.
>
> **Other Places Nearby:** A museum housing works by El Greco and Goya, England's highest waterfall, two ancient Roman forts.

Known as "the Gateway to Teesdale," Barnard Castle keeps guard over the beautiful valley of the **river Tees,** a peaceful waterway that emerges from a wild chain of hills called the Pennines, in the large northeastern county of Durham. This is a land of craggy riverbanks, hoary woods, fertile valleys crisscrossed with stone walls, and rolling unspoiled moorland grazed by innumerable sheep.

On the walking tour outlined below, you'll be able to sample this charming landscape that inspired a host of great writers and artists. Lewis Carroll was raised on the banks of the Tees, and Sir Walter Scott used Teesdale as the setting for his poem *Rokeby* (**Rokeby Park** is a Palladian-style country house two miles southeast of Barnard Castle). The landscape was an integral part of Charles Dickens's novel *Nicholas*

▼

Nickleby, in which Nicholas and the dim-witted orphan Smike escape over the moors from their grim boarding school. Landscape painters, too—such as John Sell Cotman and J.M.W. Turner—captured the splendor of the region in their works. Cotman, who lived from 1782 to 1842, painted *The Dairy Bridge* at **Greta Bridge,** just downstream from Barnard Castle. His contemporary, Turner, used the same bridge for his watercolor masterpiece *Greta Bridge in Yorkshire.*

reta Bridge was the site where the Romans built a fort in A.D. 200 (you can visit other ruined Roman forts in the area at **Piercebridge** and **Vinovia**). A stone from the Greta Bridge fort's doorway, inscribed with the year, is contained in the **Bowes Museum,** an impressive French-style stone chateau in Barnard Castle that stands prominently in the distance as you walk alongside the river. Opened in 1892, the museum was founded by John Bowes, a wealthy industrialist, race-horse owner, and collector, and his wife, Josephine, a Parisian actress and painter. The museum contains paintings by a wide range of artists including Goya, El Greco, and Canaletto and an 18th-century silver swan described by Mark Twain in *Innocents Abroad.*

The town of Barnard Castle has a long history. The site was inhabited since at least Saxon times, and the Normans later constructed a stronghold here. Barnard Castle, which gives the town its name, began as a small earthwork castle built in the late 11th century by a knight, Guy of Bailluel, on a picturesque site atop a cliff 80 feet above the river Tees. In 1112, his nephew Bernard Baliol, an ancestor of the founder of Oxford College, built a large stone fortress there, which for obvious reasons became known as Bernard's Castle. During the 1560s, it was attacked by rebels in the Northern Rising, a plot that aimed to overthrow the Protestant Queen Elizabeth I and put the Roman Catholic Mary, Queen of Scots, on the throne. Sir George Bowes gallantly defended the castle, and though he was eventually forced to surrender, his stalwart resistance bought time and helped to curb the uprising. The attack damaged the castle, however, and it was dismantled in 1629. Many of its stones were used in the construction of nearby **Raby Castle.**

▼

The ruin is still impressive today, with much of the outer walls left standing, spread out over nearly seven acres. You can see a gatehouse, the 14th-century Great Hall, and a 40-foot-high round tower in which the lords of the castle lived. There's a magnificent view of the beautiful countryside from the tower, a view that inspired Sir Walter Scott almost two centuries ago. During the 19th century, a hermit lived in the tower and planted vegetables inside the abandoned castle. Legend has it that the hermit's ghost today haunts the fortress.

A short distance from the castle is **Blagraves House,** where the townspeople feted Oliver Cromwell with cakes and wine in 1648 on his way to Richmond during the English Civil War. Now a restaurant (*see* Dining, below), the house retains the character of yesteryear, with its low ceilings, creaky floors, and small rooms. Farther up the street, in the middle of the road, stands the **Market Cross,** a curious little building erected in 1747 to replace a tollbooth that once stood on the site. The ground floor was used as a market for dairy products, and the town's courts and administrative offices were upstairs. Look for the two bullet holes in the Market Cross weather vane—the result of an impromptu marksmanship contest in 1804 between two men firing from the door of the Turk's Head Inn, 100 yards away.

Down the hill from the Market Cross, you can cross the peaceful river Tees on the **County Bridge,** which was rebuilt in 1569 after the rebel uprising. At one time, this bridge was the place where illicit marriages were performed.

Less than a mile downstream, ruined **Egglestone Abbey** rises as if by magic from the green fields adjacent to the river. The abbey sits atop a mound, and in certain light conditions, it appears silhouetted against the sky. Once you've climbed the mound, you can enjoy fabulous views of the countryside. Large sections of the abbey church and other buildings remain, with empty window holes gaping in the ruined walls. Founded in 1198, the abbey was in severe financial straits for much of its existence. In the 15th century, meetings were held to discuss whether the abbey should be downgraded to a priory because of its monetary difficulties; it was finally dissolved in 1536, and Henry VIII took possession four years later. Subsequent owners dismantled parts of

▼

the abbey and used them as building materials elsewhere. Buried in the abbey tomb is Sir Ralph Bowes, an ancestor of John Bowes, who founded the Bowes Museum.

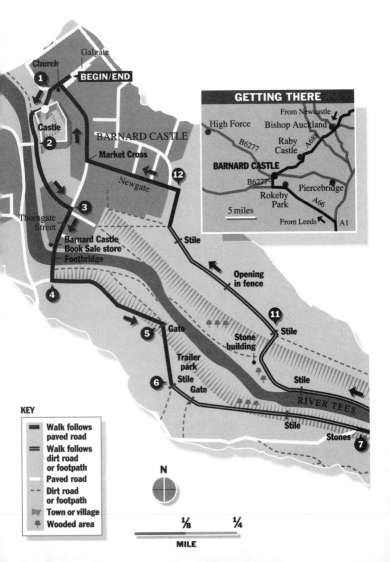

KEY

▬	**Walk follows paved road**
═	**Walk follows dirt road or footpath**
▭	**Paved road**
---	**Dirt road or footpath**
⌂	**Town or village**
♣	**Wooded area**

N

⅛   ¼

MILE

▼

GETTING THERE
By car:

From Newcastle Upon Tyne (42 miles away), take *A1* south. Connect to *A689* west toward Bishop Auckland. Near Bishop Auckland, follow *B688* southwest to Barnard Castle. Park on the main street, *Galgate,* or on one of the many adjacent streets. There are also signs directing you to public parking areas adjacent to *Galgate.*

From Leeds (70 miles away), take *A58* north to Wetherby. Connect to *A1* north and continue on to Scotch Corner. Follow *A66* west to *B6277.* Follow *B6277* north for less than two miles into Barnard Castle. Park on the main street, *Galgate,* or on one of the many adjacent streets. There are also signs directing you to public parking areas adjacent to *Galgate.*

Walk Directions

TIME: 2 hours
LEVEL: Easy
DISTANCE: 3 miles
ACCESS: By car

This walk prowls around the town on paved roads and sidewalks, then it moves into the countryside, where you walk on dirt paths and grass fields. There are several stiles to cross. Stop for a picnic at Egglestone Abbey or alongside the river Tees just beyond Point 7 or Point 10. The town of Barnard Castle is full of shops for picnic supplies.

TO BEGIN

Start on *Galgate,* the wide commercial street in the heart of Barnard Castle. Walk along *Galgate* to a Methodist church at the end of the street. Follow a paved path to the right of the church.

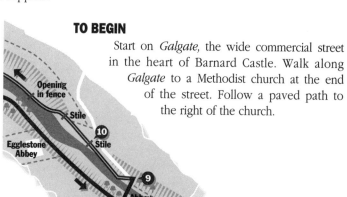

▼

1. At an intersection of paved paths, follow the path to the left, alongside the castle. Circle behind the castle, ignoring a dirt path (on your right) leading down to woodland.

2. When you reach a cobblestone sidewalk (a sign that says "Bridgegate" is on the wall to your left), continue straight on the sidewalk, with the river Tees to your right. Pass the castle, and walk until the sidewalk ends at *Thorngate Street* (in the middle of the street you will see a blue arrow directing cars to keep left).

3. Make a right onto *Thorngate Street*. Proceed on the street toward a footbridge to the left of the Barnard Castle Book Sale store. Cross the river on this footbridge and walk straight ahead up a paved path.

4. Turn left at the end of the path, onto another paved path. Continue on the paved path which leads into a paved road, ignoring the dirt road on your left. (A wooden fence is on your left.) Walk straight past some houses, ignoring a paved road going down to the left. At a stone wall, go through a gate, which takes you into a trailer park.

5. At a paved road in the trailer park, turn right onto the road. Walk on the road between the trailers and follow the road upward as it curves to the right and ascends a hill. About 35 yards ahead on the left—just before you reach the trees—there is a wooden gate that has a tiny sign saying "Please Keep Dogs On Leads."

6. Go left over a stile that crosses a wooden gate. Cross a field, keeping a hedge to your left. Go through an opening to the right of a metal gate and go across the next two fields (always keeping the hedges on your left). Go over a stile and continue across a third field.

7. Exit onto a paved road through an opening between two large stones. Turn left and walk along the road until you reach the ruins of 12th-century *Egglestone Abbey* on your right and the peaceful river Tees on your left. *You may want to visit the ruins or picnic on the grass fields sur*

▼

rounding the abbey. Follow the road straight toward Abbey Bridge.

8. Turn left over Abbey Bridge and cross the river.

9. A few steps after you cross the bridge, go through a tiny gap in the stone wall to your left. Follow a dirt path through thick woodland—the river is now on your left.

10. Use a stile to cross a wooden fence. Go across a field. *This is an excellent picnic spot with soft grass and lots of shade under the trees alongside the riverbank.* At the far side of the field, beside a metal gate, is a stile. Cross the stile and walk across the next field. Go through an opening to the left of a stone fence and walk across the next field until you reach a dirt path on the left. Follow the path (a high wooden fence is on your right), cross the next wooden fence, and continue on. Cross another wooden fence and walk across a field toward a small stone building. Turn right just before the building, leaving the building on your left and heading for a stile to the left of a stone wall.

11. Cross the stile, turn left, and follow a grass path at a 45-degree angle up a hill (walk to the left of a telephone pole). Head across a field at the same angle toward an opening in a barbed-wire fence (located to the right of the goalposts on a playing field). Go through the opening and follow a footpath across the field. Continue across this field (a stone wall is to your right) and cross a stile. Turn right after the stile and walk between two stone walls on a paved lane toward a main road.

12. At the main road, turn left and walk straight back into town. The road ends at *Market Cross, a small 18th-century building in the middle of the road that once housed a dairy market and the town's administrative offices and courts.* At Market Cross, make a right and proceed along another road to *Galgate.* Turn right onto *Galgate* and return to your car.

PLACES ALONG THE WALK

■ **Barnard Castle.** *Tel. 0833-38212. Open daily 10-6 Apr. 1-Sep.*

▼

30; open daily except Mon. 10-1 and 2-4 Oct. 1-Mar. 31. Closed Dec. 24-26 and Jan. 1. Admission.

■ **Egglestone Abbey.** *Open anytime.*

OTHER PLACES NEARBY

■ **Bowes Museum.** In a spacious French chateau dating to 1860, it has a collection that includes paintings by El Greco and Goya, ceramics, textiles, and other art objects. *Barnard Castle, tel. 0833-690606, fax 0833-37163. Open Mon.-Sat. 10-5:30 (10-5 Mar., Apr., Oct. and 10-4 Nov.-Feb.) and Sun. 2-5. Closed a few days before Christmas through Christmas Day. Admission.*

■ **High Force.** The beautiful river Tees cascades over a basalt cliff in a lush glen, creating England's highest waterfall. An area with picnic tables is nearby. *7 mi. northwest of Barnard Castle off B6277. Admission.*

■ **Rokeby Park.** This Palladian-style country house was the setting for Sir Walter Scott's ballad *Rokeby*. Scott visited the house in the early 19th century. Today it has a collection of 18th-century needlework pictures and elegant antique furniture. *2 mi. southeast of Barnard Castle, north of A66, tel. 0833-37334. Open Mon.-Tue. 2-5 May 25-Sep. 8 and one day in early May during the spring bank holiday. Admission.*

■ **Raby Castle.** A 14th-century fortification stands amid park land with lovely gardens. There are extensive remains: nine towers, a 136-foot-long Barons' Hall, an octagonal drawing room, and a medieval kitchen. The stables house a collection of horse-drawn carriages. *7 mi. northeast of Barnard Castle, on A688 near Staindrop, tel. 0833-60202. Open Easter Sat. through the Wed. after Easter; Wed. and Sun. May 1-Jun. 30; daily except Sat. Jul.-Sep.; bank holiday weekends Sat.-Tue. Castle open 1-5; park and gardens open 11:30-5:30. Admission.*

■ **Piercebridge.** A large Roman fort built about A.D. 270 and abandoned 30 years later stands next to the Roman road that crosses the river Tees. Remains include defensive ditches, dirt mounds that made up the wall, a circular oven, and a 28-person lavatory. *12 mi. east of Barnard Castle, Piercebridge.*

■ **Vinovia.** Constructed about A.D. 80, this Roman fort guarded the main road between York and Hadrian's Wall. The commanding officer's house and the most complete Roman bathhouse in Britain remain. *14 mi. northeast of Barnard Castle, less than 2 mi. north of Bishop Auckland, Binchester, tel. 0388-663089. Open daily except Thu. and Fri. 10:30-6 Apr. 1-Sep. 30.*

DINING

■ **Blagraves House** (moderate). In 1648, Oliver Cromwell stayed at this 14th-century building—the oldest in Barnard Castle—where he shared wine and oatcakes with local residents. Today the fare is more elaborate, with entrées like escalope of venison with green peppercorn sauce, sautéed monkfish in a cream sauce with stem ginger, and fillet of beef stuffed with blue cheese on burgundy sauce. For the best value, come Tuesday through Thursday, when a set-price three-course dinner menu is available. A statue of Charles I stands in the courtyard. *30 The Bank, Barnard Castle, tel. 0833-37668. Dinner only.*

■ **The Rose and Crown Hotel** (moderate-expensive). Locals rave about the food in this friendly 1733 hotel that looks out on one of three village greens in the most beautiful village in the Teesdale region. Choose between moderately priced bar meals and more expensive four-course dinners. Expect such pub meals as traditional steak-and-mushroom pie or halibut baked with Gruyère and grain mustard. In the smart oak-paneled dining room, you sit at pink tablecloths under a candelabra and enjoy such entrées as poached monkfish tails with prawn mousse and pan-fried beef entrecote cooked in red wine and black peppercorns. Save room for hot, sticky toffee pudding with fudge-toffee sauce or banana-and-toffee pie. *5 mi. northwest of Barnard Castle, Romaldkirk DL12 9EB, tel. 0833-50603. Closed Christmas Day and Boxing Day.*

■ **The Fox & Hounds** (moderate). Sit near the log fire at this 200-year-old coaching inn and enjoy specialties like roast duckling with hedgerow (blackberry-and-apple) sauce; chicken breasts with bacon, cheese, and mushroom sauce; and fresh salmon with orange and ginger. The kitchen bakes its own bread daily. *4 mi. northwest of Barnard Castle on B6277, Cotherstone DL12 9PF, tel. 0833-50241.*

■ **Morritt Arms** (inexpensive-expensive). You can choose

▼

between expensive dinners and inexpensive pub meals at this laid-back 17th-century coaching inn. The owners like to call their cooking in the dining room "nouvelle cuisine with Charles Dickens-size helpings." Expect such entrées as rack of lamb in a light tarragon cream sauce and lemon sole stuffed with prawns. The pub is full of character, with life-size murals of Dickens scenes on the walls. *3 mi. southeast of Barnard Castle on A66, Greta Bridge, tel. 0833-27232.*

■ **Kings Head** (inexpensive). The favorite dish in this 1704 wood-paneled pub is steak-and-Guinness pie, but out-of-towners come here more for the Charles Dickens connection: The adjacent small building and coffee shop, owned by the proprietors of the pub, was where Dickens stayed while writing *Nicholas Nickleby. Market Pl., Barnard Castle, tel. 0833-690333.*

■ **The Tan Hill Inn** (inexpensive). At an elevation of 1,732 feet, England's highest pub has impressive views over miles of moorland. The 13th-century building is situated in a very remote location on the Pennine Way, one of England's longest walking trails. *18 mi. southwest of Barnard Castle, Tan Hill, tel. 0833-28246. From Barnard Castle, take B6277 south to A66. Go west on A66 for less than 1/2 mi. and make a left onto a road heading south for The Slang, Kexwith Moor, and the village of Whaw. Follow the road for about 8 mi. and then turn right toward Whaw. Pass Whaw and continue on about 5 mi. to Tan Hill.*

LODGING

■ **Headlam Hall** (very expensive). This creeper-covered country mansion offers peace and quiet on three acres of land in a tiny hamlet. The Lord Gainford Suite overlooks the lawn and features a four-poster bed and a spacious sitting area. Or try the elegant Lyme Room, which also has a four-poster bed and overlooks the main courtyard. Amenities include an indoor pool, sauna, and tennis court. Meals are served in a cozy wood-paneled dining room or at marble-topped tables in the conservatory. The kitchen has a fine reputation, offering entrées like poached salmon in white wine served with fresh dill and cream sauce. Keep an eye out for toffee-and-banana flan. *10 mi. east of Barnard Castle, Headlam DL2 3HA, tel. 0325-730238.*

■ **Marwood View Guest House** (inexpensive). A well-furnished Victorian house more than 100 years old, this guest house has friendly owners. Book Room 3 and leave some time to relax next to the fireplace in the guest lounge. The cellar has been converted into a fitness room and features a sauna. Dinner is available on request. *98 Galgate, Barnard Castle DL12 8BJ, tel. 0833-37493.*

■ **The Homelands** (inexpensive). A friendly four-bedroom bed and breakfast operates in this high-ceilinged stone house, built in the 1860s and conveniently located near the heart of town. The back twin-bedded room overlooks the garden. The inexpensive home-cooked dinners are popular with locals as well as guests. *85 Galgate, Barnard Castle DL12 8ES, tel. 0833-38757.*

FOR MORE INFORMATION
Tourist Office:
43 Galgate, Barnard Castle DL12 8EL, tel. 0833-690909, fax 0833-37269.

For Serious Walkers:
The above walk can be found in Ordnance Survey Sheet NZ 01/11 (Pathfinder Map 599). For other short walks in the area, pick up the "Waymarked Walk" pamphlets provided free-of-charge at the local tourist office. If you're looking for a longer walk, the Pennine Way, one of Britain's longest walking trails, passes through this region. Bookshops in Barnard Castle sell guidebooks about the trail, which can be joined near the High Force waterfall (*see* Other Places Nearby, above).

Hadrian's Wall

EXPERIENCE 16: GILSLAND

O utside the tiny village of Gilsland, next to the river Irthing, you can walk through a countryside of wild uplands and deep green valleys. The sites of former Roman forts, camps, and roads surround you, including Rome's most spectacular monument in Britain, mighty **Hadrian's Wall,** which runs just north of the village. Built between A.D. 122 and A.D. 130 by the legions, Rome's elite citizen soldiers, this great wall stretched

The Highlights: A great wall and a fort built along the northern frontier of the Roman empire; deep green valleys; the place where Sir Walter Scott met and proposed to his wife.

Other Places Nearby: Ruins of an ancient castle and a secluded priory that was ransacked in the Middle Ages; a country park and lake; an intimate, friendly market town.

from England's east coast, at Newcastle upon Tyne, to the west coast at Bowness-on-Solway. Standing on the wall, you can gaze out at England as the invading legionnaires saw it almost two millennia ago.

For 80 years, the Romans tried to conquer all of Britain but met stiff resistance. Emperor Hadrian finally decided to abandon the effort and ordered a wall built east to west across northern England, to mark the northern barrier of the Roman Empire. The wall, he said, would separate the Romans from "the barbarians."

In Gilsland itself, two Roman altars were once unearthed, one with an inscription praising Jupiter. Near the village's railway bridge stands **Poltross Burn,** one of the wall's best-preserved "mile castles"—small

▼

forts stationed every mile along the wall, once manned by about a dozen Roman soldiers, next to a gateway.

Many centuries after the Romans departed, Gilsland developed a reputation as a spa. Leisure travelers were drawn to the chalybeate and sulphurous springs just upstream from the village, where the Irthing comes rushing down from the moors. A small spa developed, consisting of a pavilion, a bathhouse, and a hotel. The original hotel burned down in 1859 and was replaced by an opulent building, now a convalescent home. In 1797, at the age of 26, novelist Sir Walter Scott came to the spa on vacation and met his future wife, Charlotte Carpenter, the daughter of a French immigrant. Scott supposedly proposed to her just up the Irthing Gorge at the Popping Stone, so called because he popped the question to her there.

M ost of your walk will be just west of Gilsland. In the remote village of Chapelburn, a suspension bridge leads you across the river, where you walk peacefully along its bank. After you pass through a farmyard, you ascend a hill and then walk on a path right through a missing section of Hadrian's Wall. To your left and right, the wall now consists primarily of turf, though you can also find stones that were used to build the barrier. As construction of the wall progressed eastward, the Romans found themselves short of limestone building materials when they reached Gilsland, and they had to complete the wall with turf. Later, an order went out to rebuild the turf section with stone.

Hadrian's Wall was built north of a pivotal Roman road called Stanegate, which had various forts along it. A ditch was dug on the north side of the wall, except where there were crags. Between the mile castles, turrets were erected as lookout towers, each manned by about six soldiers. During construction, Rome decided to dig another ditch, called the Vallum, on the wall's south side and to add 17 north-facing forts sited at five-mile intervals. Twenty feet wide and flanked by earthen banks, the flat-bottomed Vallum was a formidable barrier; causeways leading from the south provided the only access over the ditch.

Your walk along Hadrian's Wall takes you to one of the ancient forts, **Birdoswald,** which the Romans occupied for 300 years. The fort was built next to Irthing Gorge atop the old turf wall that dates to A.D. 122. A stone wall was later constructed along the fort's northern edge. Originally garrisoned by cavalry and later by foot soldiers, the fort was attacked during the Roman occupation and had to be rebuilt. The north and west gates now lie beneath a road and a farm, but there are substantial remains of the east and south gates. (In the 12th century, stones were removed from Birdoswald and Hadrian's Wall and used to build nearby **Lanercost Priory**). About one-quarter mile east of the fort, on a steep wooded slope above the river Irthing, you can find the remains of the walls of **Harrow's Scar Milecastle.** The south side of Hadrian's Wall between the fort and the mile castle contains Roman carvings and inscriptions.

When Hadrian's Wall was completed in A.D. 128, it represented the most complex engineering accomplishment of all the defense lines that protected the Roman empire. Built of more than one million yards of stone, it stood 20 feet high with a 6-foot parapet along the top. It was 8 feet thick in some places and 10 feet thick in others, and it stretched 73 1/2 miles.

Although the wall was such an architectural achievement, the Romans were quick to abandon it. Just 17 years after the wall was built, the Romans evacuated it and established a new wall, and a new northern frontier, in Scotland. The new frontier in Scotland lasted about 18 years, until A.D. 163 when the Romans were forced to retreat south, back to Hadrian's Wall. For two more centuries the native Picts, who lived in the land that's now called Scotland, attacked the wall—usually when Roman troops were elsewhere—and inflicted a lot of damage. Several times the wall was rebuilt and, finally, in A.D. 400 the Romans withdrew and abandoned their empire's northern frontier.

GETTING THERE

By car:

From Carlisle (16 miles away), take *A69* east toward Brampton. Continue on *A69* past Brampton to the Denton/Gilsland exit. To exit,

▼

you turn left. When you reach the intersection in the heart of Gilsland, turn right and cross a small bridge next to a phone booth and a sign pointing to Northumberland. Park on the side of the road.

Walk Directions

TIME: 3 hours
LEVEL: Moderate
DISTANCE: 6 1/2 miles
ACCESS: By car

Most of the walk is on paved roads through tiny villages in the countryside, but you will also traverse some dirt paths and a grass field. The walk is simple, with no severe inclines, but quite long. Picnic along the riverbank at Point 5 or next to Hadrian's Wall just beyond Point 6. You can pick up unbelievable apple scones and other bakery goodies at the Capon Tree in Brampton.

TO BEGIN

At a small bridge next to a telephone booth in Gilsland (there's a Northumberland sign at the bridge), look for a sign indicating the road to Low Row and Brampton. Bear left, following that road.

1. Pass a Methodist church on your right. Follow the paved road up a hill and then down. Cross a railroad crossing and follow the road as it slopes upward.

2. At a Y intersection (on your right a sign points to Hadrian's Wall, Willowford, and Poltross Burn), take the road to the right. At the next junction (the town of Upper Denton), continue straight.

3. Cross a railroad crossing and keep following the paved road a few thousand yards.

4. At the first house on the right (there's a stone fence around it) in the town of Chapelburn, turn right onto a gravel road. (You've gone too far and missed the house if you reach a phone booth alongside the road in Chapelburn.) Proceed on the gravel road (yes, the gravel road looks like someone's driveway) as it leads between the house and a stone cottage. When the gravel road ends, take a few steps straight ahead on the grass and go through a metal gate to a footpath. This will lead you down into the Irthing valley. At a fat tree on your right, veer left and down a hill toward a suspension footbridge.

5. Cross the bridge and immediately turn right. Follow a path along the riverbank (the river is to your right). When you reach a metal gate near a farmhouse, go through it.

6. Proceed through the stone courtyard of the farmhouse. Go through the next gate to exit the courtyard and follow a dirt path uphill. Continue down the hill and over a cattle crossing and pass an embankment on your right and left. *This embankment is part of the ancient Roman barrier Hadrian's Wall.* Cross the next cattle crossing and take several steps forward toward a paved road.

7. Turn right onto the road. Walk on the road about one mile (Hadrian's Wall is to your right) to *the Roman fort of Birdoswald.*

8. After visiting the fort, return to the road and turn right. Continue on the road as it curves down the hill to the left, past a parking lot.

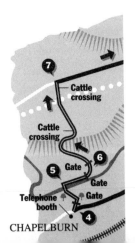

▼

9. At the next intersection, turn right onto another paved road. Walk along the road as it winds toward Gilsland.

10. When the road ends, turn right onto another paved road. Proceed one-quarter mile and walk over a bridge that crosses the river Irthing. You are now back in Gilsland—turn left at the next intersection and return to your car.

PLACES ALONG THE WALK

■ **Birdoswald.** *Tel. 0697-747602. Open 10-5:30 first week of Apr.-Oct. 31. Other times by special arrangement. Admission.*

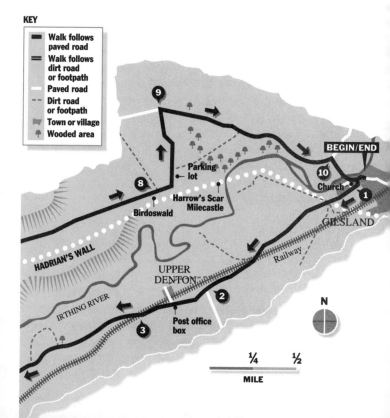

▼

OTHER PLACES NEARBY

■ **Poltross Burn Milecastle.** There's easy access to one of the most well-preserved forts on Hadrian's Wall. Remains include walls of the fort and the north and south gates. *Near the railroad bridge, south of B6318, Gilsland. Park opposite an abandoned railway station. Open anytime.*

■ **Harrow's Scar Milecastle.** This small fort alongside Hadrian's Wall stood near a much larger fort, Birdoswald. On a steep wooded slope overlooking the river Irthing, parts of the mile castle's walls remain. *2 mi. west of Gilsland on the minor road to Birdoswald, off B6318. Access by foot only, 1/4 mi. east of Birdoswald. Open anytime.*

■ **Lanercost Priory.** Stones from Hadrian's Wall and Birdoswald were used to build this secluded priory in the Irthing valley in 1169. It was repeatedly ransacked during border wars in the Middle Ages, but beautiful 12th-century arcades and a chancel containing tombs and monuments remain. *6 mi. southwest of Gilsland, Lanercost, tel. 0697-73030. Open 10-6 Apr. 1-Sep. 30. Admission.*

■ **Naworth Castle.** This fortress was built near the England-Scotland border in 1335 and has been the home of the Howard family since 1602. Fine tapestries hang in the Great Hall, the Long Gallery, and the Library. *4 mi. southwest of Gilsland, tel. 0697-73666. Open Wed., Sun., and bank holidays 12-5 Easter-Jun. 30 and Sep.; Sat. only 12-5 Jul.; Wed.-Sun. 12-5 Aug. Admission.*

■ **Brampton.** Friendliness abounds in this quaint old market town. Try to arrive on Wednesday—market day—when the center of town hums with activity. Notice the stained glass by William Morris in St. Martin's Church. A plaque on *High Cross Street* points out that Bonnie Prince Charlie made his headquarters here before he captured the nearby town of Carlisle. *7 mi. southwest of Gilsland.*

■ **Talkin Tarn.** The main attraction in this 180-acre park is a small lake suitable for swimming, sailing, and rowing. Mountain bikes can be rented, and there's a picnic area and nature trails. *9 mi. southwest of Gilsland on B6413. Small parking fee.*

■ **Housesteads.** Known to the Romans as Vercovicium, this five-acre fort for 100 infantrymen is more complete than any other surviving

▼

Roman stronghold. You can see remains of the commandant's house, gateways, granaries, and latrines. *11 mi. east of Gilsland and 3 mi. northeast of Bardon Mill on B6318, tel. 0434-344363. Open 10-6 Apr.- Sep. and 10-4 Oct.-Mar. Admission.*

DINING

■ **Fantails** (very expensive). Come here for a romantic lunch or dinner across from the village green in a quaint village. Formerly a barn and hay loft dating to the 18th century, the restaurant has oak floors, leaded windows, and a fireplace. The chef does wonders with fresh fish such as soufflé of lemon sole and crab with a cherry tomato butter sauce. The menu also includes a variety of steaks and such innovative vegetarian dishes as the peanut and spinach roast with tomato-and-herb sauce. *13 mi. southwest of Gilsland, The Green, Wetheral CA4 8ET, tel. 0228-560239. Closed Sun. lunch, Mon., and Jan. 1-4.*

■ **Crosby Lodge** (expensive). The owner of this country house is a professional chef who cooks traditionally with a modern flourish. Expect appetizers such as duck terrine served with strawberry coulis and grilled mussels stuffed with breadcrumbs and herbs. For entrées, choose between such items as the pan-fried chicken breast marinated in yogurt and mild curry, and served with a cream-and-chutney sauce, and sautéed noisettes of lamb served with a garlic-and-mint cream sauce. An assortment of desserts fresh from the kitchen are offered on a cart at tableside. *12 mi. southwest of Gilsland, High Crosby, Crosby-on-Eden CA6 4QZ, tel. 0228-573618, fax 0228-573428. Closed Dec. 24-Jan. 31.*

■ **Hole in the Wall Bistro** (moderate). Located in the heart of a friendly, attractive little village, this eatery belies its humble name. The food is well prepared—look for Angus steaks or the Pancake Romantica, a pancake filled with salmon and asparagus baked in cheese sauce. Spinach tortellini and other fresh pastas are regularly featured. On Friday, seafood special night, 10 to 20 seafood choices are on the menu. *7 mi. southwest of Gilsland, Market Place, Brampton, tel. 0697-73481. Closed Sun. Nov.-Apr. and Mon. (except bank holidays).*

▼

LODGING

Crosby Lodge (very expensive). This castellated country house sits on five acres of land adjacent to park land and the river Eden. The nine rooms in the house are decorated with fine fabrics and filled with antiques; two less elegant rooms are in an adjacent former stable. The most spacious room, Room 6, is furnished with Edwardian furniture and has a large double bed and a single bed. Room 8 is also recommended, with a half tester bed and an elegant bathroom. *12 mi. southwest of Gilsland, High Crosby, Crosby-on-Eden CA6 4QZ, tel. 0228-573618, fax 0228-573428. Closed Dec. 24-Jan. 31.*

■ **Oakwood House** (inexpensive). Set on secluded grounds, this Victorian house has fireplaces in the dining and drawing rooms. Request Room 4, which has two exposures and is the most spacious. Make use of the lovely sitting room, and ask for a breakfast table toward the front of the house, by a window. Guests may use a private tennis court. Cottages are also available. *7 mi. southwest of Gilsland, Longtown Rd., Brampton CA8 2AP, tel. 0697-72436.*

■ **Kirby Moor Country House Hotel** (inexpensive). This country hotel was a private house until just a few years ago. Room 2 is the largest, with a four-poster bed. Meals are served in the conservatory, which provides views of the rolling countryside and the cattle grazing in the fields. During World War II the Germans shot down a Lancaster bomber, and the plane crashed into a garage adjacent to the hotel. *7 mi. southwest of Gilsland, Brampton CA8 2AB, tel. 0697-73893.*

FOR MORE INFORMATION

Tourist Offices:

Moot Hall, Market Square, Brampton CA8 1RA, tel. 0697-73433.
Old Town Hall, Carlisle CA3 8JH, tel. 0228-512444.

For Serious Walkers:

The above walk can be found on two Ordnance Survey maps: Pathfinder 546 (NY 66/76) and Sheet NY 46/56 (Pathfinder 545). Rivers and private lands prevent you from walking the length of Hadrian's Wall, but there are many excellent public footpaths along it. To find them, obtain Pathfinder Sheets 534, 544, and 547-550, as well as the two mentioned above.

An Outpost on the North Sea

EXPERIENCE 17: BAMBURGH

Until the 16th century, it was dangerous to travel anywhere near Bamburgh. Situated next to the North Sea in Northumberland—England's northernmost region—Bamburgh was the scene of many clashes between local warlords. The turbulence sometimes erupted into even wider conflicts: In 1513, up to 16,000 soldiers were killed in nearby Flodden Field during a battle between the English and the Scottish.

The Highlights: A wide sandy beach on the North Sea, an ancient seaside castle where *Macbeth* was filmed, a lighthouse station, sweeping coastal views, one of Britain's best pubs.

Other Places Nearby: Boat trips to the Farne Islands; Holy Island, with Lindisfarne Priory and Castle; a coastal walk to a castle defended during the Wars of the Roses.

You see no signs of such strife today as you walk around **Bamburgh Castle,** still perched on its volcanic basalt crag, towering above a small coastal village. The wide, sandy beach alongside it lures bathers and beachcombers, and the only oppressor is the strong wind that often blows in from the sea. Although few Americans journey to this isolated place, it may seem familiar to some—this is the castle Roman Polanski used for his 1971 movie version of *Macbeth*.

Standing close to the village green in the heart of Bamburgh, the

▼

castle looks astonishingly well-preserved. In fact, it was extensively restored in 1903 by Lord Armstrong, and some critics say the overhaul went too far, erasing much of the stronghold's past. Lord Armstrong had stones transported to the castle from miles away by a procession of horse-drawn wagons; if you look closely, you notice that the newer stones don't match the color of their older counterparts. The only original section of the castle that's still intact is the mid-12th-century Norman keep, a square central tower that sports a turret at each corner. But there's plenty to see inside: tapestries, an impressive weapons collection, and unique paintings and furniture, including a cradle that once belonged to Queen Anne. There are also several apartments, including one occupied by Lady Armstrong, the widow of Lord Armstrong's son.

Bamburgh Castle dates back as far as the 6th century, when Bamburgh was the capital of the Saxon kingdom of Bernicia. Its name was derived from Queen Bebba, the wife of King Ethelfrith. In 1095, William II attacked the castle repeatedly. Deciding it was impregnable, he departed south and ordered others to continue the attack. Lord Bamburgh managed to escape from the castle, leaving his young bride behind in charge of its defense. She held off the attackers until the Lord was captured and brought to the castle walls. When his captors threatened to tear out his eyes, she finally surrendered.

The broad, sandy beach you walk on outside the castle brings you face-to-face with the often-rough **North Sea** waters. When the tide is out and the wind is howling, some stretches of the beach make you feel like you're in a sandstorm in the middle of the Sahara. A modern **lighthouse** stands on the shoreline, ready to guide ships in inclement weather. On a stormy night in 1838, 22-year-old Grace Darling and her father hurriedly left these sands and rowed out to rescue the nine survivors of a wrecked steamship, the *S.S. Forfarshire*. The gallant girl died four years later of tuberculosis. The **Grace Darling Museum,** which you pass on your return to the castle, contains the boat used in the rescue as well as paintings and other interesting relics. Grace Darling is buried at Bamburgh's **St. Aidan's Church,** an unusual 13th-century church with no side aisles and a crypt containing a Saxon sundial under a long chancel. Darling's grave is in the churchyard, where a memorial to her faces toward all seafarers who pass by.

Looking out across the water from the beach you'll be walking on, you can see the rugged **Farne Islands** two to five miles offshore. One of the most accessible seabird colonies in Europe lives on these islands, and you can visit them by boarding a boat in Seahouses, located three miles southeast of Bamburgh. In the 7th century, St. Cuthbert, the patron saint of animals, retreated to the Farne Islands. Even today the seals and seabirds there are remarkably tame.

Several miles north of the Farne Islands is another windswept island worth visiting: **Holy Island,** one of the most important centers of early Christianity. A narrow causeway that is covered at high tide connects Holy Island to the mainland. The island contains the spectacular ruins of **Lindisfarne Priory,** considered the birthplace of Christianity in Britain. The priory was founded by St. Aidan, a Scottish missionary, in A.D. 635 (St. Aidan's Church in Bamburgh is named after him). Holy Island is also home to **Lindisfarne Castle,** a 16th-century fort built as a defense against the Scots. The castle was made into a private home in the early 1900s and now allows visitors.

Vikings drove the missionaries from the islands in the 8th century, but monks returned in the 12th century and once again spread the Christian doctrine. Today, no monks live on the island, although any traveler stuck on the causeway to Holy Island during high tide probably wishes they were still there. Some divine intervention would come in handy if you were forced to abandon your car and take shelter in a refuge box on the causeway.

GETTING THERE
By car:

From Newcastle upon Tyne (50 miles away), follow *A1* north about 45 miles to Adderstone. Take *B1341* east to Bamburgh. Park in the castle's upper parking lot.

From Edinburgh, Scotland (60 miles away), take *A68* south. Just past Oxton, connect to *A697* east. Follow *A697* past Coldstream and Crookham to Wooler. Connect to *B6348* east. Stay on *B6348* for

▼

about nine miles to *A1* south. Take *A1* less than one mile and connect to *B1341* east to Bamburgh. Park in the castle's upper parking lot.

Walk Directions

TIME: 1 1/2 to 3 hours
LEVEL: Easy to moderate
DISTANCE: 2 1/4 to 5 1/2 miles
ACCESS: By car

Nearly half of this walk is on Bamburgh's wide sandy beach. The walk is rated moderately difficult because of its length and the slow

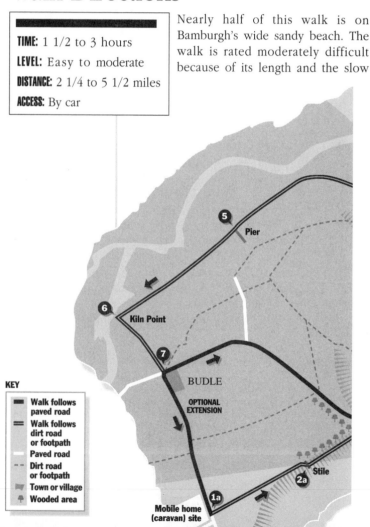

KEY

▬ Walk follows paved road
═ Walk follows dirt road or footpath
▭ Paved road
--- Dirt road or footpath
🏘 Town or village
🌲 Wooded area

▼

going on the sandy terrain. You can shorten this walk to 1 1/2 hours round-trip by proceeding to the lighthouse in Point 4 and then retracing your steps to the parking lot. If you complete the entire loop of this walk, the way back to Bamburgh from the beach is along a major road. For the best views and excellent picnic spots, take the optional 20-minute extension (on dirt footpaths and grass fields) described below.

Stop for a picnic on the lighthouse grounds, anywhere along the beach, or in the fields overlooking the castle on the walk's extension. Bamburgh has few stores in which to pick up picnic provisions, so buy them in another town or village before you arrive.

TO BEGIN

From the castle's upper parking lot, walk toward the castle and follow a path to the right leading to the shore. Remain on the path as it goes

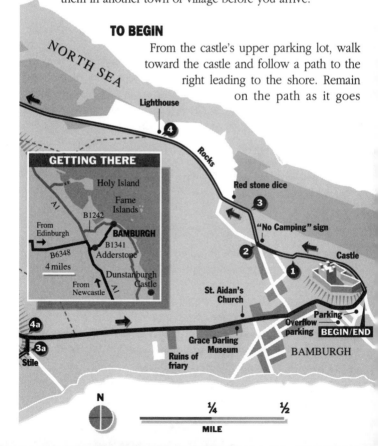

▼

around the castle. When you have circled 180 degrees around it, you will see a barbed-wire fence on your left, parallel to the path. From the beginning of the fence, continue on the path about 12 yards toward a grass footpath.

1. Turn right onto the grass footpath (ignore the dirt path on the left, which would take you through the castle's outer wall and onto the grounds in front of the castle). Follow the grass footpath until it ends next to a house on the right. Proceed forward a few yards to a paved road. Turn right and walk on the paved road.

2. At a "No Camping" sign, turn right and go toward the beach.

3. Turn left onto the beach. Walk over craggy rocks next to huge red stone dice that serve as a breakwater. Continue on the sand and then step up on a rock barrier. Continue straight and proceed toward a lighthouse. Just before the lighthouse, step up onto a path on your left. *If you want to shorten the walk, you can stop here at the lighthouse to enjoy the view or have a picnic, then retrace your steps to the castle.*

4. Pass to the left of the lighthouse. Follow a footpath alongside the rocks on your right. Pass a barbed-wire fence on your left and continue along the shore. Pass more rocks (a life preserver is on your left). *When the tide is out, the beach here seems as big as the Sahara Desert.* Continue on the beach for several hundred yards and pass yet more rocks. Proceed a few hundred yards toward an old pier that juts out at a right angle from the sand dunes, cutting across the beach.

5. Pass the pier. Walk several hundred yards toward Kiln Point, which is at a wooden signpost with a metal sign on your left. **Do not go out on the mud flats off the shoreline. Patches of quicksand exist, and there are unexploded missiles from World War II.**

6. Turn left at the signpost and leave the beach. Proceed up a path (with a barbed-wire fence to your right).

▼

7. When you reach a paved road, you have two choices. You can cross the road and follow the optional extension described below—it takes about 20 minutes longer, but you get some fabulous views—or you can turn left alongside the paved road and walk along it past the minimal remains of an *ancient friary* and the *Grace Darling Museum,* both on your right. Then pass *13th-century St. Aidan's Church* on your left. Continue along the road to the castle's upper parking lot.

Optional Extension

TIME: An extra 20 minutes
LEVEL: Easy
DISTANCE: An extra half mile

This 20-minute extension provides superb views of Bamburgh Castle, the North Sea, and the Farne Islands. You go through fields, on dirt footpaths and grass, avoiding the main road. Picnic in the fields overlooking the castle.

TO BEGIN

Follow the above walk up to Point 7. When you reach the paved road mentioned in Point 7, cross it and follow a paved road that leads away from the water. Go straight on this road for about half a mile.

1A. Turn left (just before a Waren Caravan Park sign on your right) onto a footpath that leads along the edge of a field (a barbed-wire fence is on your left). Continue along the path (trees are on your left). *Ahead are excellent views of Bamburgh Castle, the North Sea, and the Farne Islands.* Go past a wooden fence and continue straight, still with trees on your left. Proceed straight toward another fence.

2A. At the fence, cross a stile. Proceed uphill to the right of the trees and continue on with a stone wall to your left. When you reach hedges and a wooden fence, cross over them by using the stile on your left.

3A. On the other side of the hedges and the fence, turn left onto a

▼

paved road. Proceed several steps toward the main road you crossed at the beginning of this optional extension.

4A. Turn right at the main road and walk alongside it into Bamburgh. Pass the minimal remains of an *ancient Dominican friary* and the *Grace Darling Museum,* both on your right. Then pass *13th-century St. Aidan's Church* on your left. Continue along the road to the castle's upper parking lot.

PLACES ALONG THE WALK
■ **Bamburgh Castle.** *Tel. 0668-4208. Open 1-5 Apr.-Jun., 1-6 Jul.-Aug., 1-5 Sep., 1-4:30 Oct. Admission.*
■ **Grace Darling Museum.** *Tel. 0665-720037. Open daily 11-6 Easter-Oct. Donations welcome for upkeep of British lifeboats, which is not state-funded.*
■ **St. Aidan's Church.** *Open daily during daylight hours.*

OTHER PLACES NEARBY
■ **Farne Islands.** These 28 islands, between two and five miles off the seacoast, are a nature reserve owned by the National Trust. Home to cormorants, puffins, kittiwakes, oyster catchers, razorbills, and terns, the islands are also the only east coast breeding ground of the gray seal. *Boats depart from dock at Seahouses, 3 mi. southeast of Bamburgh. Contact Billy Shiel's Farne Island Boat Trips, tel. 0665-720308; Hanvey's Farne Islands Boatmen, tel. 0665-720388; Mackay, tel. 0665-721144.*
■ **Holy Island.** During two six-hour periods each day when the tide is low, you can drive over the three-mile causeway to this large North Sea island settled by missionaries from Iona in Scotland. **Check the tide tables before driving over**—they're posted on each end of the causeway and at nearby tourist information centers. If the tide comes in and you haven't made it back, you can always abandon the car and scramble into a refuge box on the causeway. The two historical attractions that follow are located on the island. *15 mi. northwest of Bamburgh. Nominal parking charge.*
■ **Lindisfarne Priory.** Founded in the 7th century, this monastery was the birthplace of Christianity in Britain and a place for Christian pil-

▼

grimages after miracles were reported. Viking raids drove out the monks, but they returned in the 12th century. Today you'll see interesting ruins, including a rainbow arch over the nave of the church. *15 mi. northwest of Bamburgh, Holy Island, tel. 0289-89200. Open daily 10-6 Apr.-Sep.; Tue.-Sun. 10-4 Oct.-Mar. Admission.*

■ **Lindisfarne Castle.** Edwardian architect Sir Edwin Lutyens tastefully converted this 16th-century fort into a comfortable home in 1902. The fort was built on a rock high above the island to defend the harbor from the Scots. *15 mi. northwest of Bamburgh, Holy Island, tel. 0289-89244. Open daily except Fri. Apr.-Sep. Admission.*

■ **Dunstanburgh Castle.** A Lancastrian fortification during the Wars of the Roses, the ruins sit on a rocky promontory next to the North Sea. There's no road access; it's an invigorating 1 1/2- to 2-mile walk to the round gatehouse towers, now the home of many seabirds. *13 mi. southeast of Bamburgh off B1339. A 1 1/2-mi. walk north of Craster or a 2-mi. walk southeast of Embleton. Tel. 0665-576231. Open daily 10-6 Apr.-Sep.; Tue.-Sun. 10-4 Oct.-Mar. Admission.*

DINING

Top restaurants are scarce in the Bamburgh area, so you may want to make this a day-trip and move on to another area for dinner.

■ **Waren House Hotel** (expensive). In a Georgian house once owned by royalty and now a small hotel, this elegant dining room offers a five-course dinner menu that changes daily. Canapés and drinks are served in the drawing room. Call for a reservation before 5 p.m. if you plan to eat dinner. *2 mi. west of Bamburgh, Waren Mill NE70 7EE, tel. 0668-4581, fax 0668-4484.*

■ **The Olde Ship Hotel** (inexpensive). One of the country's finest pubs, this seaside bar is located near the dock where you can embark on a boat trip for the Farne Islands. The Olde Ship offers good traditional food, glorious hand-drawn local ales, and nautical curios everywhere. Squeeze up to the tiny cabin bar or stretch out at the saloon bar and order a sensational new local beer, Longstone Bitter. Throw back a few brews and you may wind up a member of the Leek Club, a local society of gardeners that advertises meetings and raffles on the walls. *3 mi. southeast of Bamburgh, 9 Main St., Seahouses NE66 7RD, tel. 0665-720200.*

▼

LODGING

The pickings are slim in this remote outpost, so you may want to make this a day-trip from York or Edinburgh, or anyplace else with a better selection of hotels.

■ **Waren House Hotel** (very expensive). The area's finest hotel is situated on six acres of woodland, next to a beautiful field of oil seed rape and across the road from the wild North Sea coastline. Owned by the Third Lord of Derwentwater before he was beheaded, this handsome—but pricey—Georgian house offers two suites and five rooms with bathrooms. *2 mi. west of Bamburgh, Waren Mill NE70 7EE, tel. 0668-4581, fax 0668-4484.*

■ **The Olde Ship Hotel** (moderate). The rooms may be small and ordinary, but you come here for the atmosphere and the location next to the North Sea. The hotel, which dates to the 1850s, is an excellent place to meet a slew of friendly locals at two lively bars (*see* Dining, above). Room 2 has a four-poster double bed and a view of the harbor. *3 mi. southeast of Bamburgh, 9 Main St., Seahouses NE66 7RD, tel. 0665-720200.*

■ **Beach Court** (inexpensive). From this seaside bed and breakfast there's a good view of sandy Beadnell Harbour—the only west-facing harbor on the east coast of England. *5 mi. southeast of Bamburgh. Contact Mrs. Field, Seahouses NE67 5BJ, tel. 0665-720225.*

■ **Sandford House** (inexpensive). A modern little bed and breakfast with two small rooms, this house has one big plus: a peek at the castle from the room to the left at the top of the stairs. *20 Links Rd., Bamburgh NE69 7AX, tel. 0668-4531.*

FOR MORE INFORMATION

Tourist Offices:

Seafield Car Park, Seahouses NE68 7SR, tel. 0665-720884.
Castlegate Car Park, Berwick-upon-Tweed TD15 1JS, tel. 0289-330733.

For Serious Walkers:

The above walk can be found in Ordnance Survey Pathfinder Sheet 465. For an additional walk in the area, *see* Dunstanburgh Castle in Other Places Nearby, above.

Sir Walter Scott Country

EXPERIENCE 18: MELROSE

Many generations of readers first saw the beauty of the Melrose area through the writings of Sir Walter Scott, one of the 19th century's most popular authors. Although Scott was born in Edinburgh in 1771, his poems and novels explored the entire **Borders** region, the eastern edge of the southern uplands straddling the Scotland-England border. He lived the last 20 years of his life near Melrose, in the heart of the Borders, with its tall,

The Highlights: Stunning views from the top of a high hill over-looking countryside where several Scott novels were set, extensive ruins of a 12th-century abbey, unique lodging.

Other Places Nearby:
Abbotsford, the castellated mansion that Sir Walter Scott built and died in; a ruined abbey and a secluded picnic spot on the banks of a peaceful river.

rolling green hills, vast valleys, and plentiful rivers.

Scott was inspired by the splendor of this landscape and by tales of the Borders' turbulent past, when so many Scottish-English conflicts raged here. *Ivanhoe,* a glorious story of King Arthur's knights and chivalry, was set here, as was *The Abbot and the Monastery,* which immortalized Melrose as "Kennaquhair." In his long poem *The Lay of the Last Minstrel,* Scott wrote tenderly: "If thou would'st view fair Melrose aright/Go visit it in the pale moonlight..."

▼

Scott lived on the banks of the peaceful river Tweed at **Abbotsford House**, only three miles west of Melrose. (If you have the time and energy, you can reach Abbotsford on foot from Melrose—*see* For Serious Walkers, below.) Scott bought a farm on this site in 1811 and built the odd castellated mansion you see today, where he hosted William Wordsworth, Washington Irving, and other writers. His family still owns the house, but it's open to the public and is one of Scotland's most popular tourist stops. Five miles southeast of Melrose is **Dryburgh Abbey**, a ruined abbey next to the river Tweed, where you'll find Scott's burial place as well as that of Earl Haig, the World War I commander.

The walking tour outlined below begins in the town of Melrose, next to another ancient priory, the imposing sandstone ruins of **Melrose Abbey**. Almost nothing of the original 12th-century building stands, but the remaining 14th- and 15th-century ruins are impressive. Notice the Cistercian abbey's elaborate stonework, its pinnacles, and the stone tracery of the Gothic windows. The abbey contains the tombs of Alexander II and the 13th-century wizard Michael Scott, and legend has it that the heart of Robert the Bruce is buried before the high altar. An embalmed heart was indeed discovered in a casket nearly 75 years ago and later reburied in the abbey's chapter house.

Just outside of town are the best-known hills in the Borders, the **Eildon Hills.** About 300 million years ago, the three major hills formed beneath the earth's surface, and after millions of years of erosion three peaks were exposed—North, Mid (the tallest, at 1,385 feet), and Wester. Legend, of course, has a different explanation: a spell cast by wizard Michael Scott cut the head of Eildon Hill into three parts. The Iron Age Selgovae people realized the land's strategic importance 2,000 years ago and built a 20-acre, triple-walled fort on North Hill, the largest fort of its kind in southern Scotland. As you stand atop its windy summit, it's hard to imagine that nearly 300 Selgovae houses were crammed within the walls of the fort. The conquering Romans drove the Selgovae people out in the 1st century A.D. and established a signal station for their Trimontium garrison in the middle of the fort. The Romans remained in control until they withdrew from Britain in 422 A.D.

▼

On a clear day, the panoramic views from atop North Hill are stunning. To the east, the river Tweed winds for 30 miles to the North Sea; to the northeast stands the battlement of Hume Castle; to the southeast, the towering Cheviot Hills—including one 2,674-foot peak—form a barrier that extends for tens of miles.

Since 1018, the Borders has been part of the kingdom of Scotland. Border bandits known as reevers or mosstroopers roamed the area while the English and the Scots raided one another, fighting constant skirmishes and even full-scale wars. Fortified houses were a necessity.

Looking down at the Borders today from any of the Eildon Hills, it's impossible to sense the dangers this region presented to so many people several centuries ago. The Borders now feels so different—warm, lush, and peaceful. Even wildlife is scarce, except for some grouse and meadow pipits (small singing birds that resemble larks). But don't be lulled by the solitude, because some warriors may still remain: According to folklore, King Arthur lies deep within these hills, surrounded by an army of sleeping warriors who may awaken at any moment to defend mighty Scotland.

GETTING THERE

By car:

From Edinburgh (37 miles away), take *A7* south to Galashiels. Just past Galashiels, at the traffic circle where *A7* turns off to the right, go straight and follow *A6091* to *B6374*. Take *B6374* to Melrose. Enter the town and take the fork to the left (*Buccleuch Street*) just before you reach Market Square in the heart of town. Park on *Buccleuch Street* or in the street's parking lot.

Walk Directions

TIME: 2 hours round-trip	
LEVEL: Moderate	
DISTANCE: 3 miles	
ACCESS: By car	

This walk is moderately difficult because its first half is uphill—take your time and you can easily ascend to the summit of North Hill. Most of the walk is on dirt and grass paths that can be muddy, and winds can be strong. Parts of the Eildon Hills are used by the military, so stay out of any

▼

areas marked with red flags or red lamps. Check with the tourist office (located along the way on *Abbey Street*) to find out whether the military is practicing. Fantastic picnic spots are on the summit of North Hill or on the hillside. Provisions can be picked up opposite the abbey at Grahams Confectioners.

BEGIN/END
Abbey
Parking
MELROSE
Market Square

1
Steps
Steps
2
Stile

Double stile

Stile

N

Eildon North Hill
4
VIEWPOINT

3

Eildon Mid Hill
VIEWPOINT

KEY

▬	Walk follows paved road
═	Walk follows dirt road or footpath
──	Paved road
- - -	Dirt road or footpath
⚑	Town or village
♣	Wooded area

⅛   ¼
MILE

GETTING THERE

From Edinburgh
A7
Galashiels
B6374
A68
A6091
MELROSE
Scott's View
A72
Abbotsford
Dryburgh Abbey
A7
From Carlisle
A68
3 miles

▼

TO BEGIN

From *Buccleuch Street*, walk toward the abbey at the end of the street. Make a right turn onto *Abbey Street* and proceed to Market Square. There you'll see a sign indicating the way to Lilliesheaf; proceed uphill in that direction for about 250 yards.

1. Turn left at a sign marking Eildon Walk on the wall of a house on the left side of the street. Go down a set of steps between two buildings. Follow the path leading from those steps to another set of steps heading upward to the right. Climb this second set of steps and proceed straight.

2. Cross a stile. Follow a dirt footpath uphill (there will be a barbed-wire fence to your right) to the slopes at the bottom of the three Eildon Hills. When you reach a fence, cross one stile and then immediately another. Follow the path uphill (now there is a barbed-wire fence to your left) and cross the next stile. Proceed to a wood trail marker and continue upward on a grass path for Eildon Walk. You are heading between two peaks. **Heed the red warning sign to the right of the marker: "Danger M.O.D. Range Keep Out While Red Flags Or Lamps Are Displayed."** At the next junction of paths, follow the footpath to the right.

3. At the next trail marker (Eildon Walk), take the grass path to your left. It curves to the left toward the top of Eildon North Hill.

4. When you reach the summit, *there's a fantastic view of the Borders country from here*. Retrace your steps from the summit to the junction between the two peaks at Point 3. *To extend the walk to nearby Eildon Mid Hill, proceed straight to the summit.* Otherwise, you can return to Melrose by going to the right and proceeding down the same path you used on the way up. At the next Eildon Walk marker, continue downhill and retrace your steps to town.

▼

PLACES ALONG THE WALK

■ **Melrose Abbey.** *Tel. 0896-822562. Open Mon.-Sat. 9:30-7, Sun. 2-6 Apr.-Sep.; Mon.-Sat. 9:30-4, Sun. 2-4 Oct.-Mar. Admission. Closed Christmas and New Year's.*

OTHER PLACES NEARBY

■ **Abbotsford House.** Sir Walter Scott bought this site in 1811 and built the mansion where he lived until his death in 1832. The library contains more than 7,000 volumes, and there's a collection of Scottish antiquities, including Scottish outlaw Rob Roy's dagger and a lock from Bonnie Prince Charlie's hair. In the study, you'll find Scott's chair and the desk in which two secret drawers with letters to his future wife were found in 1935. *3 mi. west of Melrose on B6360, Abbotsford, tel. 0896-2043. Open Mon.-Sat. 10-5, Sun. 2-5 mid-Mar. to Oct. 31. Admission.*

■ **Dryburgh Abbey.** Abandoned in 1544, this ruined abbey next to the river Tweed is the burial place of Sir Walter Scott and Earl Haig, a World War I commander. A lovely, secluded place for a picnic. *8 mi. southeast of Melrose off A68, Dryburgh, tel. 0835-22381. Open Mon.-Sat. 9:30-6, Sun. 1:30-6 Apr.-Sep.; Mon.-Sat. 9:30-4, Sun. 1:30-4 Oct.-Mar. Admission.*

■ **Scott's View.** A famous viewpoint on Bemersyde Hill takes in a panorama of the Eildon Hills and the central Borders region. Sir Walter Scott favored this spot; during his funeral cortege, legend says that the horses paused here without being halted by a driver. *3 mi. northeast of Melrose on B6356.*

DINING

■ **Sunlaws House Hotel** (expensive-very expensive). The menu changes daily at this elegant country estate. Tender roast loin of pork and a heavenly dessert of warm almond crêpes with ice cream were standouts one recent afternoon. At dinner, a successful appetizer was deep-fried cannelloni stuffed with a beef-and-coriander mousse and served in a sweet pepper sauce. Winning entrées included salmon, sole, and monkfish with a fennel beurre blanc sauce and Highland venison

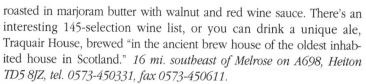

roasted in marjoram butter with walnut and red wine sauce. There's an interesting 145-selection wine list, or you can drink a unique ale, Traquair House, brewed "in the ancient brew house of the oldest inhabited house in Scotland." *16 mi. southeast of Melrose on A698, Heiton TD5 8JZ, tel. 0573-450331, fax 0573-450611.*

■ **Burts Hotel** (inexpensive-expensive). Stick with the inexpensive menu in this 18th-century inn's lively lounge—the expensive dining room tries to reach high standards but doesn't quite. Fresh salmon dishes are delightful, and order the incredible cask-conditioned Bellhaven 80 Schilling Ale, a draft rarity. A nearby college keeps the clientele intriguing. The 21-room inn fails to match the charm of its town-square setting. *Melrose, tel. 0896-822285, fax 0896-822870.*

■ **Melrose Station Restaurant** (inexpensive). An informal, friendly place frequented by those in the know, this hip eatery with good food was formerly a railway station. The menu changes weekly and is eclectic, ranging from lamb moussaka to smoked haddock pancake and from chicken baked with sweet corn and tarragon to venison in puff pastry. *Palma Pl., Melrose, tel. 0896-822546. Morning coffee (10-noon), lunch, and dinner. Closed Mon.*

LODGING

■ **Sunlaws House Hotel** (very expensive). One of the most dignified hotels in Britain, this 22-room Scottish baronial house makes a perfect place to unwind in sheer elegance after a brisk walk. Sunlaws dates to the 12th century, but it was a target of British raids and burned down several times. The present house was built in the late 19th century. Ask for Room 11, a bright space with floor-to-ceiling windows. Darker but the most spacious quarters in the house is the Bowmont Suite, which has a full living room and its own fireplace. *16 mi. southeast of Melrose on A698, Heiton TD5 8JZ, tel. 0573-450331, fax 0573-450611.*

■ **Torwood Lodge** (inexpensive). Situated in the middle of a quiet street, this modern bed and breakfast with friendly owners is a treasure. Request the upstairs room to the left of the stairs—a gorgeous room with two sitting chairs and three floor-to-ceiling windows looking out at a flower garden, horses and cattle grazing in fields, and green rolling hills. *High Cross Ave., Melrose TD6 9SU, tel. 0896-822220.*

■ **Dunfermline House** (inexpensive). This modern bed and breakfast is conveniently located at the start of the walk, about 50 yards from 12th-century Melrose Abbey. There are five comfortable bedrooms, each with a private bath. Ask for the double room with the view of the abbey. *Buccleuch St., Melrose TD6 9LB, tel. 0896-822148.*

FOR MORE INFORMATION
Tourist Office:
Abbey St., Melrose TD6 #9LD, tel. 0896-822555.
Murray's Green, Jedburgh TD8 6BE, tel. 0835-63435.

For Serious Walkers:
The above walk can be found in Ordnance Survey Pathfinder Map 461. The map will also guide you on an additional 6 1/2-mi. walk along the banks of the river Tweed to Abbotsford, the former home of Sir Walter Scott. It takes about 3 1/2 hours to walk from Melrose to Abbotsford and back. For information on the many ranger-led walks in the Borders area, contact the *Countryside Ranger Service, Planning and Development Department, Borders Regional Council headquarters, Newtown St., Boswells TD6 0SA, tel. 0835-23301, extension 433. A small fee is charged for walkers ages 10 and above.*

Where the Highlands Meet the Lowlands

EXPERIENCE 19: GARTOCHARN

Just 20 miles outside the heart of congested Glasgow, **Loch Lomond** shimmers amid a majestic setting of mountains and hills. This is Britain's largest freshwater lake—24 miles long and five miles across at its widest point—but its fame comes not from size alone. You don't have to be Scottish to know the song "The Bonnie Banks o' Loch Lomon',"

The Highlights: Britain's largest lake, surrounded by hills and mountains; a loch-side nature reserve; spectacular views atop a high hill.

Other Places Nearby:
Helensburgh, a seaside town with Victorian architecture and Charles Rennie Mackintosh's Hill House; Dumbarton Castle, former home of Mary, Queen of Scots.

composed in 1745 by a Scottish prisoner in an English jail. Condemned to be hanged for his part in the Jacobite rebellion, the prisoner imagined his soul returning—taking the "low road"—to his homeland:

> *"O ye'll tak' the high road and I'll tak' the low road*
> *And I'll be in Scotland afore ye*
> *But me and my true love shall never meet again*
> *On the bonnie, bonnie banks of Loch Lomon'."*

▼

As you walk to the shore of Loch Lomond, you realize that the banks are bonnie indeed, with the Lowlands and the Highlands meeting in a majestic panorama. The loch's southern end has its own special charm, with high green hills and shady woodlands. On the northern end, 3,000-foot mountains rise dramatically up from the shoreline, towering above the lake's ever-changing silvery ripples. On the tallest peak, 3,192-foot Ben Lomond, snow sometimes lingers as late as May—quite a sight on a clear spring day in the Scottish countryside.

William Wordsworth, Samuel Taylor Coleridge, and other Romantic poets drew inspiration from this glorious lake. On the shore at Inversnaid—a town near the loch's northern tip, with all of 100 residents today—Wordsworth met the "Highland Girl" that he later immortalized in verse. Sir Walter Scott, of *Ivanhoe* fame, used this setting for his poem "The Lady of the Lake" as well as the novel *Rob Roy*, about the Scottish Robin Hood who roamed the area in the late 17th and early 18th centuries (*see* Experience 20 for more on Rob Roy Macgregor). On the first walk outlined below, you pass **Ross Priory**, the medieval priory where Scott wrote this novel.

All of these literary associations and, of course, the scenic beauty, attract thousands of tourists in the summertime. But if you leave the traffic on the lake's bustling western shore and visit the sleepy town of **Gartocharn,** you can sample the serenity of the relatively deserted southern shore. Gartocharn also happens to be the childhood home of actor David McCallum, star of the '60s TV spy series *The Man from U.N.C.L.E.*

On the shore near Gartocharn is the **Loch Lomond Nature Reserve,** a lakeside home for wild goats, red deer, mink, whooper swans, and greylag geese that encompasses woodlands, the mouth of the river called Endrick Water, and five islands on the loch. The lake has about 30 islands, which can be visited by boat from **Balmaha,** a seven-mile drive from Gartocharn. **Inchmurrin,** the largest, is especially worth a stop, with its ancient chapel ruins and the foundations of 14th-century Lennox Castle, often visited by King James IV (who ruled from 1488 to 1513) and King James VI (who reigned from 1567 to 1625). The island later housed alcoholics and the mentally ill.

▼

On **Inchcailloch** ("the island of the nuns"), part of the Loch Lomond Nature Reserve, the remains of an ancient church still stand, a relic of the Irish Celtic saints who colonized this and many other islands on the loch. Their settlements made a natural defense against the Vikings, who savagely raided the land about 750 years ago, but the Celts were not always able to stave off the invaders. In 1263, the Norse King Haakon, who had 60 ships on nearby Loch Long, commanded his men to drag the boats over land and set them afloat on Loch Lomond. Fierce warriors devastated the ancient settlement on the Gartocharn shores. The monks never had a chance—the Vikings made off with their wealth and burned their buildings.

The history of this region, however, always takes a back seat to the scenery—the lake's most powerful attraction. For a particularly spectacular view, you may want to follow the second walk outlined below, to **Duncryne Hill,** which locals call "The Dumpling." From atop this hill, you can look out over Loch Lomond in all its panoramic glory, surrounded by both the Highlands and the Lowlands of Scotland.

GETTING THERE
By car:

From central Glasgow (20 miles away), take *A82* north past Dumbarton. Then follow *A813* north past Jamestown. Take *A811* to Gartocharn. Leave your car in a parking area alongside *A811,* a few yards past and across the road from the Hungry Monk Restaurant. *Duncryne Road* is opposite the parking area.

Walk 1 Directions

TIME: 2 hours
LEVEL: Easy
DISTANCE: 3 1/2 miles
ACCESS: By car

The walk mostly follows paved roads and dirt paths, some of which can be quite muddy. The best picnic spots are on the shores of Loch Lomond. If the weather is very warm, you might opt for a picnic in the shade of the trees in the nature reserve. For provisions, pick up a sandwich at the

▼

Hungry Monk Restaurant in Gartocharn or stop at a delicatessen or bakery in Glasgow, Dumbarton, or Balloch.

TO BEGIN

From the parking area, walk a few yards west on *A811* to the road opposite the Hungry Monk. Make a right turn

GETTING THERE

Luss • A82
Balmaha • B837
LOCH
LOMOND
B832
Helensburgh • A82
A814
Dumbarton •

4 miles

GARTOCHARN
— Balloch
Jamestown
A813
A82 From Glasgow

KEY

Walk follows paved road
Walk follows dirt road or footpath
Paved road
Dirt road or footpath
Town or village
Wooded area

LOCH LOMOND

Stile 11

Stile   Nature Reserve

Stile
10

8   9   GARTOCHRAGGAN

7

To Ross Priory of the University of Strathclyde

Post office box   Caravan site

6

12   Gate
5   Gate
4   Gate
3

Stream

WALK 1

2

GARTOCHARN   Gate   1

A811

BEGIN/END   Parking

1a

Hungry Monk restaurant   **WALK 2**

13
BURNBRAE
A811   Duncryne House
Duncryne Road

Duncryne Hill
5a

4a

3a
Stile

2a   Stile

N

¼   ½

MILE

onto the road and head into the center of Gartocharn. The road will curve to the right and take you past a church. The next building on the left is marked "Community Centre."

1. Pass the Community Centre and make an immediate left turn down the path alongside the building.

2. Go through a gate. Walk down a field, with a hedge to your right. Follow a grass path and walk over some wooden planks. Proceed toward a small gate attached to a tree.

3. Go through the gate. Proceed straight, with a stream and a barbed-wire fence on your left.

4. At a bridge and a gate on your left, go through the gate and over the bridge. Then cross a smaller bridge and go through the next gate toward a paved road.

5. Turn right onto the road. At the end of the road, turn left onto another paved road. Walk about 100 yards.

6. Turn right at the red post office box and go along a private paved road. The road will bear right. Follow the sign to the nature reserve.

7. At the next junction, take the left fork.

8. When the road bears right and runs parallel to the loch, leave the road and spend some time at the shore. *Here, looking out at the islands in the middle of the loch, you have a fabulous picnic spot.* Go back to the road and turn left onto it. Continue on toward the Loch Lomond Nature Reserve.

9. Go through a small wooden gate next to the road to enter the reserve. Follow a footpath. *The trees of the nature reserve block out the* *sun, and it seems you're in your own private forest.*

10. Cross a stile. Proceed on the footpath toward another stile.

11. Turn around at the next stile. Retrace your steps to the post office box that you passed in Point 6, above. At the intersection by the post office box, turn right onto the paved road instead of retracing your steps to Gartocharn. Follow the paved road, which will circle back into town on another route.

12. Pass the Priory of the University of Strathclyde, on your right. *This was formerly the Ross Priory, where Sir Walter Scott wrote his novel about the Scottish outlaw Rob Roy. It is now a university conference center and is not open to the public.* As you walk uphill on this road, look back over your shoulder for sweeping views of Loch Lomond. Continue on the paved road toward the main road, *A811.*

13. When you reach the main road, *A811,* turn left. Follow the road back to your car.

Walk 2 Directions

TIME: 1 hour

LEVEL: Easy to moderate

DISTANCE: 2 miles

ACCESS: By car

This second walk in Gartocharn leads you away from Loch Lomond on a paved road. You then walk through a short stretch of woodland on a dirt path and proceed across a field to the base of Duncryne Hill. The path and the field can be very muddy. The ascent to the top of the hill is steep, so go slow and stop a few times to catch your breath. The hilltop makes a perfect picnic spot.

TO BEGIN

Start in the same place as in the previous walk—at the parking area alongside *A811* in Gartocharn.

1A. Cross *A811* to *Duncryne Road.* Proceed on the paved road for half a mile, or about 10 to 15 minutes. You pass open fields on the left and right and then, on the left, Duncryne House and Duncryne Cottage. About 100 yards past the cottage, at the end of a line of trees, walk toward an iron gate and a stile on your left. (If you reach another open field, you have gone too far.)

2A. Go left and cross the stile. Follow a footpath. **Beware of mud** as you go through the woodland.

3A. Cross another stile into a field. Go straight along the path with a barbed-wire fence to your right. Proceed toward a small picket gate.

4A. Go through the gate and make an immediate right onto a footpath. Follow the path up the hill.

5A. *Atop the hill, sit down and enjoy the spectacular view of Loch Lomond.* When you can tear yourself away from the view, retrace your steps down the hill to the starting point.

PLACES ALONG THE WALK
■ **Loch Lomond Nature Reserve.** *Limited area in Gartocharn open anytime to visitors. For information, contact Balloch Castle Country Park, tel. 0389-58511.*

OTHER PLACES NEARBY
■ **Balloch Castle Country Park.** A castle built in 1808 sits in this peaceful country park in a bustling town along the southern shores of Loch Lomond. The park offers great views up the loch, wide grassy areas for picnics, beautiful woodland, a nature trail, and a lovely walled garden. *4 mi. southwest of Gartocharn, Balloch, tel. 0389-58511. Open sunrise-sunset all year. Visitors center open daily 10-6 Easter-Sep.*
■ **Helensburgh.** Where Highland and Lowland converge and meet the open sea, Victorian architecture abounds in this town of broad streets, a promenade, and restful parks. In springtime, cherry and apple blossoms

▼

add to the beauty. For a contemporary touch, stop at Charles Rennie Mackintosh's Hill House, a modern architectural treasure now in the care of the National Trust. *12 mi. southwest of Gartocharn. Hill House is on Upper Colquhoun St., tel. 0436-73900. Open daily 1-5. Admission.*

■ **Luss.** On the western shores of Loch Lomond, this quaint village has Victorian sandstone cottages, a sandy beach, and a lively pier. It's the setting for *Take the High Road,* a popular Scottish television series. *12 mi. northwest of Gartocharn on A82.*

■ **Balmaha.** From this village on the wooded eastern shore of Loch Lomond, you can take a small mail boat to the islands on the loch or walk through the forests on the West Highland Way. *7 mi. north of Gartocharn on B837.*

■ **Dumbarton Castle.** Mary, Queen of Scots, lived in this medieval castle before leaving to become the child bride of the French Dauphin. There are some fabulous views of the loch from Dumbarton Rock, which was first occupied as a stronghold in the 4th century. *8 mi. south of Gartocharn, Dumbarton, tel. 0389-32828. Open Mon.-Sat. 9:30-6:30, Sun. 2-7 Apr.-Sep.; Mon.-Wed. and Sat. 9:30-4, Thu. 9:30-noon, Sun. 2-4 Oct.-Mar. Admission.*

DINING

■ **Cameron House** (very expensive). The finest and most luxurious restaurant in the area is this hotel's Georgian Room. Beneath chandeliers, you dine on entrées like pan-fried fillet of wild Tay salmon or breast of Gressingham duck garnished with pear, apple, bacon, and caramelized orange sauce. The set-price three-course Market Menu will save you a few dollars. If you want something less expensive, head for the Brasserie, where you can get everything from tandoori chicken to fish and chips. The Grill Room serves breakfast and a Sunday lunch buffet. *6 mi. southwest of Gartocharn, on the Loch Lomond shore and off A82, Alexandria G83 8QZ, tel. 0389-55565, fax 0389-59522.*

■ **Braeval Old Mill** (very expensive). Some of Scotland's best meals come from the kitchen of this beautifully restored old stone mill. Call ahead to find out what's on the day's menu because there are no choices with the set-price four-course dinner. Recent successes have

▼

included warm rabbit salad with green lentils and halibut on a bed of spinach. *13 mi. northeast of Gartocharn, Aberfoyle, tel. 0877-2711. Open for dinner Tue.-Sat. and lunch Sun.*

■ **Lake Hotel** (expensive). The beautiful dining area looks out on Lake Menteith, Scotland's only "lake" (a foreign map maker mistakenly used the word "lake" instead of "loch"). When we visited, Princess Anne was arriving for dinner. The dinner menu changes daily—recent entrées included fillet of shark in a fennel and cream sauce and lamb liver baked with chestnuts and port. Look for rainbow trout from the lake. *15 mi. northeast of Gartocharn on A81, Port of Menteith FK8 3RA, tel. 0877-5258, fax 0877-5671.*

■ **The Hungry Monk** (moderate). This comfortable restaurant won't win any culinary awards, but it's a great pit stop at the start or finish of your walk. The food is decent—try a steak for dinner or steak-and-mushroom pie for lunch. There's a nice bar area and a patio on the side. Rooms are also available, but they're small and expensive—you can do better at a local bed and breakfast. *Rte. A811, Gartocharn, tel. 0389-83448, fax 0389-58113. Open daily 10-noon for coffee and tea, noon-10 for lunch and dinner.*

LODGING

■ **Cameron House** (very expensive). This elegant 17th-century house on 100 acres alongside Loch Lomond has an attached sports and entertainment complex with loads of facilities: an indoor swimming pool with water slide, squash courts, indoor badminton courts, a hair salon. Ask for a room with a sofa and a view of the loch—it costs the same as any other double and is more spacious. Or splurge and spend 275 pounds (as of this writing) for the double-Jacuzzi Katrine Suite, where such high-profile guests as Pavarotti and Cher have stayed; the suite has dual views of the loch and Ben Lomond, the highest mountain in the area. The ultimate temptation is the Castle Suite, which offers a panoramic 360-degree view from inside a turret. *6 mi. southwest of Gartocharn, on the Loch Lomond shore and off A82, Alexandria G83 8QZ, tel. 0389-55565, fax 0389-59522.*

■ **Culcreuch Castle** (expensive). This historic 14th-century castle

▼

tucked away on 1,600 acres of land offers a splendid view of reddish hills. Like many castles, it can get a bit cold and gloomy, but you can always head for the dungeon bar for good cheer. And where else can you find six-foot-thick walls and rooms with 250-year-old wallpaper? Both the Baron's Suite—a favorite of honeymooners—and the Napier Suite have four-poster beds. *13 mi. east of Gartocharn, Fintry G63 OLW, tel. 0360-86228.*

■ **Lake Hotel** (expensive). Although the price is high, you're paying for a lovely lakeside setting and a great view of the Trossachs hills. The rooms are otherwise basic in this refurbished 19th-century manse. Suites 1 and 2 are spacious and have the best views. *15 mi. northeast of Gartocharn on A81, Port of Menteith FK8 3RA, tel. 0877-5258, fax 0877-5671.*

■ **Lomond Bank Guest House** (inexpensive). You'll have impressive views of the loch from this late-Victorian red sandstone home set on 12 acres of land. Ask for the room with the private bath—it's spacious and has a king-size bed. Dinner is served on request. *7 mi. north of Gartocharn, Lomond Bank, Balmaha G63 OJQ, tel. 0360-87213. Open Mar.-Oct.*

FOR MORE INFORMATION
Tourist Offices:

Old Station Building, Balloch Rd., Balloch G83 8LQ, tel. 0389-53533.

The Clock Tower, E. Clyde St., Helensburgh G84 8AU, tel. 0436-72642.

41 Dumbarton Rd., Stirling FK8 2LQ, tel. 0786-75019.

For Serious Walkers:

The two walks above can be found in Ordnance Survey Pathfinder Map 391. For a real challenge, experienced walkers may want to try the West Highland Way, a 95-mile walking trail extending from the outskirts of Glasgow to Fort William. The trail runs along Loch Lomond's eastern shore and connects the Highlands and the Lowlands. A comprehensive book and map called *West Highland Way* can be purchased from: *West Highlands and Islands off Argyll Tourist Board, Albany St., Oban, Scotland PA34 4AR, tel. 0631-63122.*

The Den of a Notorious Outlaw

EXPERIENCE 20: BALQUHIDDER

Although one member of the family ruled Scotland in the 9th century and another served as an army lieutenant for King Charles II 800 years later, upstanding civic duty and allegiance to government were not the legacy of the Macgregor clan. Possibly Scotland's most famous bloodline, the Macgregors were better known as outlaws who stole cattle, fought viciously with their neighbors, and defied authority. And

The Highlights: A peaceful glen with high mountains and two pristine lochs, an intimate gourmet dinner at an inn in the middle of nowhere, excellent country bed and breakfasts.

Other Places Nearby: One of Scotland's most well-preserved castles; Callander, a lively town on the edge of the Scottish Highlands next to a high mountain and a deep gorge.

there was no Macgregor more notorious than Rob Roy, the Robin Hood of Scotland.

This experience takes you to beautiful **Balquhidder Glen,** where Rob Roy lived, fought, and later died. You will walk on a bank of **Loch Voil,** a 3 1/4-mile-long lake surrounded by the hills and mountains of the Scottish Highlands. The views across the loch are breathtaking: the houses of Balquhidder set against grass-covered mountains, the gorgeous valley of **Monachyle Glen,** and towering 3,800-foot Ben

185

▼

More, a peak that's sometimes still snow-covered in May. Along the north bank of Loch Voil, you'll see the wooded slopes known as the **Braes of Balquhidder**. When you reach the end of the loch, you can peer over another lake, tiny **Loch Doine**, and a private estate where Rob Roy spent part of his life. Set up a picnic on the bank above the loch and you can absorb all this Highland splendor at leisure.

ob Roy began his career at age 19 by recovering some stolen cattle for the Earl of Breadalbane. He was then paid to protect various owners' herds. Soon, however, he was ambushing other people's cattle drives, and he eventually spearheaded a thriving family business—regulating the flow of cattle through the narrow passes of the Trossachs hills around Loch Katrine and Loch Vennachar, just south of Balquhidder and east of Loch Lomond. Trossachs means "the bristly country," an apt name for this rugged landscape, a patchwork of heather, woodland, and rocky outcrops. Although most beautiful in autumn, the district is rich in color from early spring onward, with the variegated greens of birch, oak, and hazel trees, the grays and blues of the crags, and the browns and purples of bracken and heather. Punctuated by mountains and lochs, it is perfect country for cattle-rustling.

The Macgregors, who approved entirely of Rob's exploits, weren't motivated solely by greed. As Jacobites, supporters of the deposed Stuart kings, they relished taunting the detested new lowland government. During an autumn cattle sale in Crieff, a few miles east of Balquhidder, Rob and 30 of his men openly defied King George I by drinking to the health of James Stuart, who was then living in exile in France.

The Duke of Montrose, a government loyalist who ruled the lowland area of Loch Lomond (*see* Experience 19), was one of Rob Roy's greatest foes thanks to a business deal that went awry between them in 1712. The duke had paid 1,000 pounds for some of Rob's cattle, but one of Rob's men took the money and vanished. Rob was faced with a serious predicament: He had offered his property as collateral, and the Edinburgh newspapers were speculating that Rob had the duke's money and was using it to arm the Jacobites in an uprising against the

▼

government. The duke, figuring that he had Rob over a barrel, tried to use him as a political pawn. He told Rob to announce publicly that the duke's rival, the Duke of Argyll, was planning a revolt with the Jacobites. Rob refused, so the duke sent one of his men, Grahame of Killearn, to seize Rob's land and possessions and to throw the outlaw's family out of their house despite the freezing winter weather.

Seeking revenge, Rob ordered his men to steal cattle and grain from Grahame of Killearn. In addition, he extorted rents from the duke's wealthy subjects, brashly handing out signed receipts for the diverted rent money. Yet Rob spared the poor and even came to their aid. He gave money to one bankrupt villager who was about to be evicted from her home, warning her to get written proof that her debts were paid. In typical fashion, Rob's band then hid in the woods and stole the money back from the debt collector. When the Duke of Montrose and the Duke of Atholl teamed up to capture Rob (hoping to thus gain favor with King George), the grateful local villagers helped to hide him, in Balquhidder and at other homes in the region.

Rob Roy's adventures were daring and romantic indeed. At one point, Montrose's men captured Rob as he slept inside a cottage in Balquhidder, but as they were leading the bound captive away on horseback, he pulled out a knife, cut himself loose, and escaped. On another occasion, two of Montrose and Atholl's officers met near Loch Katrine to plot Rob's capture and decided to spend the night in a cave. The men unknowingly chose one of Rob's favorite hideouts and were shocked to see him emerge from the back of the cave with his guns blazing. Rob spared their lives and sent them back to their lords with words of defiance.

Government cavalry troops made a surprise attack on Balquhidder Glen and seized Rob at his cousin's farm in Monachyle Tuarach, but while the posse was fording a river near Sterling, Rob slipped out of his saddle, scrambled through the water, and escaped into the woods. After the king recalled his troops (he didn't want to incite a revolt from other Highland clans), Rob returned to Balquhidder Glen, bought land, and devoted time to his cattle business.

At the age of 63, Rob became embroiled in a dispute between the

▼

Macgregors and a neighboring clan, the MacLarens, over land rights in Balquhidder. In an attempt to avoid major clan warfare, the aging Rob offered to duel the MacLarens's best warrior and received his first-ever wounds in battle. Eventually he agreed to meet the leader of the MacLarens clan in peace talks. Although he was ill, his wife (Mary of Comar, another member of the Macgregor clan) outfitted him in ceremonial dress and armed him with a gun and a dagger. When the meeting was over, Rob turned to his wife and said: "Now all is over. Put me to bed. Call the piper. Let him play 'Cha Till Mi Tuille,' for my time is come. As the piper plays the old lament, I shall return no more." He died and was buried in the Balquhidder churchyard, where his wife and two of his four sons were eventually laid beside him. Outside the old parish kirk that dates to 1631 and is now a ruin, you can visit **Rob Roy's gravestone,** which bears the tragic arms of the Macgregor clan, an uprooted pine tree.

GETTING THERE

By car:

From central Glasgow (27 miles away), take *A879* north to *A81* north. Stay on *A81* to Callander. Take *A84* to the Balquhidder exit. Go

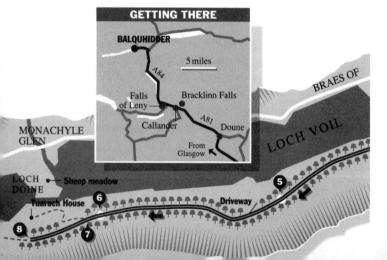

▼

under a bridge and follow the road to Balquhidder. Make the first left after the church, at the red telephone booth. Go over a stone bridge. Bear right onto a dirt road and follow it as it winds to the right and passes a pond. At the next junction of dirt roads, take the dirt road to the left, following a sign on the left for Stronvar Country House Hotel. Turn into the parking lot on your left.

Walk Directions

TIME: 1 to 3 hours round-trip
LEVEL: Easy to moderate
DISTANCE: 1 to 6 1/2 miles
ACCESS: By car

This leisurely stroll on a single dirt road above Loch Voil has no severe inclines and is rated moderate only because of its length. The walk can be shortened to any time or distance by simply turning around at any point and retracing your steps to the parking

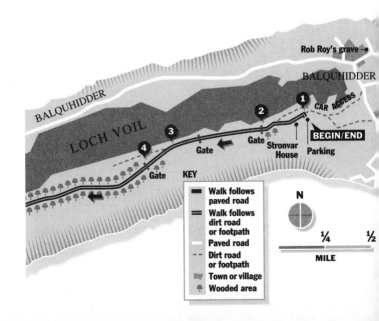

▼

lot. Picnic anywhere alongside the road. Provisions can be bought in Callander, at the Four Seasons grocery and delicatessen, *72 Main Street.*

TO BEGIN

From the parking lot, walk toward the road.

1. Turn left onto the road. Pass the Stronvar House and Bygones Museum on the left, *or stop in for a drink and a snack.* Follow the dirt road as it bears to the right and passes Stronvar Farm.

2. Go through a metal gate. Pass a Muirlaggan Farm sign on the right and proceed through another metal gate.

3. At the next junction of two dirt roads, take the road to the left, following "Hikers This Way Please" and "Muirlaggan Forest" signs.

4. Go through a big wooden gate. Follow the dirt road uphill. Stay on this road for about 1 1/4 mi..

5. You eventually reach a clearing that is scattered with rocks but looks like a car turnaround. Continue straight and look to your right at the red-tinged banks across the loch. Then pass a driveway on the right. Proceed about 3/4 mi.

6. Stop to savor the view at the next car turnaround area. Continue about 100 yards.

7. At a junction of dirt roads, bear left (don't take the dirt road to the right for Tuarach House, *a private residence that used to be the home of Rob Roy).* Continue another 100 yards or so.

8. You are now at the end of Loch Voil. *To the right, you overlook a sheep meadow between Loch Voil and Loch Doine. On the opposite bank, you look up Monachyle Glen and over a pink country hotel at its mouth.* Retrace your steps to your car.

▼

OTHER PLACES NEARBY

■ **Rob Roy's grave.** The outlaw is buried next to his wife, Mary, and two of his sons in front of Balquhidder Church. The headstone reads: "Macgregor Despite Them." *In Balquhidder. The grave can be viewed at any time.*

■ **Doune Castle.** This 14th-century castle, with a moat and a 95-foot-high gatehouse tower, is one of the best-preserved in Scotland. *18 mi. southeast of Balquhidder off A84, Doune, tel. 0786-841742. Open Mon.-Sat. 9:30-7, Sun. 2-7 Apr.-Sep.; Mon.-Thu. and Sat. 9:30-4, Sun. 2-4 Oct.-Mar. Closed alternate Sats. Admission.*

■ **Callander.** At the edge of the Scottish Highlands, next to 2,800-foot-high Ben Ledi (Mountain of God), this bustling small town has lots of shops and a large tourist center that shows a Rob Roy film. *12 mi. southeast of Balquhidder. Tourist center closed Christmas, New Year's, most of Jan., all of Feb. Admission for film.*

■ **Bracklinn Falls.** From a bridge, you look down at a deep gorge with a series of shelves over which the waters of the Keltie Burn fall en route to the river Teith. The gorge is a pleasant 1/2-mile walk from the parking lot. *13 mi. southeast of Balquhidder, Bracklinn Rd., Callander.*

■ **Falls of Leny.** A raging waterfall is located in the Pass of Leny, a major route to the Highlands for thousands of years. *2 mi. northwest of Callander off A84.*

DINING

■ **Roman Camp Country House Hotel** (very expensive). Specialties at this elegant hotel include salmon from nearby waters and such freshly shot game as venison, roasted with shallots and juniper berries on a red-cabbage-and-apple compote. Appetizers range from ravioli of Melleigh fish with leek-and-tomato stew to Angus beef marinated in sherry vinegar. You dine by candlelight and next to a fireplace. *12 mi. southeast of Balquhidder. Main St., Callander FK17 8BG, tel. 0877-30003, fax 0877-31533. Closed Jan. 5-Mar. 1.*

■ **Monachyle Mhor** (moderate). Chef Jean Lewis and her husband, Rob, create country cooking with a gourmet flair in this intimate setting looking out on the lush mountains alongside two lochs in the heart of the Braes of Balquhidder. Recent culinary winners were smoked Scottish salmon with lemon and marigold leaves and breast of duck with raspberry piquant sauce. Don't miss the white-chocolate-and-Cointreau mousse. Dinners are a good value, and there's a lively bar. *4 mi. west of Balquhidder, Balquhidder FK19 8PQ, tel. 0877-4622, fax 0877-4305. Breakfast and dinner only.*

LODGING

■ **Roman Camp Country House Hotel** (very expensive). A short walk from Callander's shops, this 14-room pink-turreted hotel on the site of a Roman encampment was designed in 1625 as a hunting lodge for the Dukes of Perth. All rooms have a view of the 20-acre garden, contain Victorian and Edwardian furniture, and are provided with fresh flowers. Reserve the Yellow Parlour or the Barrie Suite, both of which have a double bed. *12 mi. southeast of Balquhidder. Main St., Callander FK17 8BG, tel. 0877-30003, fax 0877-31533. Closed Jan. 5-Mar. 1.*

■ **Monachyle Mhor** (inexpensive). This unpretentious country inn on 2,000 acres of farmland in the middle of nowhere is the perfect place to unwind and breathe in the gorgeous beauty and isolation of Balquhidder Glen. The warmth of the fun-loving Lewis family, together with the inn's spectacular setting and excellent restaurant, draws you in. Don't be surprised if you're toasting them into the wee hours of the morning. Request Room 4 for its spacious bedroom and bathroom (with a large tub but no shower). The farmhouse has five bedrooms (all with private bath) and three self-catering cottages. *4 mi. west of Balquhidder, Balquhidder FK19 8PQ, tel. 0877-4622, fax 0877-4305.*

■ **Leny House** (inexpensive). This spacious, elegantly restored country mansion sits on many acres of well-manicured farmland. The house, which dates to 1513, was used during the Jacobite Rebellion for secret meetings and arms storage. Self-catering lodges are also available, but the house has all the character you desire. Ask for the Big Pink Room. *11 mi. southeast of Balquhidder on A84, Callander FK17*

▼

8HA, tel. 0877-31078. Bed and breakfast open one week before Easter-Sep.; lodges open all year.

FOR MORE INFORMATION
Tourist Office:
The Rob Roy & Trossachs Visitor Centre, *Ancaster Square, Callander FK17 8ED, tel. 0877-30342.*

Books:
The Braes O'Balquhidder, An Historical Guide to the District, by Elizabeth Beauchamp, Heatherbank Press, Milngavie, Glasgow.

Rob Roy Macgregor—His Life and Times, by W. H. Murray, Richard Drew Publishing Ltd., Glasgow.

Rob Roy Macgregor: Rogue or Romantic Hero? Jarrold Colour Publications, Norwich, Great Britain (available in the Callander Visitor Centre).

For Serious Walkers:
The above walk can be found in Ordnance Survey Pathfinder Map 347 and Sheet NN 41/51 (Map 358). Numerous other public footpaths lead into the mountains and hills. Check with the Visitor Centre in Callander for maps and suggestions. The best access to the summit of 2,800-foot Ben Ledi is from Corriechrombie in the Pass of Leny (on *A84).*

The Castle on the Rock

EXPERIENCE 21: STONEHAVEN

Most of the traffic in the **Grampian Highlands** flows to and from Aberdeen, a vital North Sea port for the fishing industry and for off-shore oil and natural gas developers. Just a 20-minute drive south, in the little town of Stonehaven, you can escape to a snug harbor that

The Highlights: Sweeping clifftop views overlooking a fishing port and the North Sea; 14th-century Dunnottar Castle.

Other Places Nearby: A historic church where the crown jewels were hidden; an art gallery, museums, and an old castle.

moves a lot slower and brings you back to a time of centuries past.

Stonehaven lies at the head of a sheltered bay on Scotland's storm-strewn, craggy east coast. Facing toward Norway, the coast is one long line of plunging cliffs, sweeping bays, and sandy beaches tucked between precipitous headlands. Attacked by gales sweeping down from the Arctic, ancient sandstone and rocks jut out above the foamy surf.

This experience takes you through the town to the cliffs above **Stonehaven Harbour,** where you'll watch boats pass as you gaze out across the wide expanse of the **North Sea.** You'll then proceed on a dramatic path atop the high, rugged cliffs while the surf pounds against the rocks below. Out of nowhere, a castle comes into view, seemingly floating on a rock island just off the coast. Probably the most spectacular

▼

ruin in Scotland, **Dunnottar Castle** was used as the principal setting in a movie version of *Hamlet*. Surrounded on three sides by water, the castle sprawls over four acres on the level grassy surface of a gigantic red-sandstone rock that protrudes sharply from the cliffs into the North Sea.

On this spot, St. Ninian founded a chapel in the 5th century. A monastery was later built here, and then a castle in the 12th century. The English occupied Dunnottar Castle in the late 13th century, but in 1297 it was won back by the great Scottish hero William Wallace, who burned down the castle chapel with the English still inside. Mary, Queen of Scots, visited Dunnottar, as did her son King James VI, who became James I of England in 1603.

The remains of the present castle date to the 14th century. The only access to the castle then was by a narrow rock-and-turf path that plummeted from the clifftops down almost to the sea and then ascended to the gatehouse. This approach enabled the castle's defenders to easily spot and shoot the enemy.

The castle's lasting fame came in 1652, at the end of the English Civil War, when Dunnottar, loyal to the king, refused to yield to the victorious Parliamentarian forces led by Oliver Cromwell. It was the only place in Scotland still waving the royal flag. Hidden inside the fortress were Charles II's private papers and the Regalia of Scotland (crown, scepter, and royal sword). The Parliamentarians repeatedly besieged the castle, but it resisted for eight months, defended by only 69 men under the direction of Ogilvy, the governor of Dunnottar. Finally, Cromwell's army was able to use its big guns to overtake the castle.

The Parliamentarians, however, discovered no papers or Regalia inside. During the siege, it turned out, a minister's wife who had been given permission to visit Ogilvy's wife had secretly carried the crown out in her apron, while her servant had smuggled out the scepter and sword in a bundle of flax. These items were hidden under the pulpit of **Kinneff Church,** eight miles south of Stonehaven, until the king was restored to the throne. Another woman made away with King Charles's papers by stitching them into her clothing.

Dunnottar was dismantled in 1718, yet there's still plenty to see as

▼

you walk through it today. Notice the 14th-century keep, with its L-shaped tower and walls of rubble. The gatehouse, chapel, and various other buildings date to the 16th century. But the truly memorable part is the route by which you approach the castle—high above the pounding North Sea, on a winding clifftop trail void of tourists.

GETTING THERE

By car:

From Aberdeen (14 miles away), take *A92* south to Stonehaven. Follow signs to the town center. When you reach Market Square, pull into the Stonehaven Square Car Park.

From Dundee (55 miles away), take *A929* north, which becomes *A94* north of Forfar. Follow *A94* north to Stonehaven. Proceed into town following signs marked "Town Centre." At Market Square, in the heart of town, park in the Stonehaven Square Car Park.

By train:

Take Scotrail from Glasgow (two hours and 20 minutes), Edinburgh (two hours and 8 minutes), or Aberdeen (17 minutes) to Stonehaven. For rail information, call 0412-042844 in Glasgow, 0315-562451 in Edinburgh, or 0224-594222 in Aberdeen. Exit the train station and walk straight ahead to *Arouthie Road*. Turn left onto *Arouthie Road* and follow it as it crosses *Queen's Road* (the same street as *Princess Road*) to *Evan Street*. Turn left and proceed on *Evan Street* to the Stonehaven Square Car Park at Market Square.

Walk Directions

TIME: 2 hours
LEVEL: Easy
DISTANCE: 3 miles
ACCESS: By car and train

You walk through the streets of Stonehaven to a paved path that leads above the harbor. A cliffside dirt path with a few stiles then takes you to steps heading to the castle entrance. The most difficult part of the walk is ascending the steps from the castle. Picnic on the cliffs overlooking the castle

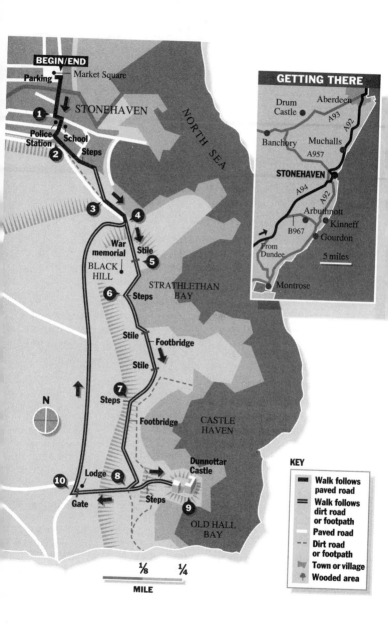

BEGIN/END
Parking — Market Square
1
STONEHAVEN
Police Station
2
School
Steps
3
4
War memorial
BLACK HILL
Stile
5
6 — Steps
STRATHLETHAN BAY
NORTH SEA
Stile
Footbridge
Stile
7
Steps
Footbridge
CASTLE HAVEN
Dunnottar Castle
Lodge
10
8
Gate
Steps
9
OLD HALL BAY
N

GETTING THERE

Drum Castle
Aberdeen
A93   A92
Banchory   Muchalls
A957
STONEHAVEN
A94   A92
Arbuthnott   Kinneff
B967   Gourdon
From Dundee
5 miles
Montrose

KEY

▬▬	Walk follows paved road
═══	Walk follows dirt road or footpath
▭	Paved road
- - -	Dirt road or footpath
▨	Town or village
♣	Wooded area

⅛   ¼
MILE

▼

and the North Sea or in the field just beyond Point 6. Pick up picnic supplies at any of the shops near the car park in the center of Stonehaven.

TO BEGIN

From the car park, walk past the telephone booths next to the Raeburn Christie Building and turn right on *Allardice Street*. Walk over a bridge and follow a sign toward the harbor.

1. When you reach a police station at the end of the street, turn left onto another street. Make the next right, between the police station and a school, and proceed alongside a paved road until it curves to the right. Follow the road for a few more steps.

2. Then immediately follow a footpath on your left. As you start uphill, a Hillcrest sign is on your left. At a fork, take the path to the left (you look over rooftops to your left). Go down some steps, then make a right onto a dirt path. Continue uphill on this path, alongside a coast road. *Enjoy the nice views of Stonehaven Harbour and the coast.*

3. At the end of the path, go through an opening in a fence (to the right of two benches) and immediately turn left onto the sidewalk that runs next to the paved coast road. Proceed along the sidewalk.

4. When the road turns sharply to the right, follow a footpath that leads to the left, away from the road. Follow the path up Black Hill (there is a war memorial to the right). *Enjoy your first glimpse of Dunnottar Castle, straight ahead on a rocky crag.* Continue on the path as it heads downhill.

5. Cross a stile over a wooden fence, above the rocky inlet of Strathlethan Bay. Continue straight, with the North Sea crashing against the rocks to your left.

6. Go down the steps and continue on the path (there is a barbed-

▼

wire fence to your right). Cross a stile and a small field. When you arrive at a footbridge, cross it and continue across the next field. Go over another stile. The path now hugs a fence on the right.

7. Go down some steps and cross a small bridge. Continue on the path.

8. Just past a bench on your left, leave the path by turning left down a long flight of steps leading toward *an entrance to Dunnottar Castle, which sits on its own rocky headland jutting out from the main cliff line.*

9. Go through the castle entrance (there's an admission charge). After exploring the castle, turn your back on the sea and retrace your steps to the cliff path at Point 8 and continue straight.

10. Just past the lodge, turn right at a paved road. Walk about 3/4 mile back toward Stonehaven. After you pass "Stonehaven" and "Give Way To Oncoming Traffic" signs and the trailhead at Point 4 (to your right), go through an opening in a fence on your right to a footpath, at Point 3. Proceed down the path. At the next intersection of two paths, take the left path; at the bottom of the hill, take the steps on the left; at a junction of two paths, stay to the right, then go down a paved path and walk between the police station and the school. At a stop sign, turn left, then make the first right and proceed to Market Square.

PLACES ALONG THE WALK

■ **Dunnottar Castle.** *Open Mon.-Sat. 9-6 and Sun. 2-5 early Mar.-Oct.; Mon.-Fri. 9-dusk Nov.-early Mar. Admission.*

OTHER PLACES NEARBY

■ **Tollbooth Museum.** Situated next to the harbor, this museum is a good place to learn about local history and the days when fishing was a major industry in town. It is in one of Stonehaven's oldest buildings and once served as a storehouse, a court, and a prison. *Old Pier,*

▼

Stonehaven Harbour, Stonehaven. Open Mon. and Thurs.-Sat. 10-12 and 2-5 and Wed. and Sun. 2-5 Jun.-Sep.

■ **Kinneff Old Church.** The Regalia of Scotland and Charles II's private papers were hidden under the pulpit of this church when Cromwell's forces attacked nearby Dunnottar Castle in the mid-17th century. Most of what remains of the church today dates from the 18th century. *8 mi. south of Stonehaven on a minor road off A92, Kinneff.*

■ **Drum Castle.** This well-preserved 70-foot granite tower house on 400 acres of land was constructed in the late 13th or early 14th century. It contains furniture and portraits of the De Irwin family, its owners from 1324 to 1975. A 17th-century mansion sits next to the castle. *15 mi. northwest of Stonehaven off A93, Drumoak, tel. 0330-811204. Open daily 2-6 May-Sep.; Sat. and Sun. 2-6 Apr. and Oct. Admission.*

■ **Aberdeen Art Gallery and Museum.** If you don't mind traveling to a nearby city, head for this museum in a mid-19th-century building. There's a large collection of 20th-century paintings and sculptures, as well as 18th-century works by Scottish portrait painters Sir Henry Raeburn and Allan Ramsay. *15 mi. north of Stonehaven, Schoolhill, Aberdeen, tel. 0224-646333. Open Mon.-Wed. 10-5, Thu. 10-8, Fri. and Sat. 10-5, Sun. 2-5.*

■ **Grassic Gibbon Centre.** This new museum commemorates the life and writings of early-20th-century novelist Lewis Grassic Gibbon, who wrote *Sunset Song,* probably the finest literary work of the Scottish Renaissance. *14 mi. southwest of Stonehaven, Arbuthnott, tel. 0561-61668. Open 10-4:30 Apr.-Oct.*

DINING

■ **Invery House** (very expensive). This country manor house cooks the best food in the area and has a cellar containing more than 500 wines. The menu recently featured an interesting warm-salad appetizer of monkfish with a basil and saffron dressing. Entrées included grilled lemon sole, prime rib of beef, and wood pigeon pie flavored with Guinness and baked with flaky pastry. *16 mi. northwest of Stonehaven, Banchory AB31 3NJ, tel. 0330-24782, fax 0330-24712.*

■ **Raemoir House Hotel** (expensive). The kitchen of this 18th-century mansion goes heavy on the game meats and fowl. Recent din-

▼

ner entrées included sautéed medallions of venison with port and black currant sauce and roast leg of spring lamb with minted apricots and a rosemary jus. *16 mi. northwest of Stonehaven, Banchory AB31 4ED, tel. 0330-24884, fax 0330-22171. Closed the first two weeks of Jan.*

■ **Tollbooth Restaurant** (expensive). Seafood is the specialty in this restaurant above a museum in a 16th-century sandstone building on the harborside. Expect such main courses as Thai-style squid with lemon grass and coriander, baked monkfish wrapped in bacon, and a North Sea bouillabaisse that includes the catch of the day, mussels, prawns, and other fish. *Old Pier, Stonehaven Harbour, Stonehaven, tel. 0569-62287. Open for dinner Tue.-Sun. Mar.-Dec.; Fri. and Sat. Jan.-Feb.; open for lunch Jun.-Aug. only.*

■ **Crofters** (moderate). Stop for lunch at this friendly roadside place when you're heading to or from Stonehaven. The decor and the exterior are nothing to rave about, but the dining room offers fine views of the countryside. Don't miss the interesting selection of beers on tap or the sticky toffee pudding. For dinner, try the salmon from the nearby river Dee. *10 mi. west of Stonehaven on A957, Lochton of Durris, tel. 0330-44543. Closed Tue. Oct.-Mar.*

■ **The Marine Hotel** (inexpensive). Sit outside the hotel's pub in the summertime and enjoy a drink and a good view of the boats in the harbor. Don't expect anything more than traditional pub food inside this 110-year-old building. *Stonehaven Harbour, Stonehaven, tel. 0569-62155.*

LODGING

■ **Invery House** (very expensive). Within 47 woodland acres on the bank of the river Feugh in the Royal Deeside valley, this well-kept country-house hotel offers elegant, charming rooms. Ask for the Lord of the Isles Room, which has a couch and two chairs and a gorgeous view of the garden. Or try the lovely Ivanhoe Room, a bright corner suite with a regal bathroom. *16 mi. northwest of Stonehaven off A93, Banchory AB31 3NJ, tel. 0330-24782 or, for reservations in the U.S., 800-525-4800, fax 0330-24712.*

■ **Raemoir House Hotel** (very expensive). An 18th-century mansion on a 3,500-acre estate has been expanded to include 28 guest

▼

rooms, a sauna, and an exercise room. It's particularly charming in the off season, when log fires crackle. The Old English Suite, in which musician Cliff Richard recently stayed, has a 400-year-old four-poster bed but can be a bit dark. The Pine Suite is brighter, with windows on three sides. *16 mi. northwest of Stonehaven off A93, Banchory AB31 4ED, tel. 0330-24884, fax 0330-22171. Closed the first two weeks of Jan.*

■ **Muchalls Castle** (very expensive). This small laird's house, which dates to 1619, is renowned for its plaster ceilings and the ornamental walk-in fireplace in the Great Hall. Although this is a private residence, eight bedrooms are rented to overnight guests. Joan Rivers recently stayed in the Turret Room, with its huge silk-canopied double bed and view down the North Sea coast. King James II slept underneath the gold-plastered canopy in the Laird Room. A set-menu dinner is available to guests only. *5 mi. north of Stonehaven off A92, Muchalls AB3 2RS, tel. 0569-31170, fax 0569-31480.*

■ **Sea View Cottage** (inexpensive). Come to this 1840s Georgian-style fisherman's cottage in a small harborside village if you're looking for good value and a fine view of the North Sea. The Jacobean Room is the most spacious of the two bedrooms, each of which is equipped with a double and a single bed, a private bath, and remote-control TV. The cottage lacks gardens or a yard area, but it's only 30 paces from the sea in the area's only active fishing village. *10 mi. south of Stonehaven off A92, 2 East End, Gourdon DD10 0LD, tel. 0561-62000.*

FOR MORE INFORMATION
Tourist Offices:
5 Station Rd., Banchory AB31 3XX, tel. 0330-22066.
920 St. Nicholas House, Broad St., Aberdeen AB9 1DE, tel. 0224-632727, fax 0224-644822.

For Serious Walkers:
The above walks can be found on Ordnance Survey Pathfinder Sheet 273. For other walks in the area, purchase two pamphlets at a tourist office: "Walk Around Stonehaven" and "Hill Walks in Grampian Highlands and Aberdeen."

A Peaceful Oasis in a Land of Strife

EXPERIENCE 22: BRECON

Although fewer than 8,000 people actually reside in Brecon, the town center buzzes with activity each day, with people scurrying in and out of shops that line the street alongside the **Wellington Monument.** Once outside this ancient market town, however, you can leave commerce far behind as you explore the beautiful surrounding hills of **Brecon Beacons National Park,** a preserve of rugged mountains that have for centuries protected this part of Wales from neighboring England.

The Highlights: Majestic rolling hills inside the northern edge of Brecon Beacons National Park, unforgettable vistas and memorable picnic spots next to an ancient hill fort, a busy market town with many shops.

Other Places Nearby: An old Roman fort with well-preserved gates and sections of walls, a scenic 19th-century canal, the world's largest second-hand bookseller, a 15th-century castle.

The Welsh name for Brecon is Aberhonddu, meaning "mouth of the Honddu," one of the two rivers that converge here. The town's English name, Brecon, commemorates Brychan, a 5th-century Irish prince who was supposedly related to King Arthur. Not far from town, atop a high grass hill in the Brecon Beacons National Park, you walk to the spot where Brychan's daughter, Elyned, was supposedly martyred,

▼

among the earthen remains of an Iron Age fort, **Slwch Tump.** A chapel dedicated to Elyned once stood on the north side of the hill.

F rom the hillside next to the fort, there are magnificent views of expansive rolling hills, with the buildings of the town jutting up between the trees. To the south stands the heart of the park, the Brecon Beacons mountain range, including the highest peak in south Wales—2,907-foot Pen y Fan. The red sandstone or brownstone of these mountains has been used in the construction of many local houses.

Encompassing 519 square acres of land, the national park includes Brecon and other small towns and villages within its boundaries. But the park's reputation rests primarily on its natural wonders: the largest natural lake and the highest waterfall in south Wales, as well as Britain's deepest cave, Dan-yr-Ogof, and the tree-lined **Monmouthshire & Brecon Canal,** Britain's only canal on national park land, where you can enjoy a leisurely boat ride or a canal-side stroll. The park's lakes and reservoirs offer good fishing for pike, perch, carp, and eels.

Although it's a peaceful spot today, this area has had a turbulent history. Roman troops were garrisoned to the west at nearby **Y Gaer,** so the native Welsh carefully guarded their own hill forts. Centuries later, King Edward I, who reigned from 1272 to 1307, swept brutally through this land as he conquered Wales, and many English-Welsh skirmishes ensued in this border region.

One famous war hero may forever be a part of Brecon. The center point of Brecon is the Wellington Monument, a late-19th-century sculpture of the Duke of Wellington, who defeated Napoleon at the Battle of Waterloo in 1815 and later became prime minister.

Near the Wellington Monument, stop in at **St. Mary's Church,** a red sandstone cathedral that dates to the 13th century. The church's 90-foot Buckingham Tower was named after Edward Stafford, Duke of Buckingham, who was beheaded by Henry VIII in 1521. Another relic from a previous era is the town's castle, once the most important fortress in this border area between England and Wales. Unfortunately, most of it was destroyed long ago, and the few remains now form part

▼

of the Castle Hotel. The first castle was built on this site in 1090, and a walled settlement sprang up in the 13th century—fragments of the wall can still be seen.

Brecon, of course, doesn't come alive only through its history. In the summer months, locals stroll on The Promenade along the river Usk or rent a rowboat at the boat house. In August, jazz musicians and their fans flock to the city's popular annual jazz festival.

But you don't have to wait for the special events to feel the pulse of this market town. Its essence comes forth twice each week: on Tuesdays, when the produce market sets up shop, and on Fridays, when both the produce and the noisy livestock market are open for business.

GETTING THERE

By car:

From Abergavenny, Wales (18 miles away), take *A40* west to Brecon. Park in the public lot next to the tourist information center.

From Cheltenham, England (65 miles away), take *A40* west to Brecon. Park in the public lot next to the tourist information center.

Walk Directions

TIME: 1 3/4 hours

LEVEL: Easy

DISTANCE: 3 miles

ACCESS: By car

On this walk in the Brecon hills, you only break a sweat once—on an initial sharp dirt incline up through woodland. You then step over a low fence and cross a stile, and the rest is clear sailing. Set up a picnic on the hillside in Point 5. Buy picnic provisions at one or more of the many shops on or off *Bulwark Street,* Brecon's main street.

TO BEGIN

With your back to the tourist information center, walk away from the center and across the parking lot. Proceed on a street that passes

▼

the public toilets. Turn left on the next street, then make the next right.

1. At the next street, *Bulwark* (on your left is the Wellington Monument), turn left. Walk down the street, past the monument and away from St. Mary's Church. Continue straight past an intersection.

2. At *Free Street,* turn left and walk on the right side of the street. Go uphill and pass the Breconshire War Memorial Hospital on you right.

3. About 40 yards past the hospital, turn right and proceed up a dirt path. Ignore the stiles and a metal gate on your right, and continue uphill on the dirt path.

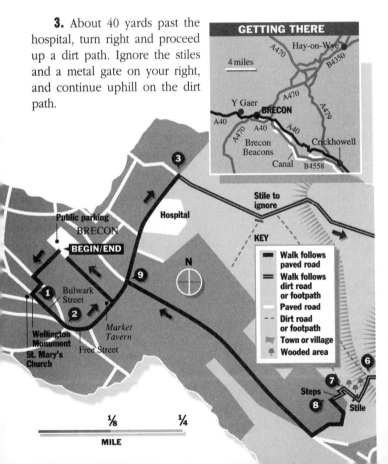

▼

4. When you reach two adjacent gates, bear right and go through the metal gate (if the gate is chained, step over the fence at the point where two fences meet on the right). Go diagonally across the field, just to the left of a hump on a hill to your right. *The hump is the hill fort of Slwch Tump.* Walk to the treeline, where you follow the trail indicated by a yellow marker. Walk straight ahead on the trail between trees on the hilltop.

5. When you reach a stile in the right-hand corner of the field, ignore it and instead pass through an opening to the right between a fence and the trees. Proceed at a 45-degree angle to your right; there will be trees on your right and a barbed-wire fence on your left. At a yellow trail marker, bear right around the hill and follow a grass path across the hillside toward a barbed-wire fence.

6. At the fence, turn left. Go downhill, keeping the fence to your right. Pass through a clump of woodland and follow a path to your right over a stile. Proceed straight through the woods, with a wire fence to your left.

7. About 20 steps after the wire fence on your left ends, turn left at a yellow trail marker. Go down a path to another wire fence. Turn right and go down steps toward a paved road.

8. Turn left at the road. Walk downhill between modern houses. Turn right at the next paved road and proceed straight toward a stop sign.

9. At the stop sign, turn left onto a major road and head back

4

Gates

SLWCH
TUMP

5

Stile to
ignore

▼

into town, retracing your steps. Just before the Market Tavern on your right, turn right to return to the parking lot or go inside the 1814 pub. *It's a great place to order a pint of Tetley or Ansells Bitter and kibitz with the locals. Farmers gather inside the pub on markets days: Tuesdays and Thursdays.*

PLACES ALONG THE WALK

■ **Brecon Beacons National Park.** *For information: Cattle Market Car Park, Brecon LD3 9DA, tel. 0874-624437.*

■ **Brecknock Museum.** Along with its collection of decorative Welsh lovespoons, the museum also exhibits a dug-out canoe, pottery, porcelain, and other local relics. *Captain's Walk, Brecon, tel. 0874 624121. Open Mon.-Sat. 10-1, 2-5 and same hours on Sun. Apr.-Sep. Closed Good Friday and Christmas through New Year's.*

OTHER PLACES NEARBY

■ **Monmouthshire & Brecon Canal.** This delightful waterway completed in 1812, has retained its charm largely because it has never served an industrial area. Its 33 miles and six locks lie within Brecon Beacons National Park. A popular place for cruising, it is Britain's only canal in a national park and arguably the most scenic canal in the country. Call the tourist office or the park office for current listings of companies renting canal boats. You can also follow a 33-mile canal-side walking path for as long as you like. There are many fine picnic spots with canal boats and canoes passing by. *The canal runs southeast from Brecon and parallels two roads: A40 and B4558.*

■ **Y Gaer.** A rectangular Roman fort, it sits in a quiet field on the northern bank of the river Usk. Its well-preserved gates and parts of walls demonstrate the precision of Roman engineering. The fort was founded in A.D. 75 and remained occupied until the Romans finally withdrew in the 4th century. *3 mi. west of Brecon off A40.*

■ **Hay on Wye.** In this old town next to the Black Mountains on the northeastern corner of Brecon Beacons National Park, there's a surprising concentration of second-hand and antiquarian bookshops. The burgeoning industry was started in 1961 when American expatri-

▼

ate Richard Booth opened a small store, and the town has grown to be the largest second-hand bookseller in the entire world. The shops huddle around the remains of a castle. *17 mi. northeast of Brecon on B4350.*

■ **Crickhowell.** On the banks of the river Usk and in the shadows of the Black Mountains, this village is notable for the remains of a 15th-century castle, abandoned after it was raided by Owain Glyndwr, who tried to liberate Wales from English rule. An oddity can be seen on *Tower Street:* A castle tower stands in the front garden of a house. Picnic by the river, next to a 13-arched stone bridge. *14 mi. southeast of Brecon on A40.*

DINING

■ **Llangoed Hall** (very expensive). Head chef Mark Salter's five-course creations make dinners a pleasure in the elegant blue-and-yellow dining room at this grand Edwardian country house. Recent winners included char-grilled breast of guinea fowl on braised salsify with a ravioli of chicken and mushroom, accompanied by a sherry sauce. Such culinary complexity is carried over to desserts, too: Try the filo parcel with apple, sultana raisins, and almonds served with vanilla and caramel sauces. Men are requested to wear a jacket and tie. *11 mi. northeast of Brecon on A470, Llyswen LD3 0YP, tel. 0874-754525, fax 0874-754545.*

■ **Gliffaes Country House Hotel** (expensive). Cold buffet and pub lunches, afternoon teas, and five-course dinners are served at this 29-acre hotel. The dining room has a terrace looking out at beautiful gardens, the countryside, and the river Usk. The emphasis is on traditional English cooking, using local game and fish. *14 mi. southeast of Brecon off A40, Crickhowell NP8 1RH, tel. 0874-730371, fax 0874-730463. Closed Dec. 31 to end of Feb.*

■ **The Griffin Inn** (moderate). Dinners in this historic inn taste home-cooked and feature fresh ingredients, though they lack flair and seasoning. You'll be served good-sized portions of such entrées as roast duck and apple sauce and fresh trout with almonds. Don't miss the charm of the sitting room and the bar area. *10 mi. northeast of Brecon*

▼

on A470, Llyswen LD3 0UR, tel. 0874-754241, fax 0874-754592. Drinks only Dec. 24-26.

LODGING

■ **Llangoed Hall** (very expensive). Designed by Clough Williams-Ellis in 1912, this beautifully restored house is now a hotel owned by Sir Bernard Ashley, chairman of Laura Ashley. When we visited recently his helicopter was on the front lawn and he was settled in a 275-pound-per-night suite. There are 23 rooms and suites decorated with antiques, Oriental rugs, and (of course) Laura Ashley fabrics. Room 7 is quite spacious and has fine views. Lovely grounds, views of the Black Mountains, and open fields add to the charm. A chauffeur-driven car is available for touring. *11 mi. northeast of Brecon on A470, Llyswen LD3 0YP, tel. 0874-754525, fax 0874-754545.*

■ **Gliffaes Country House Hotel** (very expensive). On 29 landscaped acres overlooking the river Usk, this vine-draped stone hotel was built in 1885 as a private residence. It's now an informal family owned 22-room hotel popular with salmon and trout fishermen. The large gardens contain rare species of trees and shrubs. *14 mi. southeast of Brecon off A40, Crickhowell NP8 1RH, tel. 0874-730371, fax 0874-730463. Closed Dec. 31 to end of Feb.*

■ **The Griffin Inn** (moderate). There are no exceptional views from this sporting inn located on a tiny parcel of land next to a road in the upper Wye Valley, but the eight-bedroom property overflows with historical charm. In the downstairs sitting area next to the bar, notice the 146 bread oven and the original ceiling beams made from the wood of old ships. There are nice, modern bedrooms and a quaint, private lounge with a fireplace for guests. *10 mi. northeast of Brecon on A470, Llyswen LD3 0UR, tel. 0874-754241, fax 0874-754592. Closed Dec. 24-26.*

■ **Scethrog Tower** (inexpensive). No other lodging can match the history of this bed and breakfast with seven-foot-thick walls, one of only two tower houses in the county. It may have been built by a landowner who died in 1254. The house is well furnished and well decorated, with nicely restored wood-beam ceilings. It's situated in the countryside outside of Brecon, and you can fish for salmon and trout

▼

nearby. *Brecon LD3 7YE, tel. 0874-87672. Usually open Mar.-Oct.*

■ **Trehenry Farm** (inexpensive). Cattle and sheep are raised and cereals grown on this 200-acre farm that welcomes guests to its 170-year-old stone farmhouse. The house has two large Inglenook fireplaces and oak-beam ceilings. Request one of the two double rooms with views of the farmland and the Black Mountains. Home-cooked dinners are available. *4 mi. northeast of Brecon, Felinfach LD3 0UN, tel. 0874-754312.*

FOR MORE INFORMATION

Tourist Offices:

Cattle Market Car Park, Brecon LD3 9DA, tel. 0874-622485.

Brecon Beacons National Park Office, *7 Glamorgan St., Brecon LD3 7DP, tel. 0874-624437, fax 0874-622574.*

For Serious Walkers:

To follow the above walk, use Ordnance Survey Pathfinder Sheets 1038 and 1062. If you plan to walk elsewhere within Brecon Beacons National Park, you will also need Ordnance Survey Outdoor Leisure maps 11, 12, and 13, or Landranger maps 160 and 161.

To scale the park's highest peak, 2,900-foot Pen y Fan, drive on *A470* to Storey Arms. The walk from your car to the summit and back is about four miles.

From April through October, the Brecon Beacons National Park Office conducts a full program of ranger-led walks, from easy strolls to difficult hikes. Contact the park office: *7 Glamorgan St., Brecon LD3 7DP, tel. 0874-624437. A small donation is requested.*

The Path of Dylan Thomas

EXPERIENCE 23: LAUGHARNE

A Norman castle stands on the shoreline, but most of Laugharne (pronounced "Larn") brings you back to a more recent era: the early 1950s. That's when this unpretentious, sleepy town alongside the Taf estuary inspired Dylan Thomas to write some of his most memorable poems and, in the process, make his indelible mark on literary history. Some critics believe the town Llareggub in *Under Milk Wood* represents Laugharne, though

The Highlights: An unspoiled seaside town where poet Dylan Thomas lived, worked, and is buried; a ruined castle on the shores of a huge estuary; attrac tive picnic spots in deserted grass fields.

Other Places Nearby: A pret ty village with a castle and a pub where Dylan Thomas use to drink, nice beaches, a bustling market town.

Thomas fiercely denied any connection. (The 1971 movie version of the radio play was shot in nearby Fishguard, starring Elizabeth Taylor, Richard Burton, Peter O'Toole, and Glynis Johns.)

You will walk next to Laugharne's crumbling 12th-century castle, currently under renovation but expected to reopen in June 1994. **Laugharne Castle** was painted in the 19th century by the great British landscape artist J.M.W. Turner. In the late 1930s, Welsh writer Richard Hughes, who wrote *High Winds in Jamaica,* rented a house inside the

▼

fortress, and Dylan Thomas came here to visit. Thomas described the stronghold as a "castle brown as owls." Hughes offered Thomas use of the castle's gazebo for his work, and there the poet wrote *Portrait of the Artist as a Young Dog* and a few of his best short stories. But this creative period was cut short when serious debts forced Thomas and his family to sell many of their possessions, including **Sea View,** their narrow three-story home alongside the castle grounds. (The mustard-colored house still stands today, but it is a private residence.) The financial difficulties drove Thomas out of Laugharne; for the next decade, he lived many places around the world but he always longed to return.

T hat wish was fulfilled in May 1949 when Margaret Taylor, a wealthy friend of the poet, bought the **Boat House,** a house on stilts at the foot of red sandstone cliffs overlooking the **Taf estuary**. She gave it as a gift to the appreciative Thomas family, who still had little money and were expecting a third child. Dylan spent the final 16 years of his life here. You can visit the house today, ascending a stairway from the beach. Originally a boat-building facility, the Boat House is a three-story cottage with a catwalk running halfway around and every window providing a water view. When Dylan lived here, signed photographs of broadcasting and literary stars hung on the parlor walls; today, you can see pictures of him and his family.

On the cliff near the Boat House, stop by Dylan's **work shed**, in an old converted garage originally built for Laugharne's first car. You can peer in, but visitors are not allowed to enter. Dylan spent the most productive days of his prolific career here, writing most of his play *Under Milk Wood,* as well as various radio broadcasts and several of his best poems and short stories. He usually worked every afternoon for five hours, leaving the mornings free for time with his family and for walks into town from a clifftop path next to the shed.

The path, which was renamed **Dylan Walk** in 1963, gives you a good view of the Taf estuary. You may see fishermen setting out in their coracles—small boats made from hides stretched over a frame—to catch salmon in nets, following a tradition that began before Roman times. The path leads you to the quiet of the woods and through near-

▼

by fields where there are many private picnic spots.

When Dylan lived in the Boat House, his works were well known, but sales were sluggish. So following the lead of his idol, Charles Dickens, Thomas took off on a reading tour of America. It was an enormous financial success and his book sales rose. This was a mixed blessing, however, for government tax officials soon swooped into Laugharne—the poet had been saddled with debt for so long that he never realized his new-found wealth was taxable. His debts became greater than his U.S. earnings.

So Dylan Thomas began annual tours of the United States. Without his wife, Caitlin, to keep him in check, however, he went on wild drinking sprees and partied excessively after his well-received readings. Double-digit shots of whiskey in a single evening quickly wore the Welshman out. Before his final U.S. tour, he had experienced blackouts in Laugharne, but he left anyway—and never returned. He died in New York City in November 1953, at the age of 39; alcohol and an experimental drug for blackouts were found in his system. Some say Dylan consumed at least 18 shots of booze on his last night.

Caitlin received permission to bury Dylan's remains facing the water in the Boat House garden, but she never followed through with this plan. She buried him instead in the yard of **St. Martin's Church,** which you'll walk through on your way back into town from the Boat House. The church was built in the 15th century; a 10th-century Celtic cross stands inside, as well as a replica of the plaque that commemorates Dylan Thomas in Westminster Abbey's Poet's Corner. In a graveyard next to the church, stop at **Dylan Thomas's grave,** a humble site marked with a white cross.

When he moved to the Boat House, Dylan also relocated his parents to Laugharne, putting them in a cottage called **The Pelican.** After his death, Dylan's mother moved into the Boat House and was the last person to live there year-round. She died in 1958, on the final night of *Under Milk Wood's* first performance in Laugharne.

The Pelican was handily located across the street from **Brown's Hotel,** a watering hole where the poet spent all too many hours. This pub has changed little since Dylan's time, and it's easy to imagine him

▼

here, playing bar games, hoisting a pint, or engaging in animated conversation with fellow patrons. He's featured in photographs on the wall, sharing space with the local fishing champ and other locals. Considering the way he died, it may seem a bit eerie to toss back a drink in his honor, but the gifted poet probably would be glad to join you if he were here today.

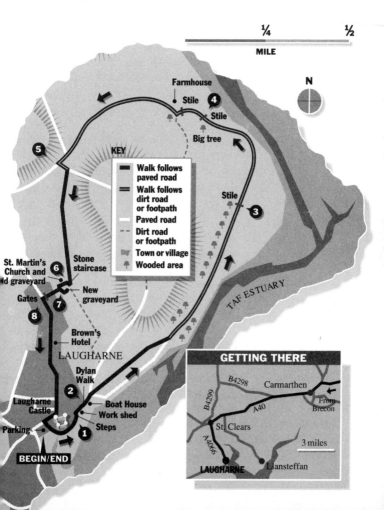

▼

GETTING THERE

By car:

From Brecon (*see* Experience 22), which is 55 miles away, take *A40* west to Carmarthen. Continue on to St. Clears. Connect with *A4066* south to Laugharne. Park in the public parking lot next to the castle.

From Swansea (40 miles away), take *M4* west to *A48*. Follow *A48* to Carmarthen. Connect to *A40* west. Follow the directions above.

Walk Directions

TIME: 2 hours
LEVEL: Easy
DISTANCE: 2 1/2 miles
ACCESS: By car

You walk along the seashore, then up stairs to a clifftop path. You proceed through the countryside on paved lanes, dirt paths, and grass, with some stiles to cross. The best picnic spots are by the shore at the beginning of the walk or in the soft grass fields in Point 3. Laugharne's food stores have slim pickings for picnic provisions, so you may wish to pick up supplies in another town.

TO BEGIN

Cross a bridge next to the castle parking lot and step onto a path that leads around the castle and along the shoreline (the castle will be to your left, the estuary to your right). Continue straight on the path toward Dylan Thomas's Boat House, following a sign pointing the way (ignore another path that goes left). Follow the rocky path as it winds around rocky red cliffs along the shoreline.

1. Climb up the steep steps that ascend from the rocks. Make a right turn. *Immediately on your right is the work shed where Dylan Thomas wrote* Under Milkwood *and other famous works. The inside of the shed is not open to the public. Proceed on a paved path that is now called Dylan's Walk.*

2. Make a right down the steps to visit *the Boat House, where Dylan Thomas lived with his family.* Then return to the paved path and continue along (the shore will be on your right). Ignore a path to the right that goes down to the shore; continue straight on the paved path and proceed through woodland. The path will cross a paved road that heads down to the beach; stay on the path, which continues straight through woodland.

3. Cross a stile. Go straight into a field (a barbed-wire fence and the *Taf estuary* lie on your right). Walk through the field and then follow a dirt path that hugs a fence. Go through a small stretch of woodland and continue alongside the fence through the next field.

4. Just behind a big tree, cross over a stile. Head straight across a field toward a farmhouse (there's a barbed-wire fence to your right). A metal gate and a stile are next to each other; use either one and then bear left through the farm's courtyard. Walk to the left of the farmhouse and follow a path uphill through the trees. At a junction, ignore a road to the right; continue straight on the path toward the next junction.

5. At the junction, turn left onto a gravel road. Proceed about 50 yards before bearing right onto a paved road heading downhill. Continue down the shady lane for several hundred yards.

6. When you reach a stone staircase to your right and a dirt road to your left, go right up the staircase. Follow a path to the left into *St. Martin's churchyard*. Turn left onto a paved path, then left again onto another paved path that leads past gravestones. Make a third left onto a paved path that heads toward a footbridge.

7. Cross the footbridge and turn left, walking along the gravestones in the new graveyard. Go uphill to the seventh row of stones and turn right. *A white wooden cross in the middle of the graveyard marks the final resting place of Dylan Thomas.* Go back over the footbridge, turn left, and head down a paved path. Go through the church gates.

8. At a main road, turn left. Proceed straight on the sidewalk; within a few minutes, you will be in the heart of Laugharne. *On your left will be Brown's Hotel, the poet's favorite drinking haunt. Go inside the*

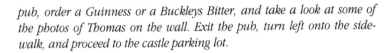

pub, order a Guinness or a Buckleys Bitter, and take a look at some of the photos of Thomas on the wall. Exit the pub, turn left onto the sidewalk, and proceed to the castle parking lot.

PLACES ALONG THE WALK

■ **Laugharne Castle.** *Closed for renovation until at least June 1994. For exact opening date, contact the tourist office in Carmarthen* (*see* For More Information, below).

■ **The Boat House.** *Tel. 0994-21420 in summer, 0792-465204 other times. Open 10-6 Easter-last week in Oct.; 10-3 the rest of the year (closed Sat.). Closed Christmas Day and New Year's. Admission.*

OTHER PLACES NEARBY

Since Laugharne sits in a very isolated area of Wales, you have to travel more than ten miles to see most of the notable places nearby.

■ **Llansteffan.** This pretty seaside village, perfect for walkers, has a magnificent Norman castle that can be visited anytime, free of charge. It looks particularly impressive under its nighttime floodlights. Dylan Thomas used to drink in the village at a pub, Yr Hen Dafarn (*see* Dining, below). *13 mi. east of Laugharne (to cross the estuary, drive north to St. Clears, take A40 east toward Carmarthen for less than two miles, then turn right onto the minor road signposted to Llansteffan).*

■ **Tenby.** An attractive walled town, Tenby has a small fishing harbor, beautiful beaches and clean waters, and interesting crafts shops. It's a popular summer retreat for British vacationers, but even in the height of the season the town retains its charm. From Easter through September, you can board a boat at the harbor and take a 20-minute trip to Caldey Island, an active monastery that makes candles, chocolates, and perfumes. *21 mi. southwest of Laugharne.*

■ **Pendine.** Although this resort town on Carmarthen Bay attracts too many recreational vehicles in the summertime, it offers a fine swimming beach, part of the eight-mile-long Pendine Sands, which hosted land-speed trials in the 1920s. *4 mi. southwest of Laugharne on A4066.*

■ **Carmarthen.** This strategic regional Roman capital where an ancient amphitheater was excavated in 1936 has lost its luster, but it's *the*

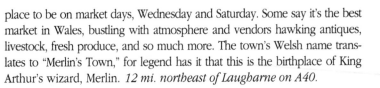

place to be on market days, Wednesday and Saturday. Some say it's the best market in Wales, bustling with atmosphere and vendors hawking antiques, livestock, fresh produce, and so much more. The town's Welsh name translates to "Merlin's Town," for legend has it that this is the birthplace of King Arthur's wizard, Merlin. *12 mi. northeast of Laugharne on A40.*

DINING

Don't expect anything resembling haute cuisine in this isolated Welsh region. For fine dining you can drive about 55 miles northeast to Brecon (*see* Experience 22).

■ **Yr Hen Dafarn** (moderate). Salmon, lobster, sea trout, skate, and other fresh fish—sometimes caught by the owner—can always be found on the menu at this 1804 stone pub beloved of locals. Other choices include steak, pheasant, and other game fowl. Dylan Thomas used to come here to drink pints of ale; he mentioned the pub (formerly called "Edwinsford Arms") in his work *A Visit to Grandma's.* The pub owner runs a boat service for ten pounds an hour that will shuttle you the five miles to or from Laugharne. *13 mi. east of Laugharne (to cross the estuary, drive north to St. Clears, take A40 east toward Carmarthen for less than two miles, then turn right onto the minor road signposted to Llansteffan), Llansteffan, tel. 0267-83656.*

■ **The Stable Door Wine Bar** (moderate). Locals appreciate this bistro near the castle because of its wine list, well-prepared food, and entertainment. You can expect live music or a performance of *Under Milk Wood. Market Lane, Laugharne, tel. 0994-427355. Open daily in summer; Fri.-Sat. evenings the rest of the year.*

■ **Brown's Hotel** (inexpensive). Stop in to soak up the atmosphere at Dylan Thomas's favorite hangout and enjoy a traditional pub lunch or dinner. Such typical bar food as plaice and chips and scampi and chips is served. *King's St., Laugharne, tel. 0994-427320. No lunch served on Sun.*

LODGING

Lodging options are very limited in Laugharne, so you may want to consider staying in the Brecon area, about 55 miles east (*see* Experience 22). If you're not in the mood for driving that far, check into a local bed

▼

and breakfast or cottage.

■ **Brook House Farm** (inexpensive). Home to 80 cows, this dairy farm offers either cottage rentals or rooms inside a 200-year-old farmhouse. The rooms can be rented nightly, the cottages weekly during the summer and on weekends during the winter. The farm looks out on fields and, in the distance, sand dunes. *2 mi. west of Laugharne on Pendine Rd., Brook, Laugharne SA33 4NX, tel. 0994-427239.*

■ **Sir John's Hill Farm** (inexpensive). Located on a clifftop, this 22-acre farm offers excellent sea views. Equipped with refrigerators, microwaves, and VCRs, cottages can be rented by the week from late May to late September, or for the weekend when available and during the off season. This farm inspired Dylan Thomas's work *Over Sir John's Farm*—he looked out over it from the Boat House. *Sir John's Hill, Laugharne SA33 4TD, tel. 0994-427667.*

■ **Halldown** (inexpensive). At this 200-year-old farmhouse, you can enjoy a nice view of the fields and rolling hills. The Towy Room has the best view; the Taf Room is the most spacious. *2 mi. north of Laugharne on A4066, Cross Inn, Laugharne SA33 4QS, tel. 0994-427452.*

FOR MORE INFORMATION:
Tourist Offices:

Lammas St., Carmarthen SA31 1LE, tel. 0267-231557.

Carmarthen District Council, Tourism & Marketing Services, *3 Spilman St., Carmarthen SA31 1LE, tel. 0267-231445, fax 0267-236659.*

The Croft, Tenby SA70 8AP, tel. 0834-842402.

For Serious Walkers:

The above walk can be found in Ordnance Survey Pathfinder Sheets 1105 and 1081. You can buy pamphlets for other walks for less than $1 at the tourist office in Carmarthen.

The Valley of Legends

EXPERIENCE 24: ABERDOVEY

The small town of Aberdovey (Aberdyfi) sits on a thin strip of coastline in western Wales between mountains and the vast sands of the **Dovey (Dyfi) estuary,** a favorite of swimmers, windsurfers, canoers, water-skiers, and yachtsmen. Aberdovey is actually inside **Snowdonia National Park,** 800 square miles of prime territory for outdoors enthusiasts. You can fish or sail in the morning and walk in a deserted mountain valley the same afternoon. In the particular valley you visit in this experience, you'll have the added enchantment of seeing spots associated with legends about King Arthur and his knights.

The Highlights: A beautiful valley with a lily-covered lake that's part of the King Arthur legend, incredible views high above an estuary, a friendly village between mountains and sea.

Other Places Nearby: A huge national park with rugged mountains and sandy beaches, a narrow-gauge steam railway, an alternative-energy community.

You start a few miles outside Aberdovey in the green hills of, believe it or not, Happy Valley, so named by Victorian travelers who came here by train and admired the countryside. But other people who came before them are the real story of this land. In the days of King Arthur, many magical things supposedly happened at Happy Valley's

Llyn Barfog (the Bearded Lake), a small body of water sandwiched between surrounding hills. In the summer twilight, the reflections on the lake and the shadows around it can be quite poetic.

The lake's dark waters contain no fish. At the edge of the lake, you see a flowery covering of water lilies—"the beard," some say—floating on the surface. But others say the lake's name comes from "The Lake of the Bearded One," commemorating one of King Arthur's knights. According to legend, here King Arthur himself killed a monster that was terrifying the country. Another version claims that Huw Gadarn the Mighty yoked horned oxen to the monster to drag it into the lake, where it drowned.

Many Welsh stories concerning "little folk," or fairies, were also set at the Bearded Lake. The fairies were once believed to be the souls of druids too virtuous for Hell but, as non-Christians, unable to enter Heaven. They supposedly lived in lakes, their castles hidden underwater. Known as Y Tylwyth Teg (The Fair Family), they were small, good-looking, humanlike creatures who dressed in green or white. They were generous to those who treated them well and vengeful to those who didn't.

In one of these stories, a farmer from Dysyrnant (a farm one-half mile north of the lake) captured a fairy's cow and took it home. He mated the cow with one of his black Welsh bulls and it bore him several beautiful calves. Years later, when the cow had grown old, he took it to be slaughtered. But as the butcher raised his knife, a voice from the crags above Llyn Barfog called for the cow to come home. The knife fell from the butcher's hand, and he and the farmer turned to see a green woman waving her arms. The cow and the calves sped toward the lake, never to be seen again, and the farmer's luck deserted him.

After you leave the edge of this fairy-tale lake, you walk up a nearby hillside to another mythical spot, **Carn March Arthur.** A hoofprint on a rock is supposedly that of King Arthur's horse. With King Arthur on its back, the horse leapt across the Dovey estuary while being pursued by enemies, according to legend.

Proceed a little farther, to the top of the hill, and you'll see an incredible view of the estuary. Beyond it lies **Cardigan Bay,** home of the few bottlenose dolphins remaining in British waters. Here, too, legends accumulate. Just off the Aberdovey coast there's supposedly an ancient underwater city in the bay—a famous Welsh song, *The Bells of Aberdyfi,* declares that the bells of the sunken city can still be heard ringing underwater. Divers searching the sea for traces of the drowned city have in fact found piles of gray, oblong stones that look like building bricks. Some say the stones were part of the elaborate fish traps of yesteryear; others, with a glint in their eye, say you just have to believe in the legend.

GETTING THERE

By car:

From Harlech, Wales (40 miles away), take *A496* south to a wooden toll bridge. Cross the bridge and turn right onto the next major road, *A493.* Follow *A493* and go through Tywyn. Less than one mile past Tywyn, turn left at a sign for Happy Valley and proceed on this minor road toward the parking area for Llyn Barfog (the Bearded Lake). Turn right into the parking lot.

From Shrewsbury, England (80 miles away), follow *A458* west to Welshpool (Trallwng). Take *A483* south and proceed about 6 miles past Newtown. Connect to *A470* and proceed northwest past Llanbrynmair to the village of Cemmaes Road. Take *A489* south to Machynlleth. Then follow *A487* north for less than one mile to *A493.* Take *A493* west to Aberdovey. Go through Aberdovey and follow the coast road, *A493,* north for three miles. Turn right onto the minor road for Happy Valley. Follow that road toward the parking area for Llyn Barfog (the Bearded Lake). Turn right into the parking lot.

By train:

Britrail's Cambrian Coast line stops at Aberdovey. For rail information, call 0492-585151 (in Wales) or 0743-64041 (in England). To get to the beginning of the walk—a few miles outside the village—take a taxi (call Dyfi cabs, tel. 0654-767877).

▼

Walk Directions

TIME: 1 1/2 hours
LEVEL: Easy
DISTANCE: 2 1/2 miles
ACCESS: By car and train

This walk traverses dirt and grass paths in a valley of hills. There are several stiles to climb over and one tiring hill to ascend. Near the end of the walk, be sure to stay on the path, because there are some open mineshafts in the vicinity. Picnic at the lake or on the hillside at Point 5. Buy picnic

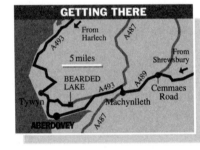

GETTING THERE

From Harlech

A493
A487
A487
From Shrewsbury

5 miles

BEARDED LAKE

A493

A489

Machynlleth

Cemmaes Road

Tywyn

A487

ABERDOVEY

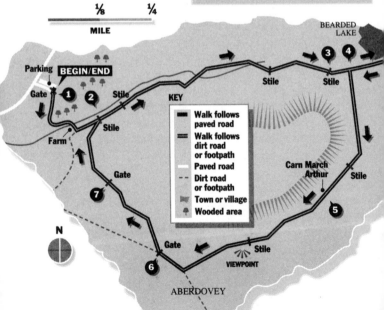

1/8 1/4

MILE

BEARDED LAKE

Parking

BEGIN/END

Gate

Stile

KEY

Stile

Stile

3 4

Farm

Stile

KEY

■ Walk follows paved road
═ Walk follows dirt road or footpath
│ Paved road
- - - Dirt road or footpath
⚑ Town or village
🌲 Wooded area

Carn March Arthur

Stile

Gate

7

5

N

Gate

6

Stile

VIEWPOINT

ABERDOVEY

supplies at one of the many shops in Aberdovey.

TO BEGIN

From the parking lot, turn your back to the road and walk toward and through a gate leading into Happy Valley.

1. Turn left immediately after the gate, onto a dirt path signposted to Tyddyn-y-briddell farm. Pass a farmhouse on your right and then walk between another farmhouse and a shed.

2. Cross a ladder stile. Go straight and then cross over a second ladder stile. Continue on a rock-strewn path up a hill until you reach a third ladder stile. Cross it and continue up a dirt track to a grass path uphill. Go toward a stile (next to a metal gate) that's to the left of a rockface on a hill.

3. Cross the stile and make an immediate left. Proceed straight to Bearded Lake. *You may want to sit on the rocks at the shoreline or find a grass patch for a picnic.* After you've finished exploring the lake, go back toward the last stile.

4. About 60 yards before the stile at Point 3, follow a grass path that forks off to the left and uphill. You soon pass a signpost on your right. Stay on the grass path (keeping the hillside on your right) as the path curves to the right. Cross a stile and follow the grass path straight up a hill.

5. On your right, pass the *Carn March Arthur headstone, imprinted with the hoofprint of King Arthur's horse.* Continue on the path (there will be a stone wall on your left), and cross another stile. *There will be a great view over the Dyfi estuary to the left.* Follow the grass path downhill (a barbed-wire fence will be to your right), and bear right on the path toward a gate.

6. Go through the gate that's behind a cottage, ignoring the signposted path to the left. Follow the path down the hill (with a barbed-wire fence to your left), past old mineshafts. **Do not venture off the wide rocky path, because there are hidden mineshafts hereabouts.**

7. Go through a metal gate. Proceed downhill on a rocky path. **Again, don't venture off the path.** At the bottom of the hill, turn left and cross a ladder stile. Follow the path through the farm buildings that you passed in Point 1 and retrace your steps to your car.

OTHER PLACES NEARBY

■ **Snowdonia National Park.** Aberdovey sits inside the southern edge of this 800-square-mile national park full of rugged mountains, hiking trails, and sandy beaches. The highest mountain near Aberdovey, 2,928-foot Cadair Idris (Chair of Idris), stands about 18 miles to the northeast. *For information, contact Mid Wales Tourism Manager, Maengwyn St., Machynlleth SY20 8EE, tel. 0654-702401.*

■ **Talyllyn Railway.** This narrow-gauge railway using steam locomotives dates to 1865. A preservation society saved the railway from shutting down in 1951 and now operates it on an inland route between Tywyn and Nant Gwernol, much of it through scenic Snowdonia National Park. *5 mi. northwest of Aberdovey, Tywyn, tel. 0654-710472. Trains run daily Easter-Oct.; otherwise, call for schedules. Admission.*

■ **Centre for Alternative Technology.** This unique working community aims to reduce pollution and to use alternative energy sources to conserve the world's resources. A seven-acre exhibition site features a water-powered cliff railway and interesting displays, including Britain's best-insulated home and organic vegetable gardens. There's also a children's playground and a natural-foods restaurant. *14 mi. east of Aberdovey off A487; 2 mi. north of Machynlleth, tel. 0654-702400. Open daily 10-5 Mar.-Dec. Admission.*

DINING

■ **Plas Penhelig** (expensive). This Edwardian country house grows its own vegetables, peaches, herbs, and flowers. In the lemon-colored dining room looking out on the terrace and river, expect such entrées as roast rack of lamb with herb crust and pepper sauce and Dyfi salmon on a bed of sorrel with lemon hollandaise sauce. Look for the peach-leaf ice cream served with a fruit coulis. *Aberdovey LL35 0NA, tel. 0654-767676, fax 0654-767783. Closed late Dec.-Feb.*

■ **Penhelig Arms** (expensive). Charles Dickens probably visited this former 18th-century inn known as Y Dafarn Fach (The Little Inn), now an 11-room hotel. The main dining room menu recently featured roasted pork fillet stuffed with sage and onion, wrapped in bacon, and served with orange sauce. There are also good bar lunches—look for fresh local crab sandwiches—and Sunday roasts. *Aberdovey LL35 0LT, tel. 0654-767215, fax 0654-767690.*

■ **Maybank Hotel & Restaurant** (expensive). The two bay windows in the dining room of this three-story Victorian hotel provide good views of the estuary. In a real departure for this part of the world, Indonesian curries and satés are offered, as well as local fish dishes (usually poached) and such entrées as strips of fillet steak in mustard and sherry sauce. *Aberdovey LL35 0PT, tel. 0654-767500. Dinner only. Closed late Nov.-Dec. 24 and Jan. 2-Feb. 14.*

■ **Wellie's Wine Bar** (inexpensive). The creative, inexpensive food here is a welcome departure from pub food. With an assortment of vegetables and fruit, the house salad is a delight. For an entrée, try the minty lamb casserole or the broccoli-and-walnut lasagna. If the apple, toffee, and pecan pie is on the menu, order it. There's a unique wine and beer list, including one of Britain's best new brews, Newquay Steam Beer. *Basement of the Harbour Hotel, Aberdovey, tel. 0654-767250.*

LODGING

■ **Plas Penhelig** (expensive). Unlike most of the hotels in Aberdovey, this country house is set back from the main road but still has estuary views. Built in 1909, it's a relaxing retreat on seven acres of grounds with landscaped gardens. Inside you'll find an oak staircase, stained-glass windows, and 11 individually decorated guest rooms—the nicest and largest is the Prince's Room, with a turret window, a double bed, and garden and estuary views. *Aberdovey LL35 0NA, tel. 0654-767676, fax 0654-767783.*

▼

■ **Maybank Hotel & Restaurant** (moderate). Built in the 1840s, this three-story, five-bedroom country house with Georgian windows enjoys a good location overlooking the estuary and the seaside village. The rooms are plain but comfortable; request Room 5, which has a double bed and a water view. Even the locals patronize the small hotel's restaurant. *Aberdovey LL35 0PT, tel. 0654-767500. Closed late Nov.-Dec. 24 and Jan. 2-Feb. 14.*

■ **Pentre Bach** (inexpensive). There are excellent views across Cardigan Bay to the Lleyn Peninsula from this countryside bed and breakfast situated on 5 1/2 acres of land. For a bay view and a double bed, request the House Oak Room. Cottages are also available, and dinner is served on request. *14 mi. north of Aberdovey on A493, Llwyrigwril LL37 2JU, tel. 0341-250294, fax 0341-250885.*

■ **Frondeg** (inexpensive). This Edwardian country house is a good value and only a three-minute walk from the village center. The bedrooms are large and elegant. *Copperhill St., Aberdovey LL35 0HT, tel. 0654-767655.*

FOR MORE INFORMATION

Tourist Office:
   The Wharf Gardens, Aberdovey LL35 0ED, tel. 0654-767321.

For Serious Walkers:
   The above walk can be found on Ordnance Survey Outdoor Leisure Map 23. On the southern side of the Dovey estuary at Ynyslas, there's a signposted trail through sand dunes and among such unusual plant species as the bee orchid, the march orchid, and the marsh helleborine.

A Stronghold Above the Sea

EXPERIENCE 25: HARLECH

A landscape photographer's fantasy becomes reality in the town of Harlech in northwestern Wales, where a historic castle clings to the precipitous slopes of a hill overlooking the wide open sea and a range of high mountains. Although the sea has receded from this quaint former port, the waters of Cardigan Bay lap the shore only half a mile away, and there are marvelous views from several hilltop vantage points around the town.

You begin this experience next to

The Highlights: A friendly town overlooking the sea and the mountains, an ancient castle where the English and Welsh battled, the remains of hut circles dating to the Roman period.

Other Places Nearby: Rugged mountains, hiking trails, sandy beaches, and large lakes in Snowdonia National Park; a fantasy village at Portmeirion; the ruins of a 13th-century castle.

Harlech Castle, built during Edward I's 1283 invasion of Wales on the site of an earlier fortress. It took six years for a huge construction crew—about 550 laborers, 225 masons, 115 quarrymen, 30 smiths, and 20 carpenters—to complete the job. The outer walls still stand, and the most prominent feature inside is a massive twin-towered gatehouse that's three stories tall with 12-foot-thick walls.

Master James of St. George, who designed three other great Welsh

▼

castles (Conway, Caernarvon, and Beaumaris) during the same period, designed Harlech Castle as a military stronghold, with Tremadog Bay protecting it on one side and a deep moat on the land side. In this rugged coastal corner, the castle inevitably became a focal point in centuries of struggle between the English and the Welsh. Having been built by an English king invading Wales, it was of course besieged a few years later when the Welsh rebelled in 1294-95. The valiant English defenders, surrounded on the land side and cut off from all communications, held out thanks to supplies brought in by sea from Ireland. (As you walk around the castle, you'll notice a fortified stairway cut into the cliff, a "way to the sea" that ensured communication to the outside world during times of siege.)

During the Welsh insurrection of the early 15th century, Owain Glyndwr took the castle after a four-year fight, proclaiming himself Prince of Wales. He only ruled for four years, however. English forces, led by the future Henry V, besieged the castle in 1408, bombarding it repeatedly with massive stone cannon balls. A blockade finally forced the starving garrison inside to surrender in the following year.

In the 1460s, when the Lancasters and the Yorks fought over the English crown in the Wars of the Roses, the castle was held by the Lancaster faction under Dafydd ap Jevan ap Einion. Offered terms to surrender, he defiantly responded: "I have held a castle in France till all the old women in Wales heard of it. Now I will hold a castle in Wales till all the old women of France have heard of it!" Starvation eventually forced him to yield the castle, the last Lancaster bastion to fall, but his deeds forever became a part of Welsh national consciousness, immortalized in the stirring song "Gwyr Harlech," or the "March of the Men of Harlech":

> *Shall the Saxon army shake you*
> *Smite, pursue, and overtake you?*
> *Men of Harlech, God shall make you*
> *Victors, blow for blow!*

The town of Harlech is pleasant to stroll around, with its quaint main street and ancient buildings, some of which date back 400 years.

▼

On a hill above the town, you can visit the ruins of a Roman-era settlement, **Muriau Gwyddelod** ("Irish huts")—native hut circles about 2,000 years old. When you head back down the hill, the view of land and sea is astonishing. Beyond the castle, a great triangle of flat land stretches from the town to the seashore. The land is **Morfa Harlech,** a delta of sand and marshland that formed naturally over the past 700 years, cutting off the former port of Harlech from the sea.

To the north and northeast of Harlech stand the towering mountains of **Snowdonia National Park,** including mighty 3,559-foot Snowdon, known to the Welsh as Yr Wyddfa. To the west, the Lleyn Peninsula juts out into Tremadog Bay between two other huge bodies of water, Cardigan and Caernarfon bays, both of which lead out to the Atlantic Ocean. On a clear evening, the sight of a sunset over the bay and the mountains brings you awfully close to paradise.

GETTING THERE
By car:
From Chester, England (70 miles away), take *A55* west to *A494*. Take *A494* south toward Mold. Stay on *A494* to Bala. Take *A4212* west to *B4391* (toward Ffestiniog). Pass through Ffestiniog and take *A496* south to Harlech. Park in the public parking lot next to the castle. If the lot is full, park in the lower lot at the bottom of the hill and pick up the walking tour just beyond Point 2.

From Llandudno, Wales (40 miles away), take *A470* south toward Betws-y-Coed. Pass through Betws-y-Coed and continue on to Blaenau Ffestiniog. Follow *A496* south to Harlech. Park in the public parking lot next to the castle. If the lot is full, park in the lower lot at the bottom of the hill and pick up the walking tour just beyond Point 2.

By train:
Take Britrail from any station in England or Wales. The Cambrian Coast line stops at Harlech Station. For information on train connections, call Britrail's London Travel Centre at 0713-880-519. From Harlech Station, join the walk just beyond Point 2.

▼

Walk Directions

TIME: 1 1/2 to 2 hours
LEVEL: Easy to moderate
DISTANCE: 2 1/2 to 3 miles
ACCESS: By car and train

At the beginning of this walk, you follow a very steep paved road for a short stretch, so be sure to stop for a few breathers. To avoid the steep road, you may choose to start the walk on *High Street,* just beyond Point 4 (although you'll miss a walk

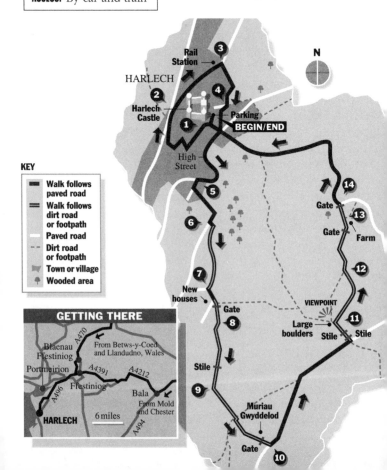

KEY

- Walk follows paved road
- Walk follows dirt road or footpath
- Paved road
- Dirt road or footpath
- Town or village
- Wooded area

N

③
Rail Station
HARLECH
②
Harlech Castle
④
Parking
BEGIN/END
①
High Street
⑤
⑥
⑦
New houses
Gate
⑧
Stile
⑨
Muriau Gwyddelod
Gate
⑩
Large boulders
Stile
Stile
⑪
VIEWPOINT
⑫
Farm
Gate
⑬
Gate
⑭

GETTING THERE

Blaenau Ffestiniog
Portmeirion
A470
A4391
From Betws-y-Coed and Llandudno, Wales
Ffestiniog
A4212
Bala
From Mold and Chester
A496
HARLECH
6 miles
A494

▼

around the castle). Also, you must climb a relatively steep grass hill, but it's not overly tiring because you cut across the hillside at a 45-degree angle. The best picnic spots, as well as remarkable views, can be found near the yellow trail marker at Point 11. Pick up picnic supplies at Bwtri Bach, a deli in the center of town (closed Sunday except in July and August).

TO BEGIN

Walk out of the castle's main parking lot (atop the hill) and turn right onto a paved road. You'll be looking out at a spectacular view of the water.

1. Follow this road as it curves to the left and goes downhill. The road bends to the right, then to the left and to the right again.

2. At a main road, turn right. Go to the railroad crossing. Take a road to the right of the railroad tracks and pass a lower parking lot for the castle. Proceed on this road past, and to the right of, the train station.

3. Make the next right after the train station. Go straight uphill on a paved road (a trailer park is on the right). Walk slowly—it's very steep—toward an intersection.

4. At the intersection, bear left. Proceed uphill on the road until it merges with Harlech's main street, *High Street*. Follow *High Street* straight ahead. Pass a post office on the right and a parking lot (in Welsh, *canolfan hysbysrwydd*) on the left.

5. Just before the road bends, at the edge of town, turn left, following a sign to the library. Bear left at an intersection and follow a road uphill.

6. Just after the road bends, turn left into a driveway. Make an immediate right onto a footpath to the right of a low stone wall: A green "Llwybr Cyhoeddus" sign directs you onto the footpath at the

▼

mouth of the driveway, but it may be partially blocked by a "Caravan Park" sign. Go up the path, turn right, and proceed toward a paved road.

7. Make a left onto the paved road and proceed uphill. Bear left (to the left of a row of modern houses) and go straight to a footpath. Bear right on the footpath (a "Gwyriad Diversion" sign is on the wall where you turn right). Follow a yellow trail marker through a metal gate and go uphill to your right at a 45-degree angle.

8. Pass through a gap in a stone wall in the right-hand corner of a field. Continue on a grass path at a 45-degree angle through the next gap in a stone wall (the rooftops of houses are to your right) until you reach a stile going over a stone wall (there will be a yellow trail marker at the stile). Cross the stile and proceed toward a wall.

9. At the wall, make a left. Go uphill with the wall on your right and then turn right through a gap. Make a sharp left turn onto a path that goes uphill between two stone walls. Continue up the path with a wall on your left, ignoring a yellow arrow to the right. Follow dirt tracks through a gap in a stone wall, ignoring a gap in the stone wall to your right. *To your left is an ancient settlement, Muriau Gwyddelod, the remains of native hut circles from the Roman period about 2,000 years ago.* Go through a metal gate between stone walls and proceed toward a paved road.

10. Turn left onto the road. Walk about 650 yards. Turn left and climb over a stile across a barbed-wire fence. Go straight across a field and over the next stone stile. Proceed straight toward a yellow trail marker and a bed of large boulders. *There are spectacular views to the northwest across a large triangle of flat land, Morfa Harlech, reaching to the sea.*

11. Turn right at the yellow trail marker. Proceed to the corner of two stone walls. Proceed straight alongside a wall to your right. At the end of the wall, turn left and head down a hill (with another stone wall to your right). Some plants and hedges block your way down, but it's

▼

easy to maneuver around them and down to a gap in the stone wall next to a stream.

12. Follow a rocky path that bears to the right and head downhill (keeping the stone wall to your right). Make a right turn and follow the path through stone walls to a farm. Bear left through a metal gate and pass between two buildings.

13. Turn left alongside a fence, ignoring a dirt path to your right. Go through an opening in a stone wall and follow a grass path down and across a hill.

14. Walk through a metal gate. Turn left onto a paved road. Follow the road as it winds back to Harlech. *Just before Harlech's High Street, you can stop in at the Lion Hotel, a friendly pub where the locals drink pints of Boddington's Bitter and hand-drawn Castle Eden Ale.* Then cross *High Street* to your car in the castle's upper parking lot.

PLACES ALONG THE WALK

■ **Harlech Castle.** *Open daily 9:30-6:30 mid-Mar. to mid-Oct.; Mon.-Sat. 9:30-4, Sun. 2-4 mid-Oct. to mid-Mar. Admission.*

OTHER PLACES NEARBY

■ **Snowdonia National Park.** Harlech sits within this 800-square-mile national park that's full of rugged mountains, hiking trails, and sandy beaches. The highest peak, Snowdon, is about 20 miles north of Harlech. *Information available at Royal Oak Stables, Betws-y-Coed LL24 0AH, tel. 0690-2426. During the off-season, contact the North Wales Tourist Commission, 77 Conway Rd., Colwyn Bay LL29 7LN.*

■ **Portmeirion.** Architect Clough Williams-Ellis created this 50-building fantasy village between 1925 and 1972 on a secluded peninsula five miles from his ancestral home. The town, which was used as the setting for the TV series *The Prisoner,* is unique but lacks old Welsh character. *8 mi. north of Harlech off A487, Portmeirion, tel. 0766-770228, fax 0766-771331. Admission.*

▼

■ **Criccieth Castle.** A ruined 13th-century castle built by the Welsh prince Llywelyn the Great, it perches on a rocky peninsula overlooking Tremadog Bay. There are exhibitions inside on Welsh princes and their castles. *15 mi. northwest of Harlech on A497, Criccieth, tel. 0766-522227. Open daily 9:30-6:30 Mar. 25-Oct. 24; daily 9:30-4:30 Oct. 25-Mar. 24. Admission.*

■ **Chwarel Hen Llanfair.** Inside this former slate mine, you can explore a network of tunnels and caverns. Bring a coat—the temperature usually stays below 50 degrees. As you emerge from the mine, you'll have one of the best views of the sea in the Harlech area. There's a pottery and crafts shop on the premises. *1 mi. south of Harlech off A496, tel. 0766-780247. Open daily 10-5:30 Apr.-Sep.; daily 11-4 in Oct. Closed Nov.-Mar., unless special arrangements are made. Admission.*

DINING

■ **Maes-y-Neuadd** (very expensive). Situated on eight acres of land on a mountainside, this elegant granite-and-slate hotel has breathtaking views overlooking Snowdonia National Park. The specialty of the excellent restaurant is Welsh lamb, and it's available even when it's not on the menu. *3 mi. northeast of Harlech, Talsarnau LL47 6YA, tel. 0766-780200, fax 800-635-3602 in the U.S., 0766-780211 in the U.K.*

■ **Cemlyn** (expensive). Chef-owner Ken Goody has been looking to retire and sell for a few years, but he's still creating excellent dishes each day for an ever-growing fan club of locals and visitors. He keeps seafood and chicken simple, yet adds the right dash of emphasis to delight diners. A picture window looks out at the castle, and there's a good wine list. *High St., Harlech LL46 2YA, tel. 0766-780425. Open for dinner; lunch by special arrangement. Closed Nov.-Easter.*

■ **Castle Cottage** (moderate). A talented husband-and-wife team run a classy restaurant in one of Harlech's oldest homes, located near the castle and alongside the steepest road in Britain. They describe their cooking as French-style traditional English cooking, with an emphasis on light, healthy meals and as much local produce as possible. The menu changes every two weeks. Look for the succulent rack

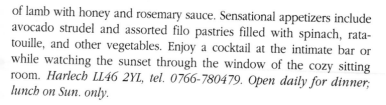

of lamb with honey and rosemary sauce. Sensational appetizers include avocado strudel and assorted filo pastries filled with spinach, ratatouille, and other vegetables. Enjoy a cocktail at the intimate bar or while watching the sunset through the window of the cozy sitting room. *Harlech LL46 2YL, tel. 0766-780479. Open daily for dinner; lunch on Sun. only.*

LODGING

■ **Maes-y-Neuadd** (very expensive). One of the best Welsh hotels, this 14th-century manor house has been modernized and expanded over the centuries. The unpretentious, comfortable guest rooms are in either the 12-room hotel or an adjoining 4-room coach house. Ask for the largest room, the Moelwyn, which has a baronial feel and a working fireplace. Or request the Wynne Room, where Jackie Onassis stayed when attending the funeral of Lord Harlech in 1984. *3 mi. northeast of Harlech, Talsarnau LL47 6YA, tel. 0766-780200, fax 800-635-3602 in the U.S., 0766-780211 in the U.K.*

■ **Castle Cottage** (inexpensive). Though small (only six rooms), this 400-year-old hotel is well situated, in the heart of town near the castle. Rooms 4, 5, and 6 on the top floor have double beds and sea views; 4 and 5 are the most spacious and have private bathrooms. There's a great atmosphere throughout, with friendly owners, a fine restaurant, and a well-stocked bar. *Harlech LL46 2YL, tel. 0766-780479.*

■ **Anne Oliver's Bed & Breakfast** (inexpensive). This home on Harlech's main street (don't worry—*High Street* is quiet at night) used to be an eight-room temperance hotel. Now the sign out front reads "Gorffwysfa" (Resting Place), and what a resting place it is if you book rooms 5 or 6, both of which have spectacular views of the sea. Avoid the only other room available—it lacks a good view. *High St., Harlech LL46 2YA, tel. 0766-780316.*

■ **Byrdir** (inexpensive). A friendly, comfortable 15-room inn built in the early 1900s, Byrdir is conveniently located on Harlech's historic main street. Room 12 is the nicest, with a double bed, private bath, and view over village houses out toward the sea. Twin-bedded Room 10 also has a sea view. Such inexpensive home-cooked English dinners as

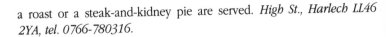

a roast or a steak-and-kidney pie are served. *High St., Harlech LL46 2YA, tel. 0766-780316.*

FOR MORE INFORMATION

Tourist Offices:

Harlech and District Tourism Association, *c/o Tom Parry Estate Agents, High St., Harlech LL46 2YA, tel. 0766-780883.*
Gwyddior House, Harlech LL46 2YA, tel. 0766-780658.

For Serious Walkers:

The above walk can be found in Ordnance Survey Outdoor Leisure Map 18. You can extend the walk by venturing north of Harlech Castle to Morfa Harlech, a region of sand dunes and marshland that has built up since the castle was constructed.